D0876104

THE DREAM SEEKERS

THE CIVILIZATION OF THE AMERICAN INDIAN SERIES

The Dream Seekers
Native American Visionary
Traditions of the Great Plains

By Lee Irwin
Foreword by Vine Deloria, Jr.

UNIVERSITY OF OKLAHOMA PRESS : NORMAN AND LONDON

Library of Congress Cataloging-in-Publication Data

Irwin, Lee, 1944–
    The dream seekers : Native American Visionary traditions of
the Great Plains / by Lee Irwin ; foreword by Vine Deloria, Jr.
        p.   cm. — (The Civilization of the American Indian series ;
v. 213)
    Includes bibliographical references and index.
    ISBN 0-8061-2643-4 (alk. paper)
        1. Indians of North America—Great Plains—Religion and
mythology.   2. Indians of North America—Great Plains—
Rites and ceremonies.   3. Visions.   I. Title.   II. Series.
E78.G73I76   1994
299´.798—dc20   93-45863
                                                                                          CIP

The Dream Seekers: Native American Visionary Traditions of the Great Plains is volume 213 in the Civilization of the American Indian Series.

The paper in this book meets the guidelines for permanence and durability of the Committee on Production Guidelines for Book Longevity of the Council on Library Resources, Inc. ∞

1 2 3 4 5 6 7 8 9 10

Contents

Foreword

READING THE EARLY MISSIONARY ACCOUNTS of tribal religions and comparing them with the effusive praise of "Indian spirituality" that is lavished on anything resembling tribal religiosity is quite an experience. Tribal religious activities have progressed from works of the devil and superstitions to highly sophisticated images of universal reality in little more than a century. It is difficult to determine whether this radical change in perspectives and interpretations is a sign that non-Indians are gaining spiritual maturity or suffering from spiritual and intellectual exhaustion. Or perhaps both.

Bookshelves today are filled with pap—written many times by Indians who have kicked over the traces and no longer feel they are responsible to any living or historic community, but more often by wholly sincere and utterly ignorant non-Indians who fancy themselves masters of the vision quest and sweat lodge. Lying beneath this mass of sentimental slop is the unchallenged assumption that personal sincerity is the equivalent of insight and that cosmic secrets can be not only shared by non-Indians but given out in weekend workshops as easily as diet plans.

It is thus with great satisfaction that I am pleased to write a short introduction to this book. For once a scholar has taken his material seriously, given it the respect it deserves, and served up a first-class analysis of one of the central themes of the Plains Indians—the dream, or vision. I met Lee Irwin some years ago when he was a graduate student at Indiana University. He showed me a mass of materials that he had accumulated and graciously made me a copy of his vision material from my tribe, the Teton Sioux—actually, to be genetically accurate, the Yankton Dakotas, but then I have lived most of my life with the western people and so tend to think more in categories that reflect plains and not woodlands and lakes.

I was somewhat skeptical that Irwin could do a decent job of analyzing and explaining aspects of the vision quest, because it is not a unique experience for me to be accosted by a non-Indian graduate student who is studying Plains religion. Indeed, the woods and libraries are filled with them, and the roads to Pine Ridge and Rosebud are clogged with their cars every summer. I have been working along similar lines—the analysis of the vision quest experience—for some time and saw many pitfalls, plus the danger that if I did publish anything it would fall into the New Age classification through the enthusiasm of a publisher's publicity department, and so I did not give Lee much encouragement.

After reading this volume I find that he was on a special and most productive scholarly quest and accomplished this task with very good results. This volume is comprehensive in many ways. It is not a mere recital of some of the popular dreams that have been printed in anthologies. Rather, it is an earnest and honest coming to grips with the difficult technical problems of understanding the material and presenting this understanding in its most substantial form.

The greatest difficulty in exploring the religious world of the Plains Indians is getting the reader and/or scholar to take the material seriously. What do we make of a vision account wherein a person experiences the transformation of a bird or animal into one of several forms in sequence, offers then a plant, root, or claw, and the dreamer, coming down from the hill, holds in his possession the *actual physical thing* granted him? It is not, of course, very believable in western intellectual circles, yet it happens, and if the scholar is going to understand the experience, he or she must grant that an event far out of the paradigm of western materialistic science has occurred. Irwin, as far as I can tell, accepts these kinds of events and is able to build up a substantial argument about them without asking his more skeptical readers to bet the farm on the reality of the event.

The second most difficult obstacle to overcome is determining exactly what kind of emotional or psychological state occurred when the individual had the experience. What does the pitiful word *dream* actually mean after all these decades of recording and interpreting Indian materials? In many instances, we may be talking about a dream comparable to those that we have at night during sleep, and nothing more. We may also be talking about different kinds of intensities of perception brought on by hunger and deprivation—experiences no less real than our relaxing day at the beach, but certainly very difficult to defend as valid expressions of the possible breadth of human potential.

And we may even be talking about a wholly unique event— an instance of an individual's walking along and suddenly entering another space-time situation in which traditional rules of causation, chains of sequence of motions, and images no longer apply. Some years ago, an acquaintance of mine had a near-death experience while undergoing an operation. Suddenly she was in a wooded valley and found herself walking up the side of a hill, where she could hear the sound of many happy voices. Reaching the crest of the hill, she saw a camp circle and many people gathered around eating. She came into the circle, greeted friends, and walked toward the western side of the group, where she saw a finely dressed man, wearing a warbonnet, handing out dishes of food. As she reached for a bowl she was told that she could not eat since, if she did so, she would have to remain there, and her time to come with the people had not yet arrived. The chief was an elder who had not yet passed on, although this gathering was obviously a feast enjoyed by the deceased in another time and place. When she used to tell of her experience, she would state that this event was the most real experience of her life. So what was it? Dream? Vision? Trauma?

This book is for the serious reader and must be read with the utmost care and earnestness. It is not a manual for fools or something for New Age exploitation. It is considerably more comprehensive than the scholarly treatments that have preceded it. The most valuable thing about the book is that it does not have a doctrinal point of view, a cherished anthropological "truth" of interpretation that labels and moves on without understanding what it was that happened—or happens. Thus, when Irwin describes the motives for enduring the excruciating experiences of the vision quest and mentions seeking "power," he is NOT talking about a New Age circle-jerk where a dozen affluent people spend all of two hours being informed that the world is round and that they can have a "power panther" at their beck and call. Indeed, as Irwin makes clear, we are talking about the enhancement of already considerable physical and spiritual powers possessed by peoples who were an intimate part of the physical world, who could run down deer and kill them with knives, who could perfectly imitate most birds and animals, and who lived in a society in which holy men could turn thunderstorms away and perform physical feats that defied any kind of rational explanation. Thus, while I hope the book is well used by its readers, I hope it is not misused by them.

Irwin has made a major contribution in this book. He has reached deep into the substance of the Plains experience and has given us enough of that substance that we can come to great understanding about the nature of life as we should be experiencing it. If even a few of these experiences are "true"—i.e., real events in the lives of a particular group of peoples on a particular landscape—then we must radically adjust our sense of what constitutes our world, start to edge away from Newtonian concepts, and begin to embrace the possibility of a substantially broader and deeper set of relationships that must constitute the world. This book is immensely helpful in placing at our disposal sets of concepts that act as orientation signposts for our journey into the unknown—but eminently knowable—aspect of life. It is a volume that I shall return to again and again, always seeing more than what first caught my eye. I am very happy to be asked to write a foreword to it, because I believe it to be a substantial work that will stand the test of time.

Vine Deloria, Jr.

Boulder, Colorado

Acknowledgments

THE WRITING of this work has a history of people who helped. First, I would like to thank Joseph Epps Brown, who initiated me into the graduate study of Native American religions and who brought the Plains Indian traditions to life for all his students as genuine expressions of deep spirituality. Both his concerns and his dedication have had a deep influence on my developing interests. Second, I would like to thank Ray DeMallie, who supported this project in particular and rode shotgun to keep me from driving off the track. Only his repeated emphasis made me finally realize how important it is to work with primary sources with scrupulous care—a trait I have yet to attain at Ray's high level of accomplishment. Third, I would like to thank Vine Deloria, whose overview of this work inspired me to think of it as worth publishing and whose keen sense of humor and no-nonsense attitude helped me feel that perhaps other Native Americans would find it useful.

I also want to thank Ken Morrison for his critical reading of the manuscript and his firm dedication to the task of giving a truly meaningful response from the perspective of current issues within comparative religion. His thorough review helped in many ways to sharpen and focus the writing and give it a more accessible form. My thanks also to Beverly Stoeltje, who insisted that I clarify and articulate my perspectives on women visionaries and dreamers—which has truly enhanced the overall work. I also want to thank my partner and wife, Catherine Evans, who has supported this project with enthusiasm and encouragement through all its many stages. I would also like to thank my parents for their generous and kind interest in this project. Finally, I thank the hardworking staff at the University of Oklahoma Press for their efforts, friendliness, and commitment to producing the highest quality publication. My thanks to all of you!

Lee Irwin

Johns Island, South Carolina

THE DREAM SEEKERS

Prologue

THE CENTRALITY OF THE ROLE of dreaming and the vision complex among Native Americans was first noted by Ruth Benedict when she called it "the largest and most basic concept of Indian religion."[1] It is this central role of dreaming in the traditional religious worldviews of Native American peoples that I explore in the following work. While I have a long-standing interest in all aspects of Plains Indian religious cultures, my concern here is to show the central importance of dreams and visions within those traditions. Further, I offer an alternative presentation of dreaming materials as they relate to the formative process of a developing and emergent religious worldview, rather than give a psychological or anthropological analysis.

The contents of the presentation are based on a selection of more than 350 dreams taken from the ethnography of the greater Plains and Prairie peoples. This area encompasses more than twenty major communities and can be distinguished into three ecological areas that give a distinctive character to their inhabitants' social and religious worldviews. There are the high plains nomads, usually distinguished by their distribution from Canada to Texas; the agricultural communities of the river valleys; and the peoples of the plains border areas to the east (woodland-prairie) and west (mountain-plains). In addition, I have used a sample of more than 200 dream accounts from areas outside the plains in an attempt to provide a broad, comparative background for the study.[2]

The central goal of this work is to illustrate the historical significance and centrality of dreams and visions in the formation of traditional Plains religious identity. While it has become an accepted tenet of ethnography to recognize the importance of dreaming in Native American communities, the exact role and relationship of dreaming to *religious* values, cosmologies, mythologies, ritual enactments, and traditional worldviews has often been only briefly defined or, more usually, relegated to a subsidiary level of interpretation. Yet dreaming and dream experiences have been central to the Plains worldview as far back as the earliest ethnographic records.[3]

Because this work is a historically situated analysis, based primarily on Native American Plains traditional religions of the nineteenth to mid-twentieth century, it is a text-dependent work. By drawing on an extensive corpus of ethnographic materials, ranging from the Jesuit Relations of the seventeenth century to contemporary field research, I have identified three levels of ethnographic reporting in the dream-related materials: firsthand descriptive texts of dreams and dreaming experiences narrated by the dreamer and directly recorded by the ethnographer; secondhand narrative texts based on dream experiences of a relative or community member known to the narrator of the account and directly recorded by the ethnographer; and thirdhand texts that usually involve the telling of a communally known dream experience of a revered ancestor or founder of a ritual society, frequently recorded indirectly by the ethnographer while gathering other types of information. Most of these texts were recorded in English and not in the original language of the dreamer. The degree to which the ethnographer may have influenced the dream report is extremely difficult to determine.

Using firsthand Plains ethnographic descriptions as the essential and primary texts, I take a broadly comparative approach. Following the historical school of descriptive phenomenology, my chief concern has been to elucidate the intentional structures of the dreaming experience as they relate to the socioreligious topology inherent in the Plains worldview.[4] Intentionality in this context refers to the lived experience of the dreamer—the way in which dreams interact meaningfully to pattern social behavior and enhance religious indentity through personal empowerment and an enhanced sense of self. This is a study of how the intent of the dreamer is shaped by both the dream experience and its social correlates. The task is not a description of a statically defined world of being, but of a dynamically charged world of transformation and becoming. Perhaps the single greatest limitation in many ethnographic accounts is the tendency to picture a specific lived world as static—as an unmoving portrait of what is, ritually and seasonally contained within unvarying cycles. Yet Native Americans were undergoing rapid transformations and cultural change during the ethnographic period under consideration, and the intentional structure of dreaming reveals this process quite clearly. In addition, I undertake an analytic description of the dynamic processes involved in dreaming and the dream experience that contribute to both cultural innovation and continuity.

The analysis may be seen as involving three interrelated concerns: the descriptive, the intentional, and the interpretative. By description, I mean the firsthand report of the immediate dream experience in a context of religious significance as given in the ethnography. How is each stage of the search and attainment of the vision carried out and directed? Answering this question involves an analysis of the shared epistemology of the visionary experience and the constructive processes involved in the integration of that experience within the sacred topology of the lived world. By intention I mean the disclosure of meaning and purpose in the life of the visionary as it is revealed through patterns of action and cultural expression representing a particular visionary experience. In this sense, the vision is seen to be a primary source of social and religious motivation.[5] What form of individual or communal behavior does the vision catalyze? Because intention involves the actualization of the will, particularly in the creation of dream-related artifacts, attention is given to these objects and the intent involved in their construction and use.

Interpretation encompasses the many-sided problem of disclosing meaningful structures of communication in a context of highly divergent perspectives. Visionary experience is best characterized in the historical period under consideration as pluralistic. A successful hermeneutics of Native American visionary texts, actions, or symbols requires a sensitivity to the multivocal nature of visionary interpretation among Plains peoples and a recognition of the many different voices speaking with varying degrees of authority and intelligibility, frequently within a single context. What is meant by the vision? Before it is possible to inquire into the rich diversity of existing indigenous interpretations as recorded in the ethnography, it is necessary to gain a clear appreciation of the processes and contents of the search and attainment of the vision itself. Therefore, in this work I have concentrated on examining the means of attaining and actualizing the vision, interpreting the ethnography in terms of widely shared patterns of behavior and the various methods of actualizing the dream experience. A future volume will be written on the subject of indigenous visionary classification or typology, the concomitant interpretive schemes used by various Plains peoples, and the rise of prophetic visionary traditions influenced by Christian missionization. Even in the simplified context of the search, attainment, and actualization of the vision, the processes are profoundly dialogical and involve the dreamer in constant, complex, interactive relationships epitomizing the underlying communal nature of the visionary experience.

Because the basic method of the analysis is comparative, the dream contents are analyzed in terms of various topological, imagistic, and intentional structures in order to disclose the shared or differential characteristics that contribute to the organization of the Plains visionary traditions. This shared set of characteristics is designated the *visionary epistemé*. This epistemé is based in religious worldviews that are enhanced and qualified according to individual visionary experiences, which are then integrated into broadly shared repertoires of behaviors, attitudes, and enactments that are found throughout the Plains area. By comparing the various dreams and their manifestations in both a communal and an individual context, it is possible to give an overview of the vision in Plains religion that is congruent with related dreaming practices in other areas of North America.

The danger of any hermeneutic analysis is the tendency to detach the phenomenon under consideration from its appropriate cultural context and to ignore issues of multilayered meaning attributed to the phenomenon by informed members of the cultural community in a context of day-to-day life.[6] Wherever possible such references have been reconstituted to give a contextual depth and meaning to the subject. My primary intent has been to present the full range and complexity of the Plains visionary traditions and to consider other aspects of religious traditions only insofar as they help broaden, on a comparative basis, a general understanding of the centrality of dreams and visions to a Plains Indian worldview.

While the relationship of dreaming to Plains religions is recognized in the early ethnography, the writers' paramount concern was to show how dreaming reinforced social organization. The present work directs itself toward uncovering a phenomenology of perception and knowledge as it contributes to religious maturity and personal empowerment rather than toward a strictly "social" presentation of the materials. The ethnographic text, functioning as a multilevel, multivalent resource, expresses religious experience primarily in terms of a mythic worldview. Part of my task has been to clarify the relationship between experience, perception, and religious thought as framed in the context of mythic discourse. Anyone familiar with Native American materials will recognize immediately the intrinsically mythical character of religious thought and action. This is perhaps one of the most interesting and challenging areas of analytic concern—to uncover the power and reality of the mythic world as the primary means for interpretive discourse. Dreaming will be shown to play an essential role in the formation and maintenance of the mythic world in Plains religions.

Finally, it is important to note that the following interpretation has arisen out of my deep interest in dreams and dreaming as religious phenomena. My stance on this issue is to support a religious interpretation of dreaming as primary and irreducible to other interpretive models of a nonreligious sort. The powerful and vivid ways in which dreams function to enhance personal awareness and ability within the Plains Indian religious context continues to be a viable model for many Native Americans in the contemporary world. This work is offered as an investigation into the primal world of dreaming, within a particular historical and ecological context, that seeks to understand the spiritual and religious significance of the dream experience without reducing it to nonreligious theories of interpretation. Through this approach, I hope to maintain a viable relationship with the continuity of the dreaming tradition among contemporary peoples both of a native and non-native background.

CHAPTER ONE

Culture, Dreams, and Theory

Dream data may hold the potential for initiating an epistemological paradigm shift in the Kuhnian sense of a scientific revolution. This claim is not made lightly . . . in order to accommodate the peculiarities of "anomalous" cognitive operations and the apparently constructive views that dream data provide, the potential exists to force, if not a cardinal paradigm shift, then at least a significant ordinal shift in conceptualizing the operations of the mind in both the sleeping and waking state.

—R. E. Haskel, "Cognitive Psychology and Dream Research: Historical, Conceptual, and Epistemological Considerations"

WE ALL DREAM. This is not a supposition, but part of our lived experience as human beings. If we forget or do not attend to our dreams, to the images and activities that come to us unbidden, it is because our cultural environment does not support a means by which dreaming could transform and revitalize our awareness. Dreams express complex moments of encounter and manifestation that surpass the constraints of purely rational thought, because dreaming engages not only the rational aspects of mind but also deeper and more enigmatic potentials. Through dreaming, the temporal immediacy of everyday consciousness is unbound from its sensory and empirical condition and flows into an altered awareness in which past, present, and future are manifested as the indefinite and powerful imagery of our shared spiritual and cultural history. This is particularly true of the mythic structures and contents of religious history. To understand the visionary world of Native American religions, it is therefore necessary to overcome the rational bias that reduces dreaming to an expression of the "irrational" mind.

Because we all dream, it would seem unnecessary to point out the continuity that exists between our dreaming and waking lives. Yet it is a mark of modern consciousness that dreaming is strongly identified with the "pre-rational" mind and with a substratum of "primitive" instinct and emotion beneath the threshold of rational conceptualization. The dreaming basis of culture must engage our attention as something far more complex and subtle than a purely sensory and empirical model of consciousness permits. The unbound depth of dreaming touches not only the immediate, lived world of everyday existence and perception, but it also enters into both our individual and our collective history. The boundaries between the immediate present and archaic past can join, merge, and such interactions can creatively result in new awareness and insight. The medium for this mergence is dreaming, uninhibited by rational suppression or denial.

A successful religious theory of dreams needs to take into consideration the long-enduring psychohistorical development of shared belief, shared imagery, and shared social and symbolic processes that underlies the experience of the dreaming individual. Such is the paradox of the dreaming experience: to bear witness to the power and depth of the psyche while simultaneously trying to mediate that power into socially recognizable channels not wholly adequate to bear the full complexity of the experience. It is important to recognize that in studying the dreaming basis of culture, we are coming to an encounter with depths of experience that cannot be contained within the normative, cognitive models of the dominant culture. The development of a fully adequate anthropology of dreaming and its relationship to any religious worldview is a task of the generations. Simultaneously, it is necessary to recognize the transformative effect that dreaming has on the dreamer—the many ways in which the shared contents of dreaming have shaped the perceptions and experiences of the "everyday." All dreamers are part of an ongoing encounter or drama of cultural enactment by which culture itself is transformed. This dynamic, transformative experience, enacted through dreaming as well as through waking, represents the challenge all dreamers and visionaries set for themselves: to unite and develop a meaningful continuity between the dreaming and waking worlds.

A THEORETICAL OVERVIEW

The history of Native American dream analysis has been intimately tied to the theoretical concerns and preoccupations of Euro-American psychologists, all of whom have developed their models in contexts divorced from the religious orientations of Native American dreamers. It is remarkable to consider that dream theory, as a form of cultural hegemony, has dominated the analytic scene in Native American studies until only very recently. The Freudian model of dream analysis gained an early foothold among a number of American anthropologists and retained its theoretical dominance in dream interpretation into the late 1960s.[1] This approach, which posits a theoretical distinction between the "latent" and "manifest" contents of the dream experience, is primarily based on a hermeneutics of suspicion.

In the Freudian model, the dream is regarded as a manifestation of a repressed, displaced, and instinctually determined content, the dream itself being regarded as a "sign" of the hypothetically constructed constituents of Freudian theory.[2] This fundamentally theoretical approach to the dream content, and its identification with predetermined instinctual contents, creates a climate of suspicion with regard to the value or significance of the manifest dream. It is not the significance of the manifest dream per se but the greater signification of the "hidden and disguised" content latent in the dream experience that matters. The radical transformation of the recognized content into a relatively narrow and limited set of "universal" instinctual paradigms tends to direct analytic attention toward theoretical constants rather than toward an appreciation of the actual, diverse experience of the dreamer.[3] This "climate of suspicion" surrounding the actual content of dreaming alienates dreaming experience from the waking state. Further, because the contents of dreams are thought of as irrational signs of bio-instinctual pro-

cesses—in contrast to the rational processes of everyday awareness—dreaming has been incorporated into the pathological
branch of the psychological sciences.[4]

A second approach to dreams, developed by a number of
anthropologists using the Boasian historical method, saw dreams
and visions as reflecting various cultural traits and "patterns."
Ruth Benedict, writing on the concept of the guardian spirit in
Native American religion, attempted to analyze the vision complex as expressive of the historical distribution of particular traits
and their psychological validity with regard to particular religious practices.[5] While this approach, like that of many other
descriptive ethnographies, is concerned with the primacy of the
dream experience, the content of dreams is strictly a secondary
issue given little attention or analysis. The early anthropological
interest in dreams and dreaming was directed toward the way
in which dreaming reinforced Anglo-American anthropological
categories (or "patterns"). The conventional idea that dreams
are a "stereotyped" means for the determination of social behavior and role identification was widely accepted. In such an approach, the specific, immediate content of the dream experience
is regarded as peripheral to the extrinsic demands of social con-
formity and adaptation. This mechanistic social model of dreaming, dependent upon its own theoretical biases, reinforces the
tendency to invalidate the individual contents of dreaming and
emphasizes the primacy of the social identity of the dreamer.[6]

By mid-century, the culture and personality school of anthropology, dominated by such figures as George Devereux (1951),
Irving Hallowell (1955), and Anthony Wallace (1958), and summarized by Roy D'Andrade (1961), had integrated both of the
previously mentioned analytic strategies into current personality models. Dream contents, while still regarded as being "inco-
herent, illogical," are taken to be expressive of *select* cultural
experience.[7] The pattern concept of dreaming is reinterpreted in
terms of over- or underdetermination, omission, and distortion
of dream materials with regard to existing cultural norms. The
analysis of latent symbols, taken over from psychoanalytic practice, is recognized but with an increasingly skeptical regard for
the symbols' "universal" contents. Devereux, a neo-Freudian,
expressed a remarkable disregard for the religious significance

of Native American dreaming by reducing all dreams to compensatory defense mechanisms.[8]

Exceptional among these writers is Hallowell, who, recognizing the formative power of the sociocultural environment, also recognized the validity of the Native American view of dreaming as a source of personal empowerment.[9] Hallowell's theory of "self" as a socially constructed reality is posited on the recognition that dreaming and the dream experience are an essential, formative process that works through the manifest contents of the dream. Furthermore, the dream as an integral part of the formation of self is recognized as an intrinsic element of the sociocultural environment and not merely as an experience in the service of determined social patterns. Wallace, while maintaining a precarious balance between behavioral theory and the psychoanalytic disavowal of dream contents, nevertheless recognized a certain "intuitive sophistication" in Iroquois dream practices.[10] While there was an increasing shift to reevaluate the manifest over the latent contents of dreams, the dominant paradigm was still strictly in the service of understanding the overall structure of culturally defined adaptation. The "deviant and distorting" structure of dream contents were regarded as expressive of their fundamentally compensatory and latent contents.[11]

During this same period, however, the experimentally oriented dream research being done by William Dement and Nathan Kleitman in the broader context of clinical sleep research had empirically validated the existence of observable dreaming cycles as normal to all their human subjects.[12] This kind of research, still being carried on as an important concern today, represents a third stream of influence in the anthropology of dreaming. While the validation of the dreaming experience, in the context of direct reports made by dreaming subjects in the laboratory and of measurable physiological correlates such as REM and non-REM (NREM) sleep states, has led to the confirmation of the unquestionable existence of the dream experience, it has simultaneously posited the experience as an expression of random—and therefore meaningless—neurophysiological activity. The gap between the dream as biology and the dream as meaningful, intentional experience has yet to be closed, and it represents a continuing area of debate among academic psychologists.[13]

Another stream of influence, strongly associated with clinical research, has come from cognitive and imagistic psychology. Roy D'Andrade noted an early, critical distinction between dream interpretation and dream analysis.[14] This distinction has been carried over into contemporary cognitive theory. Dream interpretation, early identified with psychoanalysis, involves the recognition of underlying motivations and origins of dream materials, particularly in terms of theoretically identified causes. This causal structure, intimately tied to the developmental stages of the individual, has remained limited to a narrow range of instinctually determined patterns. Jungian dream interpretation, while broadening the range of the causal structure to include collective and bipolar, archetypal patterning, has also limited itself to relatively few such processing patterns.[15]

Dream analysis, on the other hand, has concerned itself with either the social, demographic contents of dreaming or with the shared cognitive processes that characterize fundamental activities of the dream experience. This research has been carried out almost exclusively by academic psychologists among a very limited range of subjects (young Caucasian male college students). Cognitive research in dreaming has tended to concern itself almost exclusively with the process of dreaming—the "how" of dreaming as an information processing event—and has shown little interest in the sociofunctional or symbolic-cultural significance of dreams. The problem of the intention and purpose of dreaming has come to be regarded in much cognitive research as a secondary and nonessential concern.[16]

A related line of development in dream analysis has been extensive research in the area of altered states of consciousness (ASC). This research has emphasized the demographic and social dimensions of human experience. Gaining recognition in the work of Charles Tart (1972) and Erika Bourguignon (1972), this research has been carried over into the study of dreams and dreaming by a number of well-known researchers.[17] Research in ASC has been oriented to the task of developing a shared frame of reference with regard to a wide range of human experiences, including hypnogogia, dreams, visions, nightmares, trances, possession and various types of lucidity, hyperarousal, and psiconducive states (both spontaneous and induced through ritual or drugs). An important discovery of this research has been the recognition of the central role of imagery in the induction of ASCs.[18]

Imagistic research, a development within the cognitive branch of psychology, has been attempting to close the structural gap between constitutive cognitive processes and underlying intentional contents. Regarding imagery as intrinsically cognitive, the "new structuralism" attempts to analyze the image, somatic response, and meaning (ISM) of enhanced, eidetic images as a structural configuration for clinically oriented therapies. Thus the goal of imagery research, as expressed by Akhter Ahsen "is to demolish a petrified concept, to uncover what was hidden, or to discover a new form in order to instill new life where it had not been present before."[19] This research, which involves a straightforward use of phenomenological description as intrinsic to its methodology, approaches imagery on the molar rather than the molecular level.

The image, regarded as a multilayered phenomenon, directly expresses intention and meaning in a spontaneous and dramatic way that is not under the rational control of the individual.[20] Strictly rational interpretation of imagery and dream symbolism has itself come under criticism by new structuralist researchers, particularly insofar as such interpretations have tended to discredit the manifest contents and failed to analyze the imagistic contents as expressive of a wider epistemological range of human awareness. That dreams and dreaming express an inner coherency, a meaningfulness of content that is distinct from the linear, conventional world of waking life, seems subjectively conclusive and obvious.[21] Yet the analytic tendency even in contemporary research has been to devalue dreaming and dream contents because they seem to lack the socially conditioned logic of the everyday. The actual ethnographic content of the dream has either served as grist for the theoretical mills of Euro-American psychologists or has been relegated to a backwater because of the present cognitive schism over the significance of the waking and dreaming states.

COGNITIVE ASYMMETRY

The high degree of marginality of dream studies, coupled with frequently stereotypical ideas about the nature of the dream experience, significantly inhibits an in-depth understanding of the dream within Native American Plains visionary traditions. The centrality of dreaming in the formation of a Plains religious worldview is partly a consequence of the emphasis given to various types of mental and emotional experience. Such an emphasis has some important correlates with studies undertaken in contemporary research on asymmetric brain functions. The Plains visionary worlds certainly represent themselves as expressive of particular kinds of mental contents that are highly imagistic, nonverbal, spatially defined, and emotionally laden. These qualities express characteristic activities of identifiable mental processes. The functional asymmetry of brain activity has been heavily researched and documented, and although a fully synthesized interpretation has yet to be developed, a number of general conclusions are broadly shared among holistic dream researchers.[22]

While earlier research focused on an attempt to distinguish between hemispheric differences in brain functioning, later research has developed a more integrated view of this differentiation by developing an interactive model of cognitive processing.[23] The general distinctions between hemispheric functions have emphasized the left hemisphere as verbal, analytic, linear, rational, and involving the sequential processing of experience and an active, pragmatic interaction with the environment. The right hemisphere has been characterized as imagistic, synthetic, spatial, imaginative, and involved with a holistic and symbolic processing of experience—that is, with a nonlineal, simultaneous or parallel processing of perceptual events. It is characterized by a more passive or receptive mode; its function is "perceiving the world as it is rather than subjecting it to some purpose or design."[24] Furthermore, right-hemisphere activity tends to be strongly associated with altered states of consciousness, such as hypnosis, dreaming, possession, and visionary trance.[25] This cognitive asymmetry, characterized as a "verbal-visual" tension, seems clearly subject to cultural learning processes that have resulted in the development of hemispheric dominance both individually and culturally.

While a general theory of mental processing has led to an interactive model involving an adaptive, dual hemispheric strategy for problem solving and for a potentially coexistent, creative cognitive style, the actual developmental pattern of a majority of Euro-Americans appears to be emphatically left-hemisphere dominant.[26] If we consider the centrality of dreaming and imagistic experience within the Plains religious worldview, it seems evident that Native American culture has a strong right-hemispheric emphasis in its epistemic base. Cultures outside the mainstream of Western intellectual tradition have been recognized as placing more emphasis on visual-spatial orientation and to be more emphatically imagistic and mythic in an interpretive context.[27] This emphasis has frequently been misinterpreted and either ignored or denied by the dominant cultural models used to interpret dreaming among Native American peoples. A more accurate topological description requires a deeper, more salient appreciation of imagistic processes as they contribute to a world-constructing activity in a visually oriented culture.

One way in which the fundamental nature of mental health may be framed is as the fully interhemispheric processing of mental and emotional experience—the ability to actualize several modes of cognitive processing. Not unexpectedly, however, the dominant research in cerebral asymmetry has been largely oriented to left-hemisphere activity. While this research has been primarily concerned with rational, verbal processes, additional research has shown that affective and emotional response is strongly associated with right-hemisphere activity. Imagery has the capacity, unlike mental linguistic processes, to carry strong emotional intensity linked with normally synthetic and integrative functions.[28] Furthermore, research has suggested that the accessibility of right-hemisphere activity to left-hemisphere processing is minimized in culturally left-hemispheric individuals. This is particularly true as the individual moves away from the predominantly right-hemispheric activity of childhood.[29]

Yet the imagistic processing of experience, the analogical formulation of meaning and interpretation, with its rich emotional imagery, represents a primary form of cognition and creative processing—a part-whole process representing the holistic experience of the individual.[30] The visionary dream, so expressive of the Native American religious tradition, as an imagistic processing activity is a central to the Plains visionary experience. But it would be an epistemological error to consider this processing activity a strict expression of either a physiological or a psychological fact. For Native American visionaries, the vision cannot be accurately characterized as a purely psychological event or concept. Rather, the vision is recognized as a form of encounter with mythically defined sources of personal empowerment and as a manifestation of the mysterious contents of a visionary world.

An important contribution of dream research to the understanding of Native American religious visions lies in its articulation of a model in which imagistic events are an emphatic part of all cognitive processes. The distinctive contribution of Native American dreaming traditions to dream research lies in the powerful and dramatic range of the visionary event—a range that lifts dreaming out of its culturally bound research environment and demonstrates the potency and potential of the visionary experience. The Native American dreaming epistemé refers neither to the problem of dream origins nor to how dreams are "constructed" but to the macrolevel of analysis: specifically, how visionary dreams motivate significant behavior, shape belief, thought, and other types of cognitive processing, and influence communally patterned experience and interpretations.

THE VISIONARY EPISTEMÉ

In the Native American context, there is no distinct separation between the world as dreamed and the world as lived. These are states integral to the unifying continuum of mythic description, narration, and enactment. In contemporary, nonindigenous culture, the distinction between waking and dreaming is largely a consequence of culturally reinforced rational theories of mind and has resulted in a bifurcated worldview for most Euro-Americans.[31] The popular notion is to regard dreaming and waking as two distinct and separate types of awareness, the former being largely ignored or having its import reduced to that of a primarily pathological index. A strong majority within the intellectual community continues to regard dreaming as epiphenomenal—a nonessential concomitant of mental health—or as a manifestation of mental activities supporting universalized theories of mental development.[32]

Among traditional Plains peoples, dreaming is given a strong ontological priority and is regarded as primary source of knowledge and power. The visionary dream in Native American religion appropriates a wide spectrum of mental and emotional experiences. There is little evidence to support the claim that the dreams' contents are structured by either rational, sensory modes of awareness or by left-hemispheric linguistic processes. The normally restricted sensory-linguistic empiricism of a demythologized, technocratic culture expresses a cultural bias of the strongest type. It is necessary to recognize that the mythic and religious basis of Native American dreaming works through an epistemé very different from the present cultural epistemé of most Euro-Americans and integrates a diversity of altered states into its normative paradigms of consciousness.

By epistemé I mean, generally, the underlying infrastructures or conceptual frames that organize shared, collective perceptions of the lived world and motivate actions and behavior.[33] Thus an epistemé is a complex, culturally conditioned and learned organization of thought, perception, and action shared within a particular community of people and sanctioned through symbols, images, objects, behavioral norms, and recognized modes of social discourse and interaction. The epistemé represents the shared knowledge of both the individual and the community. In Plains societies, this knowledge has retained a high degree of variability—a variability conditioned by the specific contents of individual dreams.

Theoretical knowledge, typical of the dominant culture, often reveals particular kinds of relations among abstract, intellectual precepts, whereas the dreamer's knowledge has a strong experiential, emotional, and imagistic base. Dream knowledge for Plains visionaries is framed as an existential encounter that participates in alternate modes of awareness and is not dependent upon "philosophic reason." Reason may order or even alter perception through processes of reflection that attempt to bring experience into line with belief so that perception, action and understanding are congruent with immediate perception. But dreaming involves a suspension or transformation of the immediate everyday awareness. While reason may also suspend this awareness, it does so only through the limited activity of rational reflections on either immediate perception or abstract relations. Dreaming experientially *transforms* our sense of the everyday world in a holistic and immediate, emotional encounter, not in a logical or abstract sense.

The distinction between waking and dreaming is dissolved and, in the developed dreamer, becomes an awareness of conscious merging with the visionary realm. The visionary experiences the world as a radically transformed environment whose ecological structures become wholly mythic and superordinate. Reasoning may be regarded as a spiritual activity, thought and analysis as creative efforts; but to epitomize reason as expressive of the highest or best in human functioning is a culturally defined bias—one that demonstrates a loss of the instinctive vitality and relatedness that are necessary for crossing over into the visionary realm through empathy and "human-heartedness." Reason, in both its synthetic and its analytic sense, represents only one epistemic ground and is limited by its frequent usurpation of other vital epistemic means, such as aesthetics, dreaming, myth making, and visionary experience. Reason has its place in the field of human experience, but it need not be regarded as the most significant means for the attainment of knowledge or understanding. Aesthetic, symbolic, and visionary capabilities deserve equal attention as sources fundamental to the formation of any epistemic world.

Mental activity, which is no longer seen as falling under the strict domination of the senses, is not only valid but paramount for the development of personal empowerment and knowledge among the traditional Plains peoples. Dreaming fills out the epistemic base of social and personal life with specific but by no means predictable contents, and its broad continuum of possible mental and emotional states cannot be easily or paradigmatically distinguished from the experience of the "everyday."[34] The visionary epistemé is one that is situated in a mythically defined environment with a unique history in terms of both the mythic contents and the means of transmission of that visionary knowledge.

Moreover, the contents of the visionary dream do not requi
a culturally consistent, rationalized, systematic interpretation.
Dreaming reflects, very strongly, the plurality and polymorphic
nature of Native American religious traditions. Plains Indian
visions participate in a rich and vital process involving both
creative transformation and cultural innovation as well as an
affirmation of cultural continuity. The visionary episteme incorporates this dynamic quality into its infrastructure as normative
and revelatory. Yet the revelatory and polymorphic quality of
dreaming is part of a highly complex and holistic environment.

Another epistemic problem is the tendency for a contemporary reader to accept the general idea of the "unconscious" as a
valid psychological construct. Such a construct is not congruent
with the general episteme of Native American dreamers and
visionaries. Although the concept of the unconscious may be a
useful proposition in certain types of theoretical analysis, it is
nevertheless frequently reified as a psychoanalytic construct. This
reification tends to claim an explanatory power that cannot be
substantiated through any means other than purely theoretical
analysis. The "power of the unconscious" represents a meta-
phorically defined attitude expressive of a modern prejudice—
one that conditions the perception of both self and others, particularly in relationship to dream experiences. A more accurate
and useful construct, in the Native American context, is the frequent distinction made between the "known" and the "mysterious" (or unknown). Because dreams bestow knowledge of both
the known and the mysterious, we can use an epistemological
description that includes the "known" structures of the lived
world—its cosmology, mythology, ecology, and so on—as they
relate to the experiences of the dreamer. This still allows for the
expression of psychic and spiritual activity arising from an "unknown" plane of experience without positing a particular description of a culturally defined psychology.[35]

In the Native American context, dreaming is a form of knowledge. It reveals the activities of the mysterious powers—their
engagement with or relationship to the dreamer. The dream is a
medium of knowing, a way of experiencing the reality of the
lived world, a faculty of perception; the religious vision might
be regarded as an intensification and heightening of this know-

ing. While many analysts have written, rather unconvincingly, about "unconscious" structures of Native American dreaming, they have written very little about the immediate content of experience and its relationship to a culturally shared epistemé. Thus, part of my analytic task is to elucidate the relationship between the "known" and the "unknown," particularly in terms of the visionary experience.

ENFOLDED ORDER

The visionary landscapes of traditional Plains religions are charged with significance and power. In such a world, meaningful events are enfolded into an ecological order that is dynamically charged with the potency of dreaming—a potency that may reveal itself suddenly and dramatically. Any object or place in the natural world might be a means through which dreaming powers are manifested to a dreaming individual. The shared contents of the visionary epistemé participate in a cosmologically and ecologically structured, but informal, world order. This process of ordering, never really dogmatized in a formal sense among the Plains peoples, is facilitated and profoundly affected by the visionary experience. The advanced practitioner, who excels in dreaming, is able to enter the visionary world at will and to unfold the implicit structure of that world in a frequently dramatic demonstration of power and ability. A useful analogue for understanding the processes of visionary experience is the "enfolded" metaphor.

The continuing late-twentieth-century intellectual shift in science and the humanities away from a rigidly Cartesian, determinative, causally conditioned, and mechanistic world order and toward a more holistic, indeterminate, interactive, and nonlocal patterned world of interpersonal events has powerful implications for visionary dream studies. Setting aside the impulse-ordered, instinctual mechanisms of classical psychology and the deterministic models of cultural conditioning, an emergent "postmodern" science of wholeness is gradually being articulated.[36]

Such an orientation begins with a fundamental concept of dynamically active and transformative "patterns of relation" that express at every level of organization a distinctive manifestation of wholeness. A greater totality of possibility and potential order is conceived as always *implicit* in any particular set of discreet, observable phenomena. Rather than seeking to understand a particular culture through a componential, piece-by-piece analysis strictly determined by mechanistic or intellectual principles of hierarchical order and causal relations between parts, one begins by analyzing the process dynamics of an undivided wholeness from which identifiable, stable, and recurrent patterns of only relative autonomy (rather than strict hierarchy) can be identified. These patterns, as *explicit* manifestations, represent "subtotalities" of meaning that can only be described in terms of their relative autonomy or relationship to other patterns of meaning. The fundamental concept is that rather than a fixed world constructed out of a limited set of known, unchanging laws and relations in a static, deterministic manner, there is a world-process of ongoing explicit manifestations of an implicit, emerging, higher-order dynamics that continues to unfold over the generations through a series of reorganized perceptions coupled with new interpretive perspectives.[37]

In this sense, the implicit order of the psyche may be regarded as including not only all sensory, rational, and emotional fields but also the vastness of the visionary realm as an expression of a higher totality or wholeness. In the visionary realms, there are no "parts" or divisions or fixed boundaries that are permanent or metaphysically absolute; there are only relative degrees of unfolding perception. Congruent with visionary experiences, new perceptions can emerge, but they can also be enfolded back into their implicit condition and vanish. The visionary dream may subsequently represent not only a participation in a more congruent, powerful order of perception and wholeness, but also the actual encoded memory of the event: an event highly characteristic of imagistic functioning.

It might be expected that, in a cultural environment strongly based on visionary experience, the central importance of dreaming would be topologically integrated into various types of holistic imagery of the lived world. If the visionary dream expresses an awareness of a higher implicit order, then the explicit or manifest content of the dream would represent an ensemble or subtotality of the visionary order, particularly as embodied in dream images and objects. To enter the dream world means, in this sense, to alter consciousness and enter into an implicit dreaming order—the enfolded, psychic potential of the visionary realm—that has a structural, morphological effect on consciousness.

A particularly important feature of any cultural ensemble or organization of meaning is its self-consistency. Yet a process view of self-consistency requires a means for change, transformation, and the emergence of new experiences and interpretations. This suggests a "bootstrap" view of culture: members of a given community attain more powerful interpretive consistency through the continual generation of diverse interpretive frames. These frames emerge through the processes of visionary experience and the subsequent integration of those experiences into unifying cultural enactments. This process allows for a fundamental pluralism at the heart of the organization of meaning in a dreaming culture and expresses a dialogical unfolding of implicit, potential forms of new or innovative order. The process is ongoing and indefinite, including within itself a quality of indeterminacy indicated by the relationship between the known (explicit) and the unknown (implicit). Among the Plains and Prairie peoples, the enfolded order is the realm of experience that is accessible to the visionary dreamer. The "bootstrap" principle refers to cultural transformation as a process carried out through the dialogical encounter between culture members, an encounter that may challenge or impact the static nature of existent cultural ensembles.[38]

The visionary episteme referred to in this work is that context of experience which, through visionary dreams and encounters, contributes diverse and pluralistic meanings, images, acts, objects, and narratives to an ongoing dialogical process of cultural unfoldment. At any given historical moment, it is expressed by a dynamic (not static) set of relations subject to change and transformation in the processes of human interaction. A characteristic feature of this interactive process may be a visionary leap of consciousness that surpasses the normative cultural forums and enhances or extends existing modes of action or interpretation. In the Native American context, the primary representation of unfolding, new horizons of perception is through manifestations of power, often embodied in the use of dream objects. Interpretations form only a secondarily developed area of concern or interest. The "reality" of the dreaming experience lies in the pragmatic demonstration of new ability and in the dreamer's capacity to unfold the potential, implicit power and drama revealed through the vision experience. The explicit cultural order of religious symbols, icons, rituals, dances, and songs represents a testimony to some form of received, inherited, or purchased power, frequently transmitted through dream experience.

The reality of personal empowerment and its sources is enfolded into the topology of the lived world. It is not an abstract, ideological condition or an expression of a more interpretive, verbal "theology," but a testimony of powerful visionary experience imagistically and emotionally encoded into the living ecology and manifested most often through nonverbal expression and action. The visionary language of belief and experience is part of a holistic relationship between the visionary and the world of explicit phenomena—the sky, the earth, this tree, that butte, this rock, that feather—all of which embody varying degrees of the visionary world and help unfold the potential of a world-revealing process. It is the experienced dreamer's role to explicate that world, to show how the part expresses the whole and how the visionary experience is the door into the hidden order of potential and personal empowerment.

CHAPTER TWO

Greater Plains Cosmography

The world always appears to us as a meaningful structure; it is not mere brute materiality, it always has a face.

—Dreyer Kruger, "The Daseinsanalytic Approach to Dreams"

A CENTRAL FEATURE of Native American Plains religions is the search for personal empowerment through dreams and visions. The sources of these visions are a complex variety of powerful beings that imbue the world with mysterious and unpredictable qualities. The vision, as a form of communication, is fully embedded in a mythic worldview that is inseparable from the natural and social environment within which the visionary enactment is carried out. To better understand the complexity of dreaming among the Plains and Prairie peoples, it is first necessary to given some account of the topology in which the primary features of the visionary world are embedded. This requires a "mapping" of cosmological realms that are congruent with the Plains ecological setting and a recognition of the relatively stable features of that landscape, particularly in terms of how a specific place relates to its social and mythical history.[1]

The meaning and significance of these features of the landscape vary among the different Plains groups (and among individuals), forming a relatively complex series of interrelated dream worlds. The stability of the features in these worlds tends to become invariant only within a particular dreamer's experience. This observation expresses a principle that is germane to the formation of a stable religious world: visionary experience does not occur autonomously but develops out of a process of communal interactions in which the individual plays a creative role. Topological structures function to organize shared perception and meaning, which takes on certain characteristic features reflective of the dreamer's own cultural synthesis. These topological features, like landmarks on a journey, communicate varying degrees of signification, depending on the interests and concerns of the traveler. Those seeking wealth and leadership in war will see certain features as more or less significant than do those who become healers or who excel in conjuring. Men will tend to see or interpret aspects of the dreaming topology in ways distinct from those of women. More specifically, certain aspects in dreaming will be highly indicative of unique and powerful abilities, although there is wide variation in what actually constitutes the truly empowered individual.

In many ways, a topological description is a description of received ideas, social interactions, and personal encounters. The ecology of visionary perception represents a particular way of "seeing" or "knowing" the lived world. The topology is not determined by the physical structure of that world, in the western scientific sense, but by the way in which that world incorporates a variety of mysterious powers, beings, and realms. Physical boundaries are not rigidly distinct, nor are they classified according to any predetermined analytical schema. Among Plains Indian visionaries, there is a strong sense of the continuum between human perception, the natural world, and the mysterious appearance of visionary events—a sense that allows features of the lived world to blend, transform, or suddenly reveal new dimensions of meaning and power. A stone might speak, an animal change into another creature, a star fall to earth as a beautiful woman. The individual's experience of the world is not limited to ordinary motor action or to the five physical senses. It is possible to experience flights into the sky or penetration into the earth or mountains; it is possible to know the future or the distant past or events occurring in faraway places. The collapse of physical boundaries is a consistent feature of the visionary topology. Thus the world constitutes itself as permeable, transformative, mysterious, and powerful.

Furthermore, the topology described here is inseparable from the spiritual or religious dimensions of Native American visionary experience. Going into the dream means going into a transformed, viable, powerful realm of immediate experience. From the dreaming point of view, visionary gifts must be validated and manifested outwardly to receive full credibility. To be regarded as real, the viability of a visionary experience must manifest itself in a context that results in communal recognition. Real dreams of healing must result in acts of healing; dreams of war must lead to successful raids; dreams involving extrasensory perception must be shown to be true. The validation of the religious topology is twofold: first, direct experience in dreams and visions, and second, the demonstration of a specific result.

The result, however, is not attributed to the visionary per se, but to the power of the mysterious being who reveals the dream or vision. The Plains spiritual and religious topology is essentially interactive. The mythically charged world transfers its spiritual potential to the dreamer, who in turn manifests that power in a communally recognized situation. Thus the dream fulfills a primarily religious function by validating to the individual the reality and power of the cosmologic structures that are, in Native American culture, unbound and relative to personal experience.

Another essential feature of the dreaming topology is the specific type of dream or vision under consideration. While recognized categories of dream classifications by various Native American communities will be discussed in a later work, here I am primarily concerned with dreams that involve direct encounters with religiously defined powers and with the abilities that result from those encounters. These are fundamentally "dreams of empowerment" that are directly associated with the mysterious character of the lived world. They are the outstanding psychic events in the emotional and mental life of the individual—visionary experiences that mark the individual and have a determining impact on the dreamer's life. Dreams of empowerment are highly memorable in the social life of the individual; they stand out as important, credible, and provocative of specific actions and behaviors. The memorable dream, collected by the ethnographer, is inevitably the power-bestowing dream. The early ethnography of dreams is already selective in recording primarily this general type—the one recalled as worthy of report and remembrance.[2]

THE BASIC WORLD STRUCTURE

The Plains religious topology is strongly influenced by the shared visionary experiences of dreamers in a context of mythic and religious discourse. The exact relationship between this discourse and the experience of the dreamer remains highly variable and expressive of an open and indeterminate lived world. I have derived the basic structures of this world order primarily from the dreaming ethnography rather than from more general religious conceptions, because my aim is to disclose the shared structures of the dreaming world. Although the following analysis does not represent a particular community's religious worldview explicitly, it nevertheless does represent a widely shared topological orientation, one that reflects many (if not all) traditional Plains religious communities. The degree of explicitness should not be taken to indicate a systematic or rigorously structured topology among a particular group. An essential element of the following description is that it expressives particular types of *experience* that provide the substantive basis for a topological analysis.

One of the most fundamental aspects of the Plains religious topology is its implicit, undivided wholeness. This wholeness constitutes the interactive relationships between many beings, both visible and invisible, whose "homes" are identified with particular ecological environments.[3] The center of this wholeness is the earth itself, regarded as a living being—usually (but not always) a life-giving female. Human beings, the "two-leggeds," live on the earth in shared relationships with all other living creatures, particularly grazing and herding animals—the "four-leggeds" or "grass-eaters." Below, or perhaps more accurately, within both the earth and the water, is another group of beings with special or unique abilities. Above, yet another group of beings extends from the earth up through the sky, the home of the "wingeds," and into the celestial realm of the sun, moon, and stars. Thus there are three interpenetrating strata and their respective realms that constitute the wholeness of the natural world: the above realm, the middle realm, and the below realm. The relationship between these realms can best be described topologically as a distinctive contrast, more or less emphasized, between the above and the below, with the middle representing the mysterious realm in which all beings meet and interact.

Among some communities, particularly the Plains Algonkian-speaking peoples, the distinction between the above and below is more sharply drawn than it is among other Plains groups. For example, E. Adamson Hoebel makes the following comments about the structure of Cheyenne topology:[4]

The universe [*Hestenov*] is multilayered. Human beings view the universe from the Earth's surface. All above the Earth's surface is *heammahestonev*. All that lies below it is *aktunov*. Along the surface of the earth is a thin layer of air, the atmosphere as perceived by the Cheyenne. Called *taxtavo*, it is a special gift of the spirit beings to humankind, for it makes breathing and life possible. Above the air-layer is *setovo*, the Nearer Sky Space. . . . Above everything else is the Blue Sky Space, *aktovo*. Here are visible the sun, the moon, the stars, and the Milky Way. The Earth itself consists of two layers. The first is the very thin strip which supports life. It is only as deep as the roots of plants and trees can penetrate. It is known as *votoso*. Beneath it is the stratum called *aktunov*, the Deep Earth.

A similar classification of this type can be found among the Algonkian-speaking Blackfoot of western Montana as recorded by Edward Curtis: "*Spómitapi*, People-Above, including all visible objects of the heavens . . . and *Kshá'kom-mitapi*, Earth-People, including all the spirits of the creatures of the earth and air."[5] In some cases it is possible to find this topology to be explicitly delineated within the context of a particular Native American community.[6]

A similar contrast can be found among the Siouan-speaking peoples as embodied in a more conflictive tension or opposition between the *Wakinyan*, or thunder powers, above and the water-dwelling Unktehi, or Water Monster, below. The Teton Sioux George Bush Otter narrated the following to James Dorsey about the thunder beings:[7]

Some of these ancient [Thunder] people still dwell in the clouds. They have large curved beaks resembling bison humps, their voices are loud, they do not open their eyes except when they make lightning. . . . Their ancient foes were the giant rattlesnakes and the prehistoric water monsters."[8]

The three strata were even more finely distinguished by the Omaha, who delineated seven distinct spirit worlds.[9] Through the power of dreaming it is possible to be in communication with any of the beings that inhabit these many different worlds and to contribute to the shared discourse on the nature of these realms. In advanced dreaming, it is possible to move and journey through those realms and to return with extraordinary knowledge or abilities.

Many geographic features of the topology are experienced as living beings of all types. These beings, including both known animals and natural objects as well as many unknown powers, inhabit the various strata of the lived world and may be encountered at any time. Dreams and visions are one of the most fundamental means for discovering the "living" quality of the natural world, and this quality frequently leads to a conscious shaping of objects that are intended to communicate power to others. A prominent feature of the topology is the tangible, sensory immediacy of the visible dream world. The landscape of the real, lived world is also the landscape of the dream world. A constant topological feature is the interpenetration of the natural environment of visible presences—the specific and real object— and the visionary world of dreaming that embodies the potency and power conveyed to the dreamer. And this manifest aspect of the dream world is visible not only to the dreamer but to anyone initiated into the primary, enfolded order of dreaming.

The most fundamental feature of the visionary epistemé is the richness of its mythic contents and the vitality of its dynamic powers. Sacred figures that appear in visions, called here *dream-spirits*, can be said to inhabit any feature of the waking or sleeping continuum. To be in a visionary state is essentially to have contact with those powers that inhabit the living ecology of the world strata. The topological structure of that ecology, its rough division into upper, middle and lower strata that are intimately connected and dynamically related, expresses something of the type of power associated with each stratum. Yet, a dream-spirit is an embodiment of a particular power, interpreted differently according to the experience of the dreamer. The mutability of the world structure, its metamorphic characteristics, and the heterogeneous nature of mythic discourse about those powers do not allow for a rigorously determined typology of such dream-spirits. The most accurate summary would suggest that individual dreamers come to understand the nature and power of visionary figures in terms of their own personal encounters, of the ways in which these encounters come to be interpreted both by the dreamer and by knowledgeable elders, and of the way these encounters and interpretations impact the life of the community.[10]

THE MIDDLE POWERS

While the general topology of the Semitic religious traditions has tended to posit the existence of divinity as synonymous with the "heavenly" or "celestial" realm, the middle realm is the more primary arena of religious manifestation and empowerment in Plains religious topology. Visionary dreams of all types generally begin (and often remain) in a recognizable, natural environment. They contextualize, in the simplest form, an extension of the normal, lived world into the visionary realm. David Mandelbaum, writing about the adolescent vision quest of the Plains Cree of central Canada, gives a good description of the most fundamental form of the visionary dream in the context of a natural setting:[11]

While the boy slept, he might see a person coming toward him. It was the power that was to be his spirit-helper. The visitor identified himself, often changing into the guise of its namesake. The boy was led to an assemblage of spirit-powers, all in human form, who sat around a great tipi. There the youth was told the gifts that had been granted him. Very often he was informed that he would be able to cure the sick. The procedure he must follow and the song to be used were then revealed.

This dream experience takes place in a context that recreates both the natural and the social environment of the dreamer. The boy fasts away from camp in the natural environment where he is met by an elder who leads him to another camp. There, in the company of a protective messenger spirit, a council of human-appearing dream-spirits instructs him. They meet in a normal habitation in a natural social setting, and the boy is given instructions, songs, and frequently objects to help him actualize his powers. These powers were normally quiescent until middle age, when other dream experiences would signify that the time had come to begin healing.[12]

The entire context of the vision is enfolded into the immediacy of the natural environment, but it is an environment charged for the Plains Cree by the presence of the *atayoh-kanak*, those mysterious beings that appear in visionary dreams. These powers are pervasive and might inhabit any object of the natural environment.[13] Or they might appear suddenly and unexpectedly to an individual or group, as they did to the old Cree warrior Twin Buffalo while he was out hunting with some young men. The group saw a bear attack and kill some buffalo. Subsequently, one of the younger buffalo rolled on the ground: "When it got up, it had the form of a man holding a lance. The bear was afraid of this one. When it tried to escape, the man attacked it. He stabbed the bear and killed it. Then he threw himself on the ground; when he arose, there was again that young buffalo. So that young buffalo ran away; it made for the open prairie."[14]

The narrator of the incident is Twin Buffalo's nephew, and it is reported as something actually seen and experienced. Such an incident reveals the visionary epistemé as a mutable, transformative realm in which the dream-spirits can manifest in a vivid and visionary way without any special ritual conditions having been observed or any conscious intent to dream being present. No distinction is drawn between the waking state and the visionary state: they are one and the same.[15]

Alfred Kroeber, writing in 1914 about the Arapaho of Wyoming, recorded the visionary experience of a middle-aged Arapaho man:[16]

A man fasted on a hill for four days, crying. The fourth morning, at sunrise, he saw a badger. The badger stood up on his hind legs and turned into a naked man painted red over his body. This badger-man looked like an image of the man who saw him. He was an untrue person, or spirit. He directed the faster to use a badger skin for his medicine-bag. To the badger belong all medicines that grow on the ground.

Again, the context is that of the natural environment. No journey or movement is mentioned: the vision unfolds its contents in perfect congruity with the fasting place, a place charged with potential. The middle realm is pervaded by the "four-legged" animals who are capable of manifesting themselves as powerful dream-spirits, bestowing gifts on the dreamer. Thus any animal might metamorphose into a dream-spirit that appears as human but is in fact a specific image of a particular animal power. The appearance of the dream-spirit is not confined to a single animal but can be manifested as any number of such animals.[17] Furthermore, the human form is often an image that imitates the appearance of the dreamer. This aspect of the visionary epistemé involves the symbolic relationship between the visionary and the power that he or she receives. The reciprocal relationship is expressed in a powerful vision as the self to which the vision is manifested—a type of symbolic reflexivity that is not uncommon. The dream-spirit takes the form of the dreamer as a symbolic expression of the intimate link between the power and its user.[18]

Of the many creatures of the middle realm, the four-legged herding animals such as the buffalo, elk, deer, and antelope were regarded as possessing particular qualities and powers. For example, elk power among the Sioux was explained by Shooter and Brave Buffalo to Frances Densmore:[19]

Shooter explained: "The Elk . . . is the emblem of beauty, gallantry, and protection. The Elk lives in the forest and is in harmony with all his beautiful surroundings. He goes easily through the thickets, notwithstanding his broad branching horns."

Brave Buffalo: "When I was seated [in a vision] the Elks rose and said they had heard that I was a great friend of the buffalo, and they wanted me to be their friend also. They said they had tested me by requiring me to reach this difficult place, and as I had succeeded in doing so they were glad to receive me."

Here can be seen the fundamental idea of the harmony that exists between the human beings, the animals, and the environment. In the topology of the middle realm, animal powers are seen as allies and friends who wish to assist human beings and grant them special powers. The nature of the relationship between the human and the visionary being involves testing and trial. Every creature inhabiting the visible world is a potential giver of power, but not every human being can be a recipient of that power. Fasting, prayer, trial, and testing are normative practices within the visionary epistemé. The elk is a particularly beneficent power often associated, for men, with the ability to attract women and to excel in love-magic—but elk can also grant the power to kill an enemy.[20] Dual powers are frequently among the gifts of the dream-spirits and often express a synthesis of contrasts in the world of the dreamer. The visionary topology is constantly functioning as a means for integration and reintegration of conflictive aspirations or social demands. As an intentional structure, this integrative feature symbolizes the diversity inherent in the manifestation of power by a single individual.

Dream-spirits are by no means confined to manifesting themselves as animal powers. They can also appear as any aspect of the natural environment. Clark Wissler recorded the following from an old Blackfoot of Montana and southern Saskatchewan:[21]

Near the old agency is a large rock upon the side of the hill. Once I went there to sleep and this rock gave me the power to cure diseases. It gave me a little drum. I dreamed that I was on the inside of a tipi and that the rock became a man. The rock man was about to doctor a skeleton. He had three red hot stones. He picked up one in his hands and began to lick it. . . . No injury was done him. One after another, he took up all the heated stones. . . . It was in this dream that I was given the power to handle red hot stones.

This type of manifestation is widespread over the entire plains area and throughout North and Central America. The mysterious powers of the middle realm may be manifested as any of a large variety of natural forms; stones are regarded as particularly powerful, enduring objects. Any natural object may suddenly reveal to the dreamer some extraordinary power or ability. This is an essential feature of the enfolded mystery of the lived world—its inherent capacity to reveal its concealed potential to the dreamer. Furthermore, this manifestation verifies the general structures of religious belief. The power that is given demonstrates the real existence of the enfolded or "hidden" order. The unusual ability to handle red-hot stones, for example, is a validation that occurs in a communal, social context. The efficacy of such a demonstration confirms the reality of empowerment to other members of the community. The demonstration has an important intentional structure: to validate, in an observable manner, the extraordinary ability resulting from a gift of power.

A power that is bestowed might be a general feature of the natural environment, rather than a particular object. In this sense, any place where dream power has manifested itself might come to be regarded as a topos for contact with a mysterious being. Ernest Wallace and Adamson Hoebel, collecting among the Comanche in northern Texas, recorded the following with regard to Medicine Mounds in Hardman County:[22]

A Comanche medicine man first discovered its great power when once his band came to hunt in the vicinity of the mounds. He had a young and beautiful daughter who was ill of fever and was growing weaker and weaker day by day. . . . He had mixed and tried his formulae in every way he knew. He had consulted other medicine men. But all without results. One morning he came out of his tipi and in despair was gazing silently into the distance when suddenly his eyes came to rest on the rock-capped peak of the highest mound. Here was a powerful spirit that could help him, he thought. So without touching food or water, he went apart to pray and fast until the spirit should send him a revelation. At length it came. He was instructed to take his medicines to the high rock and there to mix them so that the good spirit should enter into them. He prepared the medicine as directed by the vision, gave it to his daughter and then went out and prayed to the mound spirit. . . . From that hour she mended steadily and soon was able to return to work. Thereafter this medicine man made regular visits to the mound, made offerings to the mound spirit, and performed his cures through its aid. The fame of the mound spirit spread. Other medicine men came. From the gypsum waters of a spring at the base of the mounds, the ailing Comanche came to drink. The spirit came to be a protector for the Comanche bands.

Here can be seen the clear foundations of the visionary epistemé. A memorable feature of the landscape is recognized by the medicine man to be a potential ally for healing. After he receives the visionary instructions, the efficacy of the vision is manifested in the healing of his daughter. The dream-spirits reside, in potential, awaiting some critical event that will catalyze a visionary experience that culminates in a visible manifestation of power, which is then recognized and sought by others. The efficacy of this visionary power can act as a center for an entire corpus of beliefs and practices originating in the experience of a single visionary. The telling of the original manifestation comes to be an essential feature of the establishment of communal belief. Thus, the building up of the visionary epistemé proceeds in terms of direct experience, pragmatic validation, and shared narrative traditions. While among the Comanche, a visionary might have several such dream-spirits, the community selectively incorporates individual experiences into the shared structures of visionary rites and behavior.[23]

THE BELOW POWERS

All prominent features of the below realm are inhabited by certain animals or mysterious beings that can be known through dreams or visions. The realm's most outstanding topological features are the various buttes, river bluffs, and deep-water pools of the plains and prairie environment. The buttes are believed to be the dwelling places of specific dream-spirits, and many people go to them to seek visions. The successful dreamer is often taken inside the butte, which is conceived of as the earth lodge of a particular dream-spirit. The butte is approached carefully as a place of power, and it is considered unwise to go to the very top of Bear Butte because the degree of power there might be overwhelming.[24]

According to the Pawnee ethnography, there are seven sacred bluffs on the Platte River in Nebraska that are considered to be the homes of animals from which a dreamer could attain various powers. Gene Weltfish recorded the following narrative about a young boy named Small who, around 1850, fell asleep while hunting along the South Platte:[25]

He had had a vision and gone to the [underwater] animal lodge. The animals had taken him in. When he awoke he was sitting east of the fireplace with his bow and arrows. There were different kinds of animals all around. Near the door was a big snake. Near the altar at the west was Scalped Man, Kitsahuruksu, who was the boss of them all.

For four nights . . . each animal taught the boy a different way. After all had performed, the mole told of his power [and] . . . the weasel said, "While he is looking at me, I can eat up a man's liver." . . . In this way Small came to know that these two were bad animals and because of what he had learned about them, he was able to practice sorcery, as well as to cure sickness.

Certain earth-dwelling animals are consistently represented as dangerous or harmful powers. For the Pawnee, witchcraft and sorcery are frequently associated with the mole and the weasel. These animals as dream-spirits gave powerful ability to the dreamer to harm or even kill enemies or other Pawnee. Visionaries received various ambiguous and dangerous powers (from all strata) that could be turned against other human beings, even within the same community. Yet the visionary incorporated these destructive elements as congruent with the visionary epistemé.[26]

In this context, two chthonic dream-spirits should be mentioned: rattlesnake and Water Monster. These two beings of the below realm function in a very ambiguous way within the dream texts. For the Oto of northeast Kansas, to dream of rattlesnakes is dangerous, for it precedes the coming and probable attack of enemy tribes.[27] An identical interpretation is found among the Blackfoot.[28] Among the Mandan of North Dakota, the holy man Cherry Necklace was given power by a snake that allowed him to poison people, even though the text adds that "he poisoned through habit, not meanness, and everyone respected and feared him."[29] Robert Lowie, working among the Assiniboine of northeastern Montana, recorded the following narrative:[30]

Suddenly, in the night, he heard a sound and beheld a large number of rattlesnakes approaching him. He did not know what to do. He began cutting off strips of flesh from his own body and fed them to the snakes. Then one very large snake arose from its hole, and thus addressed him. "I am thankful to you for feeding my children. None of the other men have done this before. . . . Come, follow me, there is one that wishes to speak to you." The youth went down into the hole and was ushered to a large blue tent, encircled by two large snakes. He was welcomed by two curly-haired black men, who spoke Assiniboine to him, and from them and the snakes he received religious instructions.

Thus the ambiguous and obviously dangerous power of the snake, particularly of the poisonous type, could communicate a *positive* ability to the dreamer that enabled him to heal and from which he could receive visionary knowledge. No animal or dream-spirit is unilaterally bad or destructive; all are capable of giving knowledge and power to vision seekers. Such knowledge was also received by a famous Absarokee healer, Slippery Eyes, when he was taken to the underground tipi home of a great one-eyed horned snake.[31]

This empowering of the dreamer by the hidden powers of the earth, whose ambiguity could be transformed into either destructive or creative manifestation, helps to fill out the topological structure. The visionary world contains mysterious potential for good and for harm, not in a strictly categorically defined manner but in terms of the way in which power is received and used. Empowerment, the dialectic between destructive and creative potential, is not cosmologized into a conflict between dual forces. Yet the potential for destructive behavior is linked, through visionary experience, with certain dangerous and ambiguous animals (and mythic beings such as Scalped Man) who embody the dangerous character of the lived world. Even a destructive act such as poisoning might not be regarded as "evil" but simply as an indication of a particularly potent form of power whose use served to protect the visionary from threatening or hostile individuals.[32]

The great western rivers such as the Missouri, the Platte and the Republican are regarded as the dwelling places of another dangerous dream-spirit: Water Monster. This semimythical being, while dreaded, is also able to confer positive dreaming powers. In the visionary topology, water places and water-dwelling creatures are regarded as dangerous, for drowning was always a possibility, and mysterious, because creatures of the water dwell in a nonhuman world. Among the Siouan peoples, Water Monster is conceived of as locked in a struggle with the above thunder powers, and dreaming of Unktehi (Water Monster) could be extremely dangerous because of the type of power that the dreamer might be given.[33]

Among the Omaha of eastern Nebraska, the secret society of

the Inkugthi Athin ("those having the translucent pebble") consisted of members who had dreamed of Water Monster or of the "translucent pebble," the symbolic object used to convey the power of the vision. This giant creature that lashed and stirred up the waters of the great rivers gave protective power and healing medicine to the dreamers, who would paint their bodies with designs meant to identify them with the creature.[34] Such interconnectedness demonstrates how the mythic world and the natural topology are unified and strengthened through visionary experience. The pebble is considered to be in the body of the dreamer, and the dreamer would, under certain ritual conditions, be able to reproduce this pebble. Thus even a simple object like a pebble could be imbued with the mysterious power of a mythic presence.

Other examples of powers that dwell in the great rivers and appear in dreams can be found among the Sioux. While dreaming, Lone Man beheld nine riders coming toward him and was told by them to attack an enemy painted red and standing in the water.[35] This vision narrative is very similar to the account given by the Sioux holy man Black Elk during his great vision: "I could see the country as I went [through the sky] and I remember well seeing in the forks of the Missouri River a man standing amid a flame with the dust around him in the air. I knew then that this was the enemy which was going to attack me. I could see all kinds of creatures dying beneath me, as he had destroyed everything."[36] The man (representing drought) eventually transforms into a turtle and everyone is healed, revealing once again the ambiguity of these figures: they hold both destructive and healing power.[37]

Another example can be drawn from a Kiowa-Apache narrative having to do with the origins of the Four Quartz Crystal bundle. After fasting for many days near the Medicine Water, a hot spring located in the Black Hills, a young Kiowa-Apache warrior was tested by a number of frightening visionary beings from the waters, including the ghost of a young boy killed by Apaches, until he was invited into an underwater lodge and given special instructions.[38] The text illustrates the ambiguity of these chthonic water powers: the visionary is required to demonstrate fearlessness before he can successfully receive the powers granted by the vision.

Foremost among the inner-earth powers are the pervasive presences of the buffalo and the bear. These primal beings, whose dwelling places and origins are thought to be within the earth, are the two most prominent and consistently experienced dreamspirits. The bear is seen to retreat into its earth den during the winter and then reappear in the early spring. As an earth power, the bear is regarded by many Plains peoples as the one animal closest to human beings.[39] Seen rearing on its hind legs and speaking and gesturing in a human fashion, this powerful, erratic creature is a primary source of medicinal knowledge. The Sioux Two Shields explained bear power: "Two Shields said, 'The bear is the only animal which is dreamed of as offering to give herbs for the healing of man. The bear is not afraid of either animals or men and it is considered ill-tempered, and yet it is the only animal which has shown us this kindness.'"[40]

Respect for the healing medicine given by the bear is widespread over the Great Plains and much of North America. Native Americans, as acute observers of nature, affirm an interconnectedness of animal behavior, personal power, and visionary experience as an essential feature of the dreaming topology. Meaningful behavior is attributed to a unique, innate knowledge that is possessed by every animal and every species. This knowledge is communicated through dreaming to the individual. The topology of the dreaming continuum is inseparable from the explicit behavior of any animal and is manifested through a variable content that is shaped by both communal ideas and personal experiences. The types of power bestowed by bear are highly diverse, ranging from warrior power and courage to many different types of medicine or healing. The ambiguity of the bear's power—its fierceness, irascibility, and unpredictable behavior—contributes to this diversity.

Bear power illustrates another prominent feature of the Plains topology, its variability or its communal openness to interpretation and reinterpretation. The context of interpretation, which will be explored later, is based on diversity in experience—a diversity that is "unbounded" because there is no closure on the contents of visionary experience. Every dreamer has the potential for meaningful and varied dreams, even when the source of the dream is attributed to the same animal. Deward Walker gives the sense of this variability with regard to the acquiring of bear power among the Nez Perce of Idaho:[41]

There were marked variations in the way particular tutelary spirits manifested themselves [through dreams] to different individuals. One person might obtain self-curative power from Wounded Buffalo, and another receive bravery power from Charging Buffalo. On the other hand, a person might obtain only a small part of the total power conferrable by Grizzly Bear, whereas yet another would get all of Grizzly's power.

The underground habitation of the bear led to many visionary encounters in which the dream-spirit would emerge from the earth (or den) to grant power to the dreamer. Among the Piegan Blackfoot of Montana, some of the oldest traditions of visionary experience relate to the bear, whose image was painted on the traditional dream tipis. John Ewers gives an example of a young Blackfoot who specifically went to fast in a bear den, hoping to receive power. On the fourth night a male and female bear appeared, each giving him a painted tipi along with a blackstone pipe and a drum: "Then the mother bear gave him a knife with a bear-jaw handle. She threw the knife at him and he grabbed it before it could harm him. The bears gave him a song to go with it—'A knife is just like dirt thrown against me.'"[42]

Again we can see the intimate relationship between the social environment, the natural world, and the reality of the visionary encounter. The tipi expresses in symbols and social imagery the actual experience as empowering both the dreamer and his home. The tipi is actually owned by the bear and is a gift to the dreamer, who makes a representation of it. The visionary experience is enfolded into the social environment as dwelling, pipe, drum, and song. The knife is thrown in a ritual transfer of power; this method is also used when a bear dreamer sells his bundle to another. Consequently, a bear's den or the appearance of a real bear might be cause for cautious behavior that is motivated by a visionary orientation. The power of the dream-spirit imbues the social world with its unique presence (as imaged on the tipi), and in this way the social environment encodes a wide variety of potent and powerful forms expressive of the immediate presence of the visionary experience.[43]

Keeping strictly to the dreaming ethnography, the most frequent of all below powers to appear in visions is the buffalo. Almost half the visions recorded include the appearance of this dream-spirit. The gifts given by the buffalo tend to be gifts of healing, hunting, and leadership, for the buffalo was considered by many Plains peoples to be a strong and cooperative being. It gave its body for the feeding of the people and its strength to encourage and guide the people in the present and future. In the dream narratives, the buffalo does not appear often as war power but generally expresses life-preserving values and practices. The following example, selected from many such narratives, illustrates a number of symbolic and topological features commonly found in buffalo dreams. Frank Linderman, collecting stories among the Absarokee, recorded this remarkable first-person narrative of a youthful vision (c. 1860) from the renowned warrior and tribal leader, Plenty Coups:[44]

I dreamed. I heard a voice at midnight and saw a Person standing at my feet in the east. . . . I saw a Buffalo bull standing *where we are sitting now*. I got up and started to go to the Bull. . . . The other Person was gone. . . . On that hill over yonder was where I stopped to look at the Bull. He had changed into a Man-person wearing a buffalo robe with the hair outside. Later I picked up the buffalo skull that you see over there, on the very spot where the Person had stood. I have kept that skull for more than seventy years. . . . When I reached his side he began to sink slowly into the ground, right over there [pointing]. . . . "Follow me," he said. But I was afraid. "Come," he said from the darkness. And I got down into the hole in the ground to follow him.

I could see countless buffalo, see their sharp horns . . . smell their bodies and hear them snorting, ahead and on both sides of me. Their eyes, without number, were like little fires in the darkness. . . . "Be not afraid, Plenty Coups. It was these Persons who sent for you. They will do you no harm." My body was naked. I feared walking among them in such a narrow place. The burrs that are always in their hair would scratch my skin, even if their hoofs and horns did not wound me more deeply. . . . I felt their warm bodies against my own, but went on after the Man-person, edging around them or going between them all that night and all the next day, with my eyes always looking ahead at the hole of light. But none harmed me, none even spoke to me and at last we came out [at Castle Rock].

Out in the light of the sun, I saw that the Man-person had a rattle in his hand. It was large and painted red. When He reached the top of the knoll, He said to me, "Sit here!" Then he shook his red rattle and sang a queer song four times. "Look!" he pointed. Out of the ground came the buffalo ... without number. They spread wide and blackened the plains. . . . When at last they ceased coming out of the hole in the ground, all were gone, *all!*

He shook his rattle again. "Look!" he pointed. Out of the hole in the ground came bulls and cows past counting. . . . They stopped in small bands and began to eat the grass. Many lay down, not as a buffalo does, but differently, and many were spotted. . . . They were not buffalo. These were strange animals from another world. I was frightened and turned to the Man-person, who only shook his red rattle but did not sing. . . . All the spotted-buffalo [went] back into the hole in the ground. . . . "Do you understand this which I have shown you, Plenty-coups?" He asked me. "No!" I answered. How could he expect me to understand such a thing when I was not yet ten years old?

I followed him back through the hole ... until we came out *right over there* [pointing] where we had first entered the hole in the ground. Then I saw the spring down by those trees, this very house just as it is, these trees which comfort us today, and a very old man sitting in the shade, alone. I felt pity for him because he was so old and feeble. . . . "This old man is yourself, Plenty Coups," the Man-person told me. And then I could see the Man-person no more. He was gone, and so too was the old man. Instead, I saw only a dark forest.

This visionary experience incorporates many features of the topology of the dreaming world. First is the extraordinary concreteness, the tangible structure, of the dreaming world, which is denoted by the ability of the narrator to point out specific, actual features of the environment that encode the visionary journey. The buffalo bull is seen standing in the exact location in which the narrative is given. The nearby hill is pointed out as the actual place where the bull turned into a Man-person wearing a buffalo robe. A buffalo skull is picked up from the ground where this Man-person stood and is still owned by the dreamer seventy years later. Plenty Coups emerges "right over there," and the narrative articulates the enfolded structures inherent to the visible world. Then, opening up the temporal horizon, he sees a house, years before such a house existed, and himself as an elder. Over the years, the vision acts as a template that gives structure and content to the unfolding of his personal power.

The buffalo bull transforms itself into a human being wearing a buffalo robe, so that a buffalo robe takes on various degrees of symbolic meaning, communicating the presence of the dream-spirit. Changed into a man and thereby emphasizing the intimate link between the human and the animal, the buffalo and Plenty Coups proceed on an underworld journey. Not all buffalo dreamers, however, take underworld journeys. While the buffalo is generally associated with earth powers, exceptions can be found.[45] Thus the visionary realms of experience are by no means rigidly determined according to the nature of the animal power or to a strict topological classification. The dreamer may move into and through a wide variety of visionary environments to receive instruction.

The journey motif is a pervasive feature of many dream narratives. Only rarely do events occur in a single location. Generally there is movement toward a place of power (a local environment), the giving of various kinds of instruction, and a return to the original situation. The dream topology does not pass before the eye of a static dreamer; the dreamer experiences movement through the landscape. This movement is neither random nor without significance. Movement is intentionally structured: it is purposive and inevitably leads into the altered world of the dream-spirits, to the unfolded order of their existence and habitation. In this expanded and altered condition, the individual dreamer is given instruction that may now be beyond his ability to comprehend. Spontaneous visions by very young individuals are common. They might see into the future or past. They might behold strange appearances or beings that will only gradually become comprehensible. The vision contains, in potential, the yet unknown reality that over the course of years will slowly be integrated into actual events, objects, and encounters. Thus the topology of the visionary world is intensely symbolic and provides an expansive epistemic base for later reflection and action.

The dreamer's relationship with the dream-spirits is very vivid and has sensory tangibility. Plenty Coups feels the immediate presence and physical closeness of the buffalo through their smell and the visual impact of their eyes "like little fires"—a vivid symbol of life force and mysterious power. The danger and vulnerability of the dreamer is expressed in his fear and anxiety, as he travels naked and exposed to possible injury. The liminality of the experience opens the individual to the deeper potency of the visionary world, the overwhelming vitality of the buffalo. However, it is the buffalo that "call" the dreamer, and the threatening experience is transformed into a protective encounter that bestows power and knowledge. This is an essential feature of the powers that inhabit the visionary realm: a dramatic encounter with a potentially overwhelming reality that threatens to submerge the individual and to overcome him with the potency of visionary experience. Fear and terror are commonly expressed by Plains visionaries when encountering these openings into the visionary realm. Yet the general character of the experience is integrative and positive.

Finally, the visionary nature of the experience frequently unfolds an order of perception that is incongruent with the known structures of experience. In Plenty Coups' vision, the buffalo vanish, foretelling some inconceivable consequence to one of the most revered beings. Strange buffalolike animals—obviously cattle—appear as unknown concomitants of some other order of existence not familiar to the ten-year-old dreamer. The overall significance of this strange transformation seems wholly incomprehensible to him. This is a frequent feature of the visionary experience, particularly in a period of intensive culture contact. There is a constant appearance in dream narratives of strange, incomprehensible, and mysterious objects, events, and beings. While it is tempting to attribute certain of these phenomena to the conflict with an oppressive Euro-American cultural hegemony, they are perhaps equally expressive of the general nature of the visionary experience. There is a constant unfolding of potential through the interplay of various social, natural, and individual characteristics. The imagistic language of that unfolding is filled with visionary appearances that express the not yet known, the unseen, or the not yet visualized. The concept of the mysterious is partly a function of the process of formulating an emergent symbolic order out of the visionary potential.

THE ABOVE POWERS

The visionary realm of the sky and heavens includes all celestial phenomena as part of a unified topological stratum. The sun, moon, and stars are not conceived of as in any way separate from clouds, sky, and the various beings that inhabit the upper realm. This is not to suggest that these celestial phenomena are not distinguished or classified in unique ways according to the specific experiences of different Plains peoples. However, the contiguity of the above realm is part of an unbroken wholeness in which all celestial phenomena participate. The general structure of the visionary experience is to be taken up into the sky and introduced to a variety of celestial beings. Or, in other circumstances, the dreamer may be visited by one of these celestial beings who comes down with the purpose of bestowing a gift.

The classic example of the visionary experience of the upper realm is that of the Lakota holy man Black Elk. His extensive, detailed vision is unsurpassed in the present ethnography and is one of the most elaborately recorded visions presently available for study. Only the briefest account can be given here, as published by Ray DeMallie from John Neihardt's fieldnotes:[46]

As I lay in the tipi I could see through the tipi the same two men whom I saw before and they were coming from the clouds. Then I recognized them as the same men I had seen before in my first vision. They came and stood off a ways from me and stopped, saying: "Hurry up, your grandfather is calling you." When they started back, I got up and started to follow them. . . . I followed those men up into the clouds and they showed me a vision of a bay horse standing there in the middle of the clouds.

I followed the bay horse and it took me to a place on a cloud under a rainbow gate and there were sitting my six grandfathers, sitting inside a rainbow door, and the horses stopped behind me. . . . One of the grandfathers said to me: "Do not fear, come right in." So I went in and stood before them. The horses in the four quarters of the earth all neighed to cheer me as I entered the rainbow door. The grandfather representing where the sun goes down said: "Your grandfathers all over the world and earth are having a council and there you were called, so here you are.

The messengers take the visionary into the sky, and the clouds become a place where many different dream-spirits are encountered. The dreamer (who was nine years old at the time) plays a basically passive role as the visionary drama unfolds and carries him forward into the mystery of the visionary experience.[47] Animals who speak express a pervasive dream experience that supports the belief that animals had fully developed, and frequently superior, physical and intellectual powers when compared with human beings. The personification of the directions as wise elders is expressive of another important feature of the dreaming topology. The personification of abstract ideas, as the grandfather of the "west," frequently appears in the form of valued kinship relations. The mysterious beings of the vision frequently appear as concerned, caring elders who bestow knowledge and gifts on the recipient. The relationship is presented as a respected interactive role formed by elder and younger individuals or occasionally by siblings, creating a strongly sanctioned social bond between the dreamer and the dream-spirit.[48]

Instruction takes place in a council where many dream-spirits are gathered together to give power to the dreamer. This is a topological reflection of a widespread form of Native American social organization, the decision-making council of mature elders. The symbolic nature of the council is a presentation of various powers reflective of the particular realm in which the council is held. In the case of Black Elk's vision, the grandfathers represent the celestial directions, which are then associated with certain types of power through the gifts given to the dreamer. The personification of directionality helps to fill out the celestial topology by giving a sense of order and balance to the vision experience. Just as another visionary was taken to a power-bestowing council of the underwater lodge, here the dreamer finds himself in an upper-world sky lodge.[49] Topologically, the council lodge is the stable meeting place (often located in the center of the camp circle) for the integration of a unique synthesis of powers given structure and significance through the seating arrangements in the lodge. The rainbow tipi reflects within itself unified expression of social and celestial order, thereby giving the dreamer a sense of orientation within the vaster mystery of the lived world. The beings who are present and their gifts symbolize the unique visionary synthesis of the dreamer.

The most obvious features of the above realm are the sun, moon, and stars. All of these may be personified in the visionary experience. For example, Plenty Coups was also taken in a vision to a sky lodge in which the celestial powers of "the Winds, the Bad Storms, the Thunders, the Moon, and many Stars" were gathered.[50] Among the Blackfoot in particular, the sun, moon, and stars formed an integrated visionary that which might manifest itself to the dreamer. Clark Wissler recorded the following dream of a Blackfoot medicine man:[51]

I made a shelter wall of rock, in which I slept and fasted. [On the fourth day] there appeared to me an old couple with a son. . . . The old man addressed me, "My son, do you know me?" "No," I replied. "Well, my name is Always Visible." This I knew to be the sun man. Then the old woman addressed me, "Do you know me?" "No," I said again. "Well, my name is Moon Woman." . . . [The son said] "My name is Morning Star." The old man then addressed me, "I will give you my body. You will live as long as I." . . . Then the old woman addressed me, "My son, all the clouds in the sky are paint for my face. Now, if I paint my face, it rains; if I do not paint my face, it does not rain. This power I give to you." Then the son gave me feathers, which I now wear on this hat.

Here the interrelationship among the powers is constituted as the most fundamental of all kinship units, the nuclear family. Taken into the celestial family, the visionary is given particular rain-making power and visible objects to create a unique bond, as one "adopted," with the celestial powers. Like them, he is empowered to affect natural events. The narrative bears eloquent testimony to the holistic relationship between the celestial beings, the individual, the place (topos) of fasting, and the mythic symbols that invoke the visionary power and relate the dreamer to the natural world.

The sun is another powerful being. In the ethnography, various types of ritual fasting are undertaken to receive a vision from the sun, which is thought frequently to grant war power to the visionary. Both Gideon Pond and James Lynd, writing about the Dakota Sioux, mention the early (1850s) form of the Wiwanyag wacipi, or sun dance, as an individual quest for power given by the sun through dreams and visions.[52] These visions are often associated with bravery in battle and the ability to avenge oneself against an enemy. The Sioux medicine man Goose had a direct vision of the sun that granted him the ability to heal using certain herbs. Goose narrated the dream by which he felt himself authorized to undertake the treatment of the sick:[53]

One day I arose before daybreak to go on a hunting trip. As I went around a butte I saw an antelope. . . . The antelope looked at me and then began to graze. I took my rifle and fired several shots with no effect. I fired 16 cartridges and wondered what could be the matter. Then the animal stopped grazing and began to move slowly away. Then I heard a voice speaking three times, then a fourth time, and the voice said it was going to sing something and I must listen. The voice was above me and commanded me to look at the sun. I looked and saw that the rising sun had the face of a man and was commanding all the animals and trees and everything in nature to look up. . . . Then the voice above me told me to observe the structure of the human body. I then saw blood run into the skeleton, and a buffalo horn appeared on the back, between the shoulders, and drew the blood out of the skeleton. The voice above me said that this was a sign that I would have more than any other to cure diseases of the blood . . . a practice which I have followed ever since. I do not consider that I dreamed this as one dreams in sleep; it appeared to me when I was early in the chase.

The power of the sun, however, was not exclusively associated with male power. Among the Plains Cree the sun was regarded as a female power that gave visions and dreams to both men and women.[54] The Blackfoot visionary Mink Woman received her power in the form of a buffalo stone from the sun.[55] In this regard, James Schultz recorded a very interesting tradition concerning Blackfoot women:[56]

[The women] had always believed that they were nothing-persons beneath Sun's notice. Like the men, they occasionally, in their sleep, had visions, but they had thought it useless for them even to try to interpret their strange experiences. But now Mink Woman had proved that the Sun had as much regard for them as he had for men, and from this time on they would heed their visions. . . . From that day, women had an ever-increasing share in sacred matters, until, finally they, and not the men, conducted the ceremonies of the building of the great lodge that was given to the Sun, every summer in the Berries Ripe moon.

Here another feature of the dreaming topology emerges: the shifting gender associations based on the experiences of individual dreamers. The dream-spirits, being largely identified with animals or other, more neuter features of the dreaming environment, could take on differing gender associations according to the predisposition of the dreamer. Traditionally recognized gender distinctions usually emphasized one gender over another. The granting of power by a male dream-spirit to a female dreamer might characterize a new possibility for the expression of female power. Or, the male dreamer might receive power from a female dream-spirit rather than from another male.

Receiving female power is particularly characteristic of moon dreamers. Dreaming of the moon results in a variety of powers: among the Blackfoot such a dream might bestow the power to prevent conception in women; among the Arapaho a dream during the full moon might reveal the future.[57] For several groups, dreams of the moon meant a fundamental change in gender identity. Among the Oglala Sioux, the Winnebago, and the Dhegiha-speaking people, the dreamer might, for example, be presented with a choice by the moon of taking either the bow and arrows of a warrior or the carrying strap of a woman. If he chooses the carrying strap, he must then live the life of a woman, wearing female clothing and behaving in accordance with recognized female proprieties.[58] If a Mandan male dreamed of Village Old Woman, who is frequently identified with the moon, or a loop of sweetgrass, he would be classed with a special group of holy women.[59]

Among the Omaha, men who live like women are called *mixúga*, "instructed by the moon." Black Dog in 1898 told the following story about a young man to whom this occurred:[60]

Once a young man went to fast and was gone many days. He started home, not having had any dreams or visions, and on his way home he met a matronly woman who addressed him as "daughter." She said to the young man: "You are my daughter and you shall be as I am. I give you this hoe. With it you shall cultivate the ground, raise corn, beans, and squash, and you shall be skillful in braiding buffalo hair and in embroidering moccasins, leggings, and robes." In speaking to the woman the young man discovered that he had been using the feminine terminals of speech. He tried to recover himself and use the speech of man, but he failed. On his return to his people he dressed himself as a woman and took upon himself the avocations of a woman.

The power of the visionary encounter might profoundly affect the identity of the dreamer and reorganize and shift his or her entire pattern of social behavior. The visionary topology is charged with a power of signification that not only enhances the ability of the dreamer but can also radically shift the locus of social identity and confer an emergent spirituality on the dreamer. Moon dreamers were regarded as particularly mysterious.

Visionary experience of the stars is frequently found among the Blackfoot and the Absarokee. Blows Down, an Absarokee warrior, was given oracular power to see his enemies at a distance by the celestial power of the morning star.[61] When the Absarokee warrior Long Hair fasted on Wolf Mountain, he was taken to a lodge inhabited by a man-person whose teeth were like those of a bear and on whose forehead shone seven stars. This was Many Together, a mythic dream-spirit who granted him the ability to defeat a rival in the hoop-and-arrow game.[62] In these experiences the visionary topology is enfolded into the daily activities of the dreamers, but in such a way as to enhance the power of their personal performance. The dream-spirits are not distant or abstract entities; they are experienced in visions as living beings that appear to assist and aid the dreamer in his everyday encounters.

Among the Pawnee, various sacred bundles are believed to have their origins with the star and meteor powers. These bundles frequently originate in a visionary dream. One Pitahawirata woman dreamed of a healing method given to her by a meteorite found by her daughter. A Pawnee warrior, Riding In, also found a meteorite, surrounded by eagle feathers, from which he received a dream granting him bundle power rites.[63] A dream about the morning star is recorded as being particularly ominous, indicating the possible need for human sacrifice, particularly if the star was visible on the eastern horizon when the dreamer awoke.[64] These examples help to illustrate the inter-connectedness of the social and dreaming world, such that the dreaming topology is enfolded into the social order and may act as a catalyst for various social and religious events.

Of all the celestial powers, it is the Thunder Being who holds the most prominent place among Plains dreamers as a source of great and fearful power. The manifestations of this mysterious being are the tremendous thunderstorms that roll across the plains, booming and flashing with huge black clouds, shooting fearsome yellow, green, and red lightning. In form, the Thunder Being is frequently associated with the eagle. The following visionary encounter happened to an Absarokee warrior during an evening watch while he was trying to escape from the Sioux:[65]

I watched the hailstorm coming and saw lightning quite close to me. . . . I saw a big bird coming down among the clouds. His color was white and he was large. . . . In descending to the ground he made no noise. I saw him plainly. The lightning came from his eyes. He sat on the ground. . . . The hailstorm did not come near but left a circle free around the bird and me. I watched the eagle going back up into the heavens. He said, "I am going to adopt you, that is why I came down. Whatever you ask for, we shall hear you." This was the first time I dreamt about him.

The Thunder Being is most expressive of the dynamic encounter with reversibility, possession, and danger. Lightning, the most immediate and powerful manifestation of the Thunder Being, might directly strike people and, if not killing them, claim them as part of the order of thunder beings. This dynamic and ambiguous quality is frequently encountered where there is an overabundance of power. The topology of the celestial realm finds its most expressive manifestation of such power in the Thunder Being, who could confer truly remarkable and dangerous power. Among the Canadian Sioux, almost all medicine men were believed to have lived with the thunder powers before being born on earth. They would travel about with every thunderstorm seeking a place to be born, after which the thunder power would awaken them to their preexistence during a dream or vision experience.[66]

Dreams of lightning and other thunder associations were regarded as a call among the Oglala Sioux to become a member of the Heyoka order of dreamers, and to deny such a dream was to court death by lightning.[67] Among the Cheyenne, the Hohnuhk'e were also dreamers who had dreamed of thunder or the Thunder Lance, which expressed that power in the community.[68] Before becoming a recognized member of a thunder society, the dreamer might experience increased anxiety during thunderstorms. This frequently involved erratic behavior motivated by uncertainty or fear of the thunder power.[69] Only after the dreamer had performed certain public ceremonials and assumed the responsibilities of being a thunder dreamer would this anxiety be lifted. Women dreamers might also become Heyoka.[70]

Thunder dreamer societies consisted of individuals whose dreams required behavior regarded as foolish or contrary to social norms. The potency of thunder power is so great that its manifestation reversed the normal order of social relations. Thus the topology of the dreaming world is charged with the capacity to invert or radically transform dreamers' behavior while simultaneously granting them special status. Thunder dreamers are often regarded as particularly powerful because of their unique ability to act in an unconventional and unpredictable manner while also manifesting strange abilities. Not all orders of thunder dreamers, however, are so radically charged. Among the Dhegiha peoples, the Iñgchan Icha'eche Ma, or "Those who had interviews with the Thunder-beings," formed a religious society whose purpose was to bring rain and manifest various magical abilities.[71] This quality of the visionary topology corresponds to the dynamics of the natural environment that contained the unpredictable, the terrifying or the overwhelming power of natural events.

Finally, one of the most expressive powers of the Thunder Being is that of the war horse. In the visionary ethnography, the horse is associated almost exclusively with the above realm of thunder. The sound of thunder is like the beating of hooves, and many vision accounts contain experiences in which the dreamer rides among the clouds with other warriors.[72] In addition, the thunder powers had other associations—particularly among the Sioux—such as eagle, dog, dragonfly, nighthawk, swallow, and stone.[73] An example that demonstrates the pattern of associations was recorded by Stanley Vestal for the Sioux warrior Bull Standing With Cow, who described a vision of his childhood (c. 1858):[74]

One day he was out under the bank of a stream trying to shoot the darting black birds. . . . Because they lived near water, flew in a darting, zigzag way, and were dark like storm-clouds, these swallows were thought of as belonging to the Thunder. For some time he kept looking up and shooting with his little bow and arrow, but at last, he does not know how, he fell asleep and "died." His soul seemed to leave his body and was in another place.
  All at once he saw a man riding a black horse, his face and naked body painted with zigzag lightnings. This man addressed him: "Boy, you seem to like my birds. Look me over well, so that when you tell about me you will tell the exact truth. When I am facing anything, I do *this*." Then the man on the black horse rushed with his lance at a man who stood there and pierced him through the heart. Strangely, the dead man was transformed into a plant.

The horse plays a crucial role as one who carries or manifests the Thunder Being, thus infusing the warrior's role with fearless and celestial power that strikes down the enemy suddenly and swiftly. This vision, and others like it, demonstrate the correct behavior and appearance that sacralizes the war party. The visionary topology draws together the warrior, the war party, and the dream-spirits to enact a communal celebration of their visionary abilities. The vision lays out the pattern of significant relations between the dreamers and the use of their powers. The reenactment of the vision is the means by which that relationship is strengthened and made visible in the tangible immediacy of a warrior's life. The horse becomes not merely an animal of transport but a celestial manifestation of the Thunder Being. Painted with zigzag lightning and dressed in an appropriate manner, it becomes a powerful presence invoking the most dynamic of the celestial beings.

CHAPTER THREE

Space, Time, and Transformation

This capacity of the Native to sustain the mythological pres-
ence of the transparent world, to integrate sacred time and
geography with the ordinary time and space, gives rise to a
unique view of self in relation to all things.

—Arthur Amiotte, "Our Other Selves: The Lakota Dream Experience"

A PRIMARY ORGANIZING PRINCIPLE of the Native American visionary topology and the dreaming epistemé is the power
of direction. Directionality is not a passive, cognitive principle
abstracted from Cartesian coordinates, but a dynamic and mythically charged form of cosmological orientation. As seen in the
great vision of the Sioux Black Elk, the grandfathers of the rainbow tipi represent the six directions and express a symbolic,
topological organization of space.[1] The directions, in general,
include not only the explicit, literal direction (as north or south)
but also implicit realms of significance that are structured through
visionary experience, ritual movement, the use of objects, and
narrative traditions. Each direction enfolds a variable complex
of qualities and powers emphasizing color, particular beings
(plant or animal), and geographical landmarks. The topological
character of direction is charged with a potency that is both
immediately visible in the physical geography expressed through
behavior and actions learned in dreaming.

The Lakota spiritual leader Fools Crow, while fasting at Bear
Butte at age sixty, received a powerful manifestation of the mys-

terious Thunder Being. A voice speaking in the midst of thunder
told him to look up:[2]

So I looked up and from the west through the whirling clouds came
four riders on four running horses. The first horse was black, the
second was a bright red sorrel, the third was the palomino or yellow, and the fourth was white. The color included the mane, tail
and hooves. The Indian rider of each horse was the same color as
his horse, including his clothing. . . . They swept over me with booming thunder and flashing lightning following behind them, going
on until they disappeared in the distance.

When they were gone, the rich voice explained that the riders represented the four winds and the four storms. So they were the
powers of the four directions. The reason the riders were shown to
me was to tell me that I would be as strong with my medicine as
they were, and after this their colors would be my trade mark when
I did my ceremonies to heal the sick.

In this vision, the four horsemen appeared four times from
each of the four directions. The horsemen collectively express
not only the directions but also the mythical power of storms
and winds, as well as providing a vivid repertoire for the use of
color. The dynamic quality is captured in the moving images of
the war horses and the painted riders, fusing into one the fierce
quality of the war horse and the power of the warrior. These
powers give the visionary strength and a ritualized pattern of
meaningful actions that symbolically embody the topological order, sanctified by the presence of the Thunder Being. The existential encounter with power is also an encounter with a particular organization of the lived world, and it unfolds the
dynamic quality of that world as a gift to the visionary. The
specific nature of the pattern is individual and expresses a unique
quality of visionary synthesis.

While many Native American communities have specific associations of colors, powers, and directions, in the Plains Indian
dreaming ethnography there is no consistent pattern of such
associations. The heterogeneous nature of the dream experience
allows for great variation within a particular group or even society. Color associations tend to be based on primary colors and
thus to a limited range of possible hues. Black and white are

inevitably present in color associations and may represent a primary symbolic quality by which contrasts are reconciled and integrated into a holistic expression of the dreaming order.[3] Every dreamer has his or her own associations with colors and various powers, and a rationalized system of color symbolism on the plains is not developed with the same degree of consistency that it is among other Native American communities. Although the use of color symbolism is pervasive and an intrinsic feature of ritual behavior, it was determined not by ritual sanctions but through dreams.

The exact nature of the associations of power, color, and direction was a problem for one of the grandsons of Fools Crow:[4]

In the Indian religion, there are colors that mean different things or different directions represented by different animals, winged or four-legged and each of these medicine people—maybe they had a different color. Maybe they don't use black, for example. . . . This was the conflict I experienced, so I went to my grandfather and explained it. We had a sweat, and during that sweat he explained that not all medicine men are alike, and never put one down or above the other. Hold them at the same level and respect them. Even if the colors change or the four-legged or the winged change or the direction, it doesn't matter, it all means the same thing. It is just that their vision is different from the other, no two are alike.

Thus the nature of the dreaming topology is fluid and unbound and may best be expressed according to the nature of individual visionary experiences and in subsequent manifestations of power, warfare, or healing.

The topological principle holds that one of the most fundamental expressions of spatial order comes from the association of power with directionality. A specific pattern of organization through direction is an essential feature of almost all visionary experiences and represents a widely shared orientation in both space and time. Through the medium of visionary experience, the dream-spirits manifest a sense of place (topoi) and specific, meaningful actions that establish the macrocosm of the dreamer within the context of communal beliefs and socially recognized religious patterns.

SPACE-TIME RELATIONS

It is important to realize that the character of both space and time in Native American religious topology is relative and elastic. A direction is not something to be measured in a strict Cartesian sense as a rigidly fixed, three-dimensional spatial grid, and time is not a rigidly conceived, unidirectional linear flow from past to future.[5] Such a cognitive predisposition makes it extremely difficult to appreciate the otherness of the traditional Plains dreaming epistemé. Directionality, in the Native American context, inevitably refers to the subjective experience of the individual or the collective activities of the people as a whole. A revered mountain or butte stands as a stable but relative feature of the religious topology. The individual moves in relationship to the more stable features of the environment, which provide a sense of orientation and "direction"—but this sense of direction is not an absolute based on measurable mathematical abstractions determined by a three-dimensional code. It is, rather, the lived world of ritual movement, multidimensional visionary experience, and personal perception given structure and meaning through certain relatively stable features of both the natural and visionary landscape.

From the point of view of the dreaming ethnography, the "center" of this topology is the place of visionary or ritual instruction. Either the dreamer is taken into a center or the center becomes a place where visionary experience occurs. The dreamer journeys to a place of power and receives instruction, or else the dream-spirits come to the place where the visionary happens to be. The vision often occurs in a purely spontaneous manner without preparation or ceremony; at other times, it involves ritual preparation and careful ceremonial procedures. Any place where visionary experience occurs or is invoked becomes a center and a place of power.

The dreaming topology is thus a space filled with variable manifestations of spiritual presence. The "dream-space" is identical with the cosmological structures that constitute the world topology in its totality. It is unbound space because physical properties (such as gravity or matter) do not inhibit access to the visionary world. The boundaries of actual perception and movement participate in a mythic and liminal topography. In this sense the dream-space incorporates all possible world space. All that can be seen or sensed or known is contained within a greater cosmological and mythical reality whose boundaries are indefinite. Within that mythic space there are significant markers and directionality to give orientation without closing the boundaries. Such space is congruent with the experiences of everyday perception and action and has both social and religious characteristics. The dream-space is centered on the perceptions of the dreamer as actor; consequently, this perspective quality is highly mobile. Visionary space includes all the regions of the dreaming topology, and the center can shift to any point in that mythic totality.

In discussing Native American dream ethnography, Douglass Price-Williams, following Mircea Eliade, notes the significance of the *temenos,* or sacred place of power:[6]

The reality of the imaginative leap, the entities and the actions encountered in imaginal space, is carried out in the *temenos,* the sacred ground, the theater, the altar. This is what marks the process off from sense perception reality. . . . In other words, the imaginative process—what I am calling the mythopoetic function—is not carried on outside of the ritual space. It is not extended into the common domestic sphere, the market or the areas of ordinary work.

The problem here is in the separation of the *temenos* from the "common domestic sphere," a distinction that in no way holds for the traditional lived world recorded in the Plains ethnography. The *temenos* is the omnipresent reality of power manifested in and through the living ecology of the everyday—in objects, tipis, clothing, painted in images, and so on. The mythopoetic function may be redefined in this context as an "unveiling" or manifesting of power in the context of everyday life. Ritual space cannot be dogmatically separated from the visionary features of the immediate environment. The rigid association of "sacred space" with a purely ritual context is more a reflection of a dogmatized religious history and the use of dialectic, often antagonistic, categories in the history of religious studies than an accurate portrait of Plains religious orientation. In fact, a visionary object may define and give meaning and "sacredness" to the nature of the domestic sphere. A medicine bundle, with its aura of powerful influences, can act as an empowering agent wherever it is found or even when it is transported.

The Plains Indian nomadic pattern constitutes a "mobile center" that can sacralize whatever space is inhabited. The center is constantly being moderated between outward seasonal movement and subsequent return to the communal center, or immediate kin group. The visionary topology inevitably consists of a pattern of movement away from the communal center, an encounter with the dream-spirits in places of power, and a return to the communal center, which continues the ongoing process of sacralizing communal space and validating shared beliefs. The symbolism of the center thus comes to be associated with the actual manifestations of visionary dream power.

Maturity and spiritual vitality are characterized by memorable acts of personal empowerment, by a person's knowing how to handle sacred objects, and by one's being able to ritually recreate the appropriate conditions for the renewed manifestation of empowerment. Sacred space is relative to the perception, experience, and knowledge of the individual and the conditions necessary for the expression of remarkable ability. Such space is neither fixed nor predetermined. The visionary epistemé is such that knowledge is a function of experience and the impact of the visionary encounter alters the perception of the world order. The part-whole relationship between the visionary individual and the cosmos is encoded in both the journey into the mythic space of the vision and in the return to the socialized space of the community. The journey itself is an image of the whole because it describes the inherent potentiality of both the known and the unknown, uniting them in a single, often ritualized framework.

When the Absarokee healer Fringe went to the hot springs called Medicine Water to fast for a vision, he crossed the boiling water by means of a long pole that was removed by his friends after he crossed onto an island in the middle of the springs. Having been taken down into the water in a visionary experience, he awoke and found himself back on the shore where he had stood before crossing on the pole.[7] Visionary space, the dream-space, is nonlocal and collapses the ordinary symmetry of space and time, contracting, expanding, or transforming perception and revealing an enfolded order. An Assiniboine dreamer reports falling asleep in one lodge only to awaken in another.[8] An Absarokee dreamer moves through space rapidly, covering great distances in moments, or else seems to take days in reaching a place of visionary encounter.[9] Thus, qualitatively, visionary space is dynamic, nonlineal, multidimensional, metamorphic, discontinuous, and liminal. The visionary, in his or her journey, crosses the variable distances of the topological realms and arrives at a place of encounter, which is generally a congruent social environment. There, the correct use of objects and actions is demonstrated, and the visionary then returns with a new understanding of the visionary world.

The temporal dimension of the visionary epistemé has a very characteristic structure: the topology of dreaming is unified through a movement between discrete, structured events—a certain repetitive, formal pacing. The vision unfolds as if it were a ritual, particularly the central events involving pragmatic instructions or teachings. The journey through the dream-space culminates in a ritual of enactment that is unfolded and elaborated in a visionary time. In this sense the vision is a kind of preperformative, or prototypical, enactment through which the visionary receives a potential sanction and instruction for later social, ceremonial behavior. Although the subjective experience of time is contracted or expanded, the actual unfolding of events follows a memorable pattern that can be recreated with varying degrees of modification. The ritual recreation represents the elaboration and structuring of "real-time" events. The vision is part of an interpersonal, instructive preparation of the dreamer for the ceremonial experience. The ritual time of actual demonstration expresses a unity with the visionary time of potential actions and meanings; it is a highly charged, processual demonstration of power, beauty, and possibility.

The visionary reality of the event, however—the prototypical enactment—can still retain its primacy in the mind of the visionary above and beyond the actual ritualized expression. The enactment of the Horse Dance by Black Elk is a perfect example of this intimate relationship between the time of the vision and the time of the ritual. At the moment of ritual enactment, Black Elk sees the rainbow tipi in the thunderstorm that arises during the communal ceremony: "When I looked into the cloud, only [the] grandfathers were beholding me and I could see the flaming rainbow there and the tipi and the whole vision I could see again. I looked at what I was doing and saw that I was making just exactly what I saw in the cloud. This on earth was like a shadow of that in the cloud."[10]

Ritual time is nonlinear and coextensive with the visionary experience. There is an entelechy to visionary time; it moves toward a self-fulfilling "end"—the manifestation of positive results. The vision culminates in a transference of spiritual potential that can then be recreated through a ritual enactment, empowering others. The visionary experience inevitably leads to a dramatic apotheosis through which various potential abilities are transferred to the visionary. The later enactment in ritual recreation expresses that very same "sacred time" (or timelessness) in which the gift of power was bestowed. The unified topology of the dreaming and lived worlds can only be grasped if the "checkered tablecloth of Cartesian space-time" is pulled out from under the externally observed world, leaving the multidimensional, unbound, fluid contours of a noncausal, visionary space-time to expand or contract according to individual experience.

Visionary time is inclusive, nonabsolute, ritually structured, seasonal, climactic, and expressive of the rhythms of lived experience. It is paced according to the degree and complexity of the instruction given. It is vital, processual, formally structured, dynamic, and moving toward a specific end (entelectic)—the acquisition and manifestation of specific ability. The dream world does not represent a static world of objects fixed in empty Euclidean space, but a dynamic world of events in a multilayered, enfolded potential that can suddenly and explicitly manifest as mysterious ability and have a profound impact on the lives of an entire people. This is part of the enfolded order of dreaming by which the significance and importance of the vision bears fruit in the lived world of communal existence. This is the topological feature of recurrence: the means by which the present contains periodic manifestations confirming the visionary reality. Temporal relationships are not bound by continuity in space. A dream figure encountered by one person can be encountered by another at any time, and not just in the ritually structured circumstance. This sudden appearance of a dream figure, breaking into the world of lived experience, is part of the expressive means by which continuity is heightened between the dreaming and the lived worlds. The manifestation of the dream-spirit acts as a recurrent expression emphasizing the visionary quality implicit to the lived-world.

THE LIVED WORLD

The existential world of dream experiences is a tactile, sensory world of immediacy in which actions and events occur with vivid and intense tangibility. It is not a shadowy world of vague appearance and misty forms but a vivid, highly charged world of sensory participation, drama, movement, flight, and encounter within often highly detailed scenes that are regarded as actual and real. These encounters are congruent with the natural world of the dreamer, so that the dreaming world and the natural environment interpenetrate and complement each another. This topological feature might be called contextual continuity.

Native American dreaming tends not to take place in radically distinct or disjunctive environments alien to the natural lifeway of the dreamer. The dreamer journeys through the various strata of the world topology, but these strata are only manifestations of the variable dimensions of communally shared visionary space and time. More importantly, the visionary world of the dreamer is in no way subordinate to a strictly empirical waking world. Indeed, the meaning of "empirical" is wholly unique in the visionary context: it means not the measurable world of external perception, experimentation, and testing, but the highly valued, lived experience of dream encounter and unfolding perception. Visions are a reality base for the lived world; they are actual experiences of transformation and empowerment. This is perception based in a cosmographic totality that is unbounded and open to the vision encounter. Dreaming has a reflexive consequence in that it informs ("makes real") for the dreamer the oral, ritual, and social traditions that point to a more empowered existence. Dreams open the boundaries of perception and action, thereby contributing to an enrichment of the social and waking world of communal experience.

Weasel Tail, a Blackfoot dreamer, narrated the following dream experience that occurred during a horse raiding expedition:[11]

During the night I had a strange vision: Came to me a very old man and said, "You are to see a Coyote. Watch the animal, notice the direction his nose is pointing, and go that way, and you will find horses." Having said that, the old man vanished. . . . I told my companions of my vision, and they thought as I did, that it was without value. But while we were eating . . . a coyote appeared upon a rise of ground quite near us, and, looking straight to the south, never once at us, it raised its quavering yelp. Four times it did that—four, the sacred number—and then trotted off southward. And Bird Rattle said to me: "I was mistaken about your vision. It meant something of value to us. . . . We must go south."

The lived world is permeated with a sense of the immediacy and presence of spiritual powers. The dream experience and the events of the natural world are enfolded into one another in an intimate and inseparable way. The ambiguity of the visionary event is resolved through the observation of visible, perceptible events given special meaning through the visionary dream. Contextual continuity is based on the identification of the two experiences—the vision and the actual appearance—in a single frame of meaning as one unified reality. The mystery of the world of appearances is the vital means through which the visionary event expresses itself as knowledge of what is or of what will become. This continuity is reinforced even further by encoded and shared symbolic forms that serve to validate actions strengthening the relationship between the meaningful vision and the observed moment. The four yelps of the coyote are part of a social, semiotic network of shared meanings that validate the experience. This signification is recognized by someone other than the dreamer who shares the same general ritual associations, thereby strengthening the socioreligious dimension of the event.

Dreaming is constantly integrated into the ongoing events of the lived world. It is reflected in the social organization of the community, as in the case of the Pawnee, whose division between bundle priests and chiefs is determined by a vision of the evening star given to First Man.[12] Dreaming often sanctified the status of the individual in the community, for any unusual ability or outstanding characteristic (a particularly fast runner, a good hunter) might be attributed to various dream-spirits. These individuals might then form societies, either openly or in secret, based on the particular type of dream-spirit experienced.[13] Dreams were an important means for sanctioning ceremonial events, either in a seasonal pattern or as newly conceived celebrations.[14] They often conferred healing power on the individual and thereby affected the well-being of others.[15] They could bestow oracular or prophetic knowledge that in turn could motivate individual or collective action.[16] And they contributed to the ongoing oral tradition and were encoded in any number of visible forms. All these features contribute to the general structure of the lived world, that is, the world of immediate, existential concern and care. In general, the topology of the dreaming world pervades the entire fabric of social and personal existence and motivates, influences, and confronts both the individual and the community with an ongoing manifestation of dream-related events that are inseparable from those of the waking state.[17]

The lived world as a context for the integration of social, individual, and visionary experiences enfolds one into the other and is bound together by both ritual enactment and narrative interpretations. The constitution of the lived world must be seen as inseparable from the dialogical, performative, and interpretive events that pervade the religious contents of social existence. The time frame of this interaction is multigenerational and is contextualized through the constant interpretation and reinterpretation of visionary experience. This experience is generally sanctioned or contradicted by elders who are usually regarded as the purveyors of cultural tradition. Such an interpretive setting is highly charged with mythic contents that provide a powerful medium of imagistic and symbolic meanings. The given is primarily a narrated given—what exists and what preexists are simultaneous. The narrative basis of culture informs the lived world and is strengthened or weakened by the modulating influence of the individual dreamer or visionary. Nevertheless, the narrative totality of beliefs and paradigmatic behaviors provides a preexistent basis against which the individual can measure personal experience. Plains Indian culture in this sense is not an imperative structure of inflexible codes or beliefs but a pluralistic, thematically diverse totality of emergent and shifting ideas, actions, and narratives strengthened by tradition and given formal coherence through ritual enactment.

THE SACRED OR HOLY

To articulate fully the topological structures of visionary space and time, it is necessary to consider briefly the problem of the sacred or holy. Because this work involves the descriptive and intentional analysis of religious experience, the sacred is defined only in terms of the encounter or manifestation of mysterious power and the means by which it is known. Speculative thought or reflection on or about the holy—the development of a mythic ontology—represents a form of reflective discourse that is distinct from the actual record of dream experience. The sacred as direct encounter and the sacred as a product of intellectual speculation reflect a primary analytical distinction. The concept of the sacred as an ontological category of experience, one that bestows or reveals meaning through empowerment and understanding through a higher order of perception, is often contrasted in the mind of a non-native analyst with a concept of the sacred as nothing other than a characteristic form of social organization, a mass emotional experience, or a human psychological tendency to create a meaningful symbolic order (defensively) in the face of an otherwise chaotic and threatening existence. This profound dialectic tension and skeptical denial of the ontological significance of the sacred, perhaps a reaction to the fallibility of Judeo-Christian religious discourse and the presumptive use of Western religious categories, stands in stark contrast to the traditional understanding of the holy in Native American religion. Furthermore, the primacy of religious experience is often relegated to a minor or subsidiary area of analytic discourse, theophany being inevitably subordinate to logocentric theology.[18]

The sacred as a quality of visionary experience, expressing variation and creative transformation, movement, and encounter through space and time, is intrinsic to the dreaming ethnography. The concept is used often in the visionary narratives, perhaps in an attempt by both the visionary and the ethnographer to close the cultural gap between radically different religious traditions. Fundamental to the vision experience (and often attributed to highly developed visionaries) is the manifestation of a mysterious presence. This presence is conceived of as a concealed potency or mystery that breaks forth suddenly, generally in the context of natural events, evoking profound feelings of reverence and respect. Normally this manifestation takes the form of a remarkable human being, and it can occur in circumstances of stress, during ritual enactments, or through the conscious control of the developed dreamer or shaman. The natural world has a topological character charged with varying degrees of "immanence" at known places that is also fully capable of manifesting itself at a not yet recognized place or a not yet sanctified time. It is not constrained by either mythic narrative or the ritual cycles.

The nature of what is "holy" is such that it is a hidden potential in any environment or circumstance. Thus the Teton Sioux Lone Man could describe the world as follows: "The earth is large and on it live many animals. This earth is under the protection of something which at times becomes visible to the eye. One would think that this would be at the center of the earth, but its representations appear everywhere, in large and small forms—they are the sacred stones. The presence of a sacred stone will protect you from misfortune."[19]

Here Lone Man identifies the manifestation of the "protective spirit" with sacred stones, a specific form of that manifestation scattered throughout the natural world and tied to Sioux creation mythology.[20] But the reality of this belief is rooted in direct visionary experiences that Lone Man had regarding the "stone people" and that certainly affected his understanding of the narrative traditions. In a vision, the Thunder Being appeared to him and taught him many things: "The voice also said, 'The sacred stones will look upon you as a man whom they are to guard and protect.'"[21] This protective power is another well-attested feature of the dreaming topology. Access to this power or presence is acquired directly through dreams, which unveil the implicit ontology of the visionary epistemé. In general, the vision experience is a recognition of the concealed powers of nature, and the experience of the holy is identified with its many and often protective manifestations.

The mysterious power of visions, as an agent-contingent order, is concrete and immediate. The agency of manifestation confers specific types of detailed knowledge (generally regarded as "sacred") and thereby potentially enhances the agency of the individual or the community. The agent of the visionary presence is potentially any animal, object, or being that might dwell in the unbound strata of the lived world. Edward Curtis recorded the following observation among the Mandan of North Dakota: "All creatures, spirits, objects, and phenomena possessing . . . *hopini*, or inexplicable power, are called *mahópini*, and are thus personified and deified. All animals and birds, even inanimate objects, are *hopini*, and can transfer their spirit-power to men."[22] This observation may be regarded as generally true throughout the plains and prairie area.[23]

The special quality, *hopini* (like *wakan* among the Sioux), expresses a potency that surpasses ordinary human effort or capacity. It imbues a dreamer with extraordinary power, and its sources are various and multiple. While the mysterious beings through whom it is received are qualitatively more powerful than humans, they are sometimes conceived of as an entirely different class (like the thunder powers). Yet in the Plains ethnography there is no systemic hierarchy, no absolute valuation of rank or position.[24] Most descriptions confirm the powerful, overwhelming, and dangerous character of the Thunder Being, but no texts give a superordinate position to such a powerful being. The diversity of the more-than-human dream-spirits is based in personal visionary experience, which relativizes the relationship of the dream-spirits to one another. The key is the degree of agency that is conferred on the dreamer and his or her ability to manifest it.

It would, nevertheless, be inaccurate to assume that this individual orientation toward the holy had no other, more radically comprehensive pattern or expression. The existence of an overarching unity, a synthesis or potency that encompasses within itself all powers and manifestations is also widespread. The various concepts of the holy or the sacred held by Plains communities also express a profound belief in a single, dynamic principle inherent in the religious topology and maintained through the types of agency manifested in natural events and visionary experience. This point is well summarized by Alice Fletcher and Francis La Flesche's discussion of the Omaha concept of *Wakonda*:[25]

Wakonda is not a modern term and does not lend itself to verbal analysis. . . . There is therefore no propriety in speaking of *Wakonda* as "great spirit." Equally improper would it be to regard the term as a synonym of nature, or an objective god, a being apart from nature. It is difficult to formulate the native idea expressed in this word.

The *Wakonda* addressed in the tribal prayer and in the tribal religious ceremonies which pertain to the welfare of all the people is the *Wakonda* that is the permeating life of visible nature—an invisible life and power that reaches everywhere and everything, and can be appealed to by man to send him help. From this central idea of a permeating life comes, on the one hand, the application of the word *Wakonda* to anything mysterious or inexplicable, be it an object or an occurrence; and on the other hand, the belief that the peculiar gifts of an animate or inanimate form can be transferred to man. The means by which this transference takes place is mysterious and pertains to *Wakonda* but is not [The] *Wakonda*.

While this statement expresses an Omaha Siouan orientation explicitly, it also captures a general Native American pattern of belief. In terms of the ethnographic record, the manifestation of this mysterious presence through visions and dreams is always explicit, personal, and inseparable from often detailed forms of agency. Though the general phenomenology of religious experience does not include a record of encounter with the holy as distinct from the particular form of its manifestation, nevertheless the impact and power of the manifestation certainly include an encounter with the numinous, mysterious, and powerful. It is also true that such manifestations open the way for a more receptive understanding of various comprehensive, integrative principles. It is the religious specialist, as master visionary, who articulates these greater principles in the visionary context of interpretation, prayer, and mythic discourse, distinguishing the plurality of dream-spirits from the unity of their mutual coexistence. Ideas of a rigorously distinct "monotheism" that posit a dialectical relationship between a dependent humanity and an absolute, all-powerful God circumscribing a unique human community play little or no role in the visionary ethnography.[26]

The contemplation of this underlying unity and of the diverse relationships between the various beings and powers that populate the world, along with their relationship to human beings, is a reflective task undertaken by elders and advanced dreamers and shamans. Grounded in personal experience and explicitly manifested in ceremonial and ritual behavior, the concept of the sacred in the texts has many diverse meanings, all of which express an attitude of heartfelt reverence. The texts record a deep respect and profound appreciation by informed members of the community for the vision experience and for acts and objects associated with the vision. If the concept of the holy is not stratified into hierarchical schemes by Plains visionaries, it is expressive of a deep regard for the importance and generative processes of nature that reflect an underlying unity and vitality impinging directly upon and acting through human life. This underlying unity requires long and thorough reflection to be fully appreciated. Among the Omaha, such reflection led to the articulation of traditional ethical norms:[27]

Old men have said: "*Wakonda* causes day to follow night without variation and summer to follow winter; we can depend on these regular changes and can order our lives by them. In this way, *Wakonda* teaches us that our words and our acts must be truthful, so that we may live in peace and happiness with one another. Our fathers have thought about these things and observed the acts of *Wakonda* and their words have come down to us."

METAMORPHIC CYCLES

The principle of an underlying dynamic unity that both permeates and yet is distinct from the particular manifestation provides a phenomenological basis for understanding the processes of metamorphosis that inevitably accompany the manifestation. The metamorphic quality of the dreaming topology is a principal feature of the visionary epistemé. The mysterious, unifying power of a *wakan* reality unfolds the visionary encounter as a fluid, transformative expression of multiple powers and beings.

This pluralistic expression and its dynamic, transformative quality are normatively regarded as inseparable from a holistic view of a unified relationship between human beings, dream-spirits, and the all-pervasive, unifying, and mysterious presence.

The metamorphic aspects of the visionary experience tend to follow a distinctive pattern: first, the dreamer sees some significant object or animal; then that object or animal transforms (or metamorphoses) into a dream-spirit usually having a human form, but one that retains certain symbolic features representing the unique character of the dream-spirit; and finally, the dream-spirit returns to a form similar to the one it had when first seen, or to another related form. More formally stated, the "object-world" of visionary experience is not constituted by a tangible empiricism but by a transformative potency or potential. In this sense, it might be said that the visionary topology is one of constant becoming, a process of continuing transformation and fluidity by which the dynamic character of any object is capable of manifesting its potential to be something "other"—an otherness whose ultimate roots lie in the pervasive, unitary quality inherent in the natural and social world. This metamorphic dynamic is one of the fundamental means by which both the sacredness and the power of the manifestation can be recognized.

The issue of empowerment is discussed in a well-known article by Irving Hallowell, as it relates to the Ojibwa: "Metamorphosis to the Ojibwa mind is an earmark of power. Within the category of persons there is a graduation of power. Other-than-human persons occupy the top rank in the power hierarchy of animate beings. Human beings do not differ from them in kind, but in power."[28] While I agree with his distinction based on degrees of power, which he characterizes as a hierarchy, I find among the Plains Indian texts (and elsewhere) that in fact many "other-than-human" beings were categorically "more-than-human"—Thunder Being, Unktehi, black-tailed deer women, the stone people, the many "pipe bringers" (such as White Buffalo Calf Woman), and so on. Moreover, many animals (who appeared as humans) were thought of as superior to and different from humans. The issue here is not the development of hierarchy, which is basically a Christian idea embedded in Western religious discourse and in its political power structures, but a principle of differentiation that affirms the important, intrinsic differences between beings as well as the capacity of a more powerful being (including shamans) to become "something more," or for "something more" to manifest itself as a human being. Dream-spirits are often thought to be incapable of death or injury, or to be capable of acts no ordinary human could perform. This strongly suggests an ontological category different from that of humans, who are so weak and dependent on these more-than-human beings for empowerment. Shamans, as more powerful beings, are assimilated into the more-than-human categories, acquiring an ability to transform themselves and consequently to lose their human face.[29]

The symbolism of the dream records the potency of the dream-spirit and its more-than-human capacity to reveal transformative, multiple aspects of its supraordinate being. An outstanding mark of real power is the ability to metamorphose. Edward Curtis recorded the following narrative of a vision quest experience from the Teton Sioux Red Hawk:[30]

As he slept something from the west came galloping and panting. It circled about him, then went away. A voice said, "Look! I told you there would be many horses." . . . Then he saw the speaker was a rose-hip, half red and half green. Then the creature went away and became a yellow headed black-bird. It alighted on one of the offering poles which bent as if under a great weight. The bird became a man again and said, "Look at this!" Red Hawk saw a village into which a man threw two long-haired human heads. . . . Then the creature, becoming a bird, rose and disappeared in the south. Red Hawk slept and heard a voice saying, "Look at your village." He saw four women going around the village with their hair on the top of their heads and their legs aflame. Following them was a naked man, mourning and singing the death-song.

This vision foretold Red Hawk's ability to steal horses and the actual deaths of four Sioux warriors, accompanied by the mourning rites of their wives (women frequently slashed their arms and legs in grief). It also foretold the later deaths of two enemies. Structurally, it moves through a series of metamorphic changes that signify tremendous potency inherent in the visionary world and the beings who dwell there. This intrinsic potency is expressed by the transformations and by the observation that one of the offering poles "bent as if under a great weight." The potential, intrinsic power seems barely containable within its manifest form. The prophetic structure of the vision is expressed through dramatic series of actions that are given coherence through the metamorphic presence of the dream-spirit. The inherent meaning of those actions is directly linked to actual events in the dreamer's life. The meaning of the vision is inseparable from the lived world of the dreamer; thus, visionary events tend to confirm the validity of ongoing daily experience as manifestations linked to sacred events.

The metamorphic quality is not limited to the dream-spirit that appears to the visionary. The visionary too can undergo transformation leading to new power. Among the shell and pebble societies of the Omaha, as a result of certain visionary experiences, members claimed that "they could transform themselves into birds, animals, stones, or leaves," thereby assimilating themselves into the more-than-human categories. Similar abilities were recorded among the Lakota and other plains tribes.[31] A remarkable and representative example of this visionary metamorphosis of the dreamer was recorded by Irving Hallowell among the Saulteaux:[32]

For several nights I dreamed of an *ogima* (chief, superior person). Finally one night . . . the *ogima* began dancing around me as I sat there on a rock and when I happened to glance down at my body I noticed that I had grown feathers. Soon I felt just like a bird, a *kini'u* (golden eagle). *Ogima* had turned into a bird also and off he flew towards the south. I spread my wings and flew after him in the same direction. After a while we arrived at a place where there were lots of tents and lots of people. We stayed there all winter. It was the home of the summer birds. I shot lots and lots of birds there; ducks, geese and many other kinds. In the spring when the birds started to fly north, *ogima* came too and guided me to the island from which we had set out.

Here the individual becomes identified with the power of the *ogima* in a particular form that implies bird-hunting ability, both by the dreamer's turning into an eagle (who hunts other birds) and by the dream-spirit's enacting the same transformation.[33] Both space and time are metamorphosed: great distance is covered easily and time is vastly expanded. The journey motif completes its usual cyclical form, and the dreamer now embodies the sacred power of the eagle. The identification of the individual with the power is frequently symbolized by the belief that the dreamer has the power within his body—an actual distinctive presence as a consequence of the vision. The vision experience expresses an intrinsic bond and is inseparable from the life and body of the individual.[34] Power acquired in visions is no different from power acquired in waking life, and in most cases the power given in visions is regarded as superior.

The entire structure of the dreaming topology could be experienced by the individual in a macrocosmic visionary encounter that unifies all the diverse realms and powers into an integrated, unique whole. Among the Dhegiha-speaking peoples, this kind of unification might be accomplished in a cumulative sense, as it was for one founder of a dreamer society:[35]

He dreamed that a large number of animals appeared to him and gave him power. First, there came to him two eagles, one white and one dark. Each claimed to be the leader of the fowls, but he believed the white one because it came first. They promised him eagle powers. Next he saw a duck, which offered him the privileges of the duck people who can even walk on water. The owl came to him in the clear day and hooted for him . . . [and] gave the dreamer owl power over the night. Then it seemed to the dreamer that it was a still clear cold day, with frost on the ground, yet he saw a woodpecker seated on a mossy tree trunk and a shaft of warm sunlight played upon it and the moss steamed in the sun. "Now this is my work," said the woodpecker to him. "This nice clear day, with the streak of warmth. I give you and your children to come, power to do this." The plover next appeared, and said, "I can give you health." The prairie owl that lives in the burrows of the prairie dogs appeared and said, "I am the keeper of the day. Just at dawn you see the streaks of light appear above the eastern horizon. I bring them, I bring daylight. This power I give you and your children." Then the little owl screeched four times and disappeared in the north.

From various "winged" creatures, the dreamer successively accumulates powers associated with air, earth, and water, as well as the powers of day, night, and dawn. He is also given good health. The powers, the distinctive times, and the various realms combine to form not only a personalized vision of the whole but also a dynamic set of temporal relationships, each connected with a unified manifestation of the "holy." This vision empowers not only the dreamer but also his social role. By forming a society with other dreamers, he strengthens the pattern, and it expands to include the dreams of all the members. Thus the powers together, through the unique constellation of each dream and dream society, qualify the experience of the holy and help give it a distinctive form and meaning.

Another manifestation of topological diversity and unity can be found in the following visionary narrative of an Arapaho man, collected by Alfred Kroeber:[36]

He saw himself standing alone on a green prairie, looking to the east. On his left, to the north, he then saw a person seated, dressed entirely in black silk. He thought that this was the messenger. The man wanted to approach him and touch him; but his thoughts were not strong enough, and he was unable to move. Then this person in black spoke to him. He knew all the man's thoughts. He told him of the new world that was to be, and that they were now on a cloud. Then the informant saw the earth below him and the sky above him at an equal distance. The person in black, who was the crow, then showed him a rainbow extending from east to west, and another from south to north. The informant was then taken by him to the spot where the two rainbows crossed one another. There he stood, and the crow told him to look up. He then saw where the father was, and saw the thoughts of all mankind reaching up to him [the father]. He saw also birds of all kinds. Two of these were foremost—the eagle and the crow. He also saw the sun, the stars, and the morning star.[35]

Here the metamorphic quality of the experience is combined with the formation of a center from which the visionary may perceive his own place within the whole. The transparency of the vision opens his perceptions to a new world in which his role is that of an empowered being. The crow becomes the messenger of the transformation and acts as the means by which the individual comes to understand how the world is reborn through the visionary experience. The individual is centered at the intersection of the two rainbows, which encompass within their boundaries both directionality and the open horizon of the visionary's world. This expansive horizon includes within itself a simultaneous expression of the cosmological symbols of both day and night. Furthermore, the communication of meaning and significance is not confined to purely symbolic forms, for the visionary comes to know the thoughts of the man in black, which draw him to the center where he sees the thoughts of all mankind rising to the father. The vision gives an organized, unified picture of reality and its inherent principles and powers through specific forms. And it unfolds a new horizon of experience in the form of its purely mental contents.[37]

The unification of the topological dimensions of experience may be accomplished in a simple and straightforward manner through a highly symbolic experience. Robert Lowie collected the following narrative from the Shoshone:[38]

A medicine man, in seeking supernatural aid, went to the mountains to fast and pray. At the end of some days, an eagle, a bear, and a badger appeared to him. The eagle took off one of his talons and gave it to him, telling him that by means of it he would be able to command all the powers of the air. The bear also took off one of his claws and promised him aid from all the powers of the earth. Finally, the badger gave him a claw and told him by means of it he could command all that was under the earth. The medicine man, as a means of testimony, produced the three claws, strung on a cord to be worn about his neck.

This remarkable unification of the three topological strata clearly demonstrates both the unique variants of the visionary experience (eagle, bear, and badger) and the synthesis of those elements into a single cohesive expression of the visionary world. The shaman's necklace is a symbolic expression of this unity and of the powers through which it was manifested. The visionary encounter has its particular signs, themselves charged with the gifts of power given to the visionary, that become the personal icons of the visionary. The material form of the experience links the visionary with specific powers yet simultaneously represents the wholeness or totality of the lived world. This is an inherent topological principle: the whole is more than the sum of its parts. The dreaming topology, constantly unfolding its spiritual potential through the agency of its manifestation, transparency, and metamorphosis, simultaneously expresses the mystery of presence and its numinous fullness. In this sense, every vision expresses the totality from which it comes forth.

CHAPTER FOUR

Isolation and Suffering

In the various ways of gaining supernatural favor may be recognized three main types: the visionary may receive a revelation without seeking one or enduring any hardship whatsoever; he may be visited by supernatural beings in times of difficulty without a deliberate courting of them; and he may go in quest of a vision, generally subjecting himself to suffering in order to arouse their commiseration and thus obtain a revelation.

—Robert Lowie, *Religion of the Crow Indians*

THE ACQUISITION OF dreaming power and its subsequent integration into the life of the dreamer could occur in numerous ways and under highly divergent conditions. While the ritually structured vision quest was widespread among most of the nineteenth-century Plains and Prairie peoples, involuntary or spontaneous visions were a major source of personal empowerment. Indeed, the high percentage of spontaneous visionary experiences recorded in the ethnography strongly suggests that the vision complex for the Plains peoples was part of a ritually induced recreation of the spontaneous visionary encounter. The visionary epistemé of the Native American worldview intrinsically sustains an ongoing belief not only in the reality of dream-spirits but also in the possibility of an immediate, spontaneous encounter with them. Because the lived world is charged with potential and power, the possibility of visionary encounter is omnipresent. Many individuals had powerful visionary experiences without any ritual preparations or even a particular religiously motivated intent. The Plains vision quest ritual came to epitomize the informal quality of such experience and to heighten it through a ritualized form.[1]

The religious motivation for the undertaking of a vision quest centered on the ability of the visionary to establish a living, experiential contact with the primary sources of spiritual empowerment. The "gift of power," which could be channeled into a variety of socially recognized forms such as warfare, skill in crafts, healing, or a variety of shamanistic abilities, is, in the ethnographic texts, the ultimate religious source of personal empowerment for the Plains peoples. The visionary experience opened the doors for specific patterns of personal development, while simultaneously serving as a source for both socioreligious organization and communally patterned forms of ritual enactment. The visionary experience established a meaningful sense of religious identity both in terms of the particular society the visionary might choose to join and in terms of socially recognized abilities gained through the vision.

The knowledge gained by the individual in the vision was not theoretical but paradigmatic and capable of being communally enacted under appropriate circumstances. Among highly developed dreamers, however, this knowledge could supersede communally shared patterns of belief and take on highly esoteric and unusual forms. Often such knowledge was "secret" and only accessible to those who belonged to the various visionary societies or who had received truly remarkable and unusual powers. Many dreamers did not discuss their dreams with others, for such discussion might result in a loss of power. Those who, as a result of their dreams, practiced a harmful use of their power within the community ("witchcraft") also did not generally discuss the nature of their powers or abilities.[2]

Three basic motivational patterns can be identified as underlying the general structure of the search for personal empowerment: the quest as a socially significant rite of passage undertaken around the time of puberty; the individually or communally motivated quest as a response to a particular social condition, crisis, or cyclical event affecting the community; and the quest undertaken as a means of attaining or enhancing personal empowerment. The intentional structure of such motivation, seen from the religious viewpoint, is the same in all three cases: to attain a specific and immediate relationship with the dream-spirits and to acquire the means to transform and enhance the human situation. In most cases, the search for empowerment is open to all individuals and is consciously sought by most individuals, particularly men.

Among the Gros Ventre of Montana, the search for power is recorded as pervasive and essential for the development of personal ability: "Men and woman and even some young boys and girls, sought or accepted power, and such power was by no means confined to professional medicine men but was widely distributed. . . . Boy stated: 'Only a few men and women had ancestral helpers, but it was the usual thing for grownups, men and women, to have some kind of power. . . . Males would start questing when young, but older men would also go out to seek power.'"[3] Moreover, according to Boy, an elder Gros Ventre, the seeking of power generally resulted in the seeker's being given ritual instruction for the use of that power, a sacred song to be sung as an invocation of the power, and certain sacred objects that contained or manifested the power.[4] The intentional search for power is meant to bring about specific, identifiable results that can subsequently be used by the individual for either personal or communal benefit. Age and gender are not major considerations, although the majority of dreams recorded (by male ethnographers) are of men's experiences.

According to the visionary texts, among the Mandan, the Hidatsa, the eastern and western Sioux, the Dhegiha-speaking peoples and the Comanche, fasting for a vision was undertaken at about the time of puberty as a normative rite mostly for young males. Although the vision quest was not as institutionalized as it was among the foregoing groups, frequent references to visions experienced during youth are also found among the Assiniboine, Cheyenne, Plains Cree, and Gros Ventre. Exceptions to the male-dominant vision quest can be found among the Mandan, where both men and women fasted for power; every women fasted for a dream at least once in her lifetime, usually in her garden or on the corn scaffolds.[5] Older women among the Absarokee might seek a vision, particularly at the time of the death of a relative.[6] Vision experiences of women are mentioned for the Gros Ventre, the Apache,[7] the Arapaho,[8] the Assiniboine,[9] the Blackfoot,[10] the Cheyenne,[11] the Comanche,[12] the Kiowa,[13] the Dhegiha peoples,[14] and the Pawnee.[15] Among the Teton Sioux, a young boy might seek a vision when his voice was changing, and a young girl, during the time of her first menstrual flow.[16] Generally speaking, the ethnography supports the basic observation that women most frequently received visionary experience spontaneously and without male supervision.[17]

An excellent explanation of the complex religious symbolism of the dream fast at puberty is given by Alice Fletcher and Francis La Flesche, as found among the Omaha:[18]

The literal meaning of the word *Nózhinzhon* is "to stand sleeping"; it here implies that during the rite the person stands as if oblivious of the outer world and conscious only of what transpires within himself, his own mind. This rite took place at puberty, when the mind of the child had "become white." This characterization was drawn from the passing of night into day. It should be remembered that in native symbolism night is the mother of day; so the mind of the new-born child is dark, like the night of its birth; gradually it begins to discern and remember things as objects seen in the early dawn; finally it is able to remember and observe discriminatingly; then its mind is said to be "white," as with the clear light of day. . . . [It] is "old enough to know sorrow" . . . [and] should enter into personal relations with the mysterious power that permeates and controls all nature.

This rite is recorded as undertaken by a young male, and it could be repeated until he had married, at which time the Omaha said the individual's life "had become fixed." Only if he was to become a priest or shaman would he continue to pray and fast. The Omaha appeal made at this time is directed to the highest power, Wakonda, in the hope that the individual would receive something that would help him throughout his lifetime. The awakening mental and spiritual life of the adolescent child is believed to be particularly receptive to the influence of visionary experience, which could bestow powerful gifts on the correctly motivated individual.

Generally, among the nomadic Plains peoples, the seeking of a vision might continue throughout adulthood and even into old age. While it is a pattern usually associated with youth and young adulthood, the search for both communal and individual power continued because of crises or needs during times of stress throughout an individual's lifetime. For the Comanche, a number of examples of such crisis motivation can be given: during mourning, to face an enemy in war, for revenge, for curing severe illness, and for success in hunting or raiding.[19] These types of motivation are typical for the plains area and are very widespread.

The motivational structure could also be influenced by numerous secondary factors such as individual psychology, age, and experience; communal conditions of plenty or want; social aspiration for "place" within the communal structure; and the religious temperament or inclination of the individual who thought seriously about the centrality of religion in the overall worldview. Yet implicit in such questing is the underlying structure of the visionary epistemé, which is informed and empowered by the reality of a religiously designated cosmography. What might appear to a nonparticipant in Native American culture as purely "secular" motivation (e.g., success in war) is in fact given meaning and religious significance through the gift of power granted by the most revered sources intrinsic to the shared religious worldview. The particular result desired by the individual always relates to primary sources of empowerment in a spiritually sensitive context, even if that result is acquired through the purchase of visionary objects (or a bundle) possessed by another.[20]

Continued success in fasting for a vision in many cases resulted in the visionary's becoming a recognized shaman or master dreamer whose ability surpassed that of other members of the community. Power was concieved of as something that could be built up over the years in the form of various types of knowledge. In such a context, spiritual maturity was a function of a continually deepening understanding and ability, which results in the individual's mastering the paradigmatic structures of successful religious behavior. Individuals who had a history of successful visionary experience and are able meaningfully to demonstrate their empowerment in socially recognized forms became religious leaders. On the other hand, many individuals who sought dreams and visions were not successful in their quests and consequently were regarded as having little or no power; they often had low social standing as well.[21]

To illustrate the complexity of the questing pattern, I will distinguish a number of phases and describe the significant aspects of each in the context of a comparative analysis. The structures of the vision quest and the resulting religious experiences and instructions received have very distinctive characteristics, all of which contribute to a rebirthing of the individual in a context of developing responsibility and understanding of the visionary topology.

UNSOUGHT DREAMS

Frances Densmore, in discussing the dream fast of the Chippewa, noted that "fasting, isolation, and mediation" are the principal conditions under which a powerful dream might be attained.[22] This observation certainly holds true for the Plains and Prairie groups and a large proportion of the other indigenous peoples of North America. According to the ethnography, the most fundamental condition for the visionary, power-bestowing dream is that of isolation. While dreams did occur spontaneously, particularly among the young and the very old in the course of normal sleep, the majority of the visions recorded occurred when the individual was alone and generally separated from communal activities or companionship.

Implicit in such separation is a symbolic dimension expressing movement from socially defined activity to a more liminal condition in which social identity is subordinated to the potency and powers that imbue the visionary ecology. Separation and movement away from communal activity is, at the same time, an immersion in the enfolded realm of the mythic and visionary world. Outside the camp circle is not a wilderness but an open horizon where encounters with the mysterious beings are more likely. Furthermore, this immersion is heightened by the ever-present reality of danger, particularly in the form of hostile human beings. Movement from the socially known and nomadically defined encampment into the less secure and potentially mysterious world of the unknown is a movement into liminality. In

this sense, liminality refers to a lessening of systemically determined social relations in the face of a transformative power stimulated by a heightened sense of the mysterious character of the
natural world.[23]

Visionary origin narratives often occur in situations of spontaneity, isolation, and suffering. Such a narrative is given with
regard to the foundation of the ritual known as the march to the
tobacco gardens by the Absarokee. This ritual procession came
to form a paradigmatic element of the more general structures
of the Absarokee tobacco-planting societies. An Absarokee
woman, a captive among the Piegan Blackfoot, managed to escape and, in the process, to steal a Piegan otter medicine bundle:
"The Crow woman saw a Piegan otter [bundle], stole it and ran
away. She was overtaken by a snowstorm . . . and slept there
with the otter. The otter gave her a dream and told her that if
they got home in safety, they should join the Tobacco and take
the lead in going to the garden."[24]

Like any Piegan, the woman would have recognized the otter-
skin medicine bag as a sacred object charged with power potentially helpful to her in obtaining freedom. Also, stealing an enemy
medicine bundle would have brought her social recognition for
an act of bravery. Thus, in isolation, under stress and fatigue,
carrying a highly sacred object, she has a dream of power in
which the otter appears to her and gives her the gift of institut-
ing a sacred march to the tobacco garden during the annual
tobacco-planting rites. A fusion takes place between the woman
and the dream-spirit under circumstances of isolation, which
results in a heightened sense of religious participation and social
identity.

This general pattern of separation, visionary revelation, return, and new (or renewed) responsibility has its locus of acquisition in the liminal period of separation during which the individual encounters the dream-spirits. This period of heightened
awareness, of increased watchfulness and attentiveness resulting from isolation, is a time during which any sound, movement, or discontinuity in perception might represent danger in
the form of a human enemy, a dangerous animal, or a mysterious being. Immersion in the potency of the natural world, heightened by the constant threat of danger and strengthened through

stress, hunger, or anxiety, placed receptive individuals in a state of vulnerability. In such a condition the frequent human response, as recorded in the ethnography, was to call on all the visionary powers for help and assistance. Having no social or communal support led the individual to seek aid from the powers of the religious and mythic world. A continuum can be sketched ranging from a simple hunting expedition or a child playing alone to situations of intense stress and danger. In all these conditions, isolated individuals spontaneously encounter a manifestation that transforms their awareness of the lived world and grants new power and responsibility. The condition of separation and isolation is essential to this process because it heightens the receptivity of the individual to altered states of awareness through a suspension of socially sustained modalities of interaction.

Dreams of empowerment that come unsought are frequently associated with additional types of stress or crisis: natural disasters such as famine or extremes of weather; attack by enemies; or a variety of emotional conflicts engendered by problematic kinship relationships. Any of these could catalyze a powerful dream. This is particularly true for female visionaries. For example, frequent conflict between husband and wife could elicit a powerful, spontaneous dream. After a quarrel with her husband, an Omaha woman left the communal hunt to return to the deserted village, where she subsequently had a vision of the Haethúska warrior-society dance performed by dead warriors.[25] For the Gros Ventre, John Cooper specifically mentions that a woman might cease eating and drinking and wander away from camp as a consequence of being angry at her husband.[26] In such a condition she might well have a vision.

Coyote Woman, a Mandan married to a man who frequently beat and abused her, was sent by her husband to check his pit traps. There she discovered a wolf who spoke to her and coughed up a sacred blue stone to use for healing among her people. The wolf also told her that her husband would not return from his hunting expedition because he would be slain by wolves. The wolf's prediction subsequently proved correct.[27]

In an origin tale collected by Maurice Boyd, a young Kiowa boy named Takatahle was admonished by his grandmother for losing her rabbit-hunting stick: "After his grandmother had admonished the grandson, he lay on his little bed in the tipi and cried, for he was sorry he had lost the rabbit stick. Then a sudden vision informed him that he would deliver his people from great famine. . . . The voice said, 'I will guide you.'"[28]

All these examples reflect an emotional tension that contributes to the spontaneous unfolding of visionary contents. The conditions for the spontaneous visionary experience involve a tension that disturbs the congruence of social relations and through stress shifts the individual into a state of receptivity to the potential of the visionary world, generally in a condition of emotional, physical, or social withdrawal and isolation. It is the visionary powers, inhabiting the lived world under conditions of liminality, who frequently become a solace and an authority for redressing the structures of human relations. The sanctions for such a restructuring do not lie within the strict confines of known social relations, nor are they validated only by socially determined processes. While redress of communal tensions exists in the normative patterns of social interaction—for example, the use of the tribal pipe to heal social friction—the most powerful sanctions come directly from the vision experience (which established the pipe ritual). The vision imbues the individual with an aura of power that, if demonstrated successfully, can lead to renewed social identity. On a more interior plane, it can bestow a sense of self-worth and heighten the intimacy between the individual and the determinative, life-sustaining forces of the visionary world.

Many rites or rituals are established through spontaneous, stress-related visions. During a severe winter famine, a young Blackfoot by the name of Mink Woman heard a voice singing off away from camp:[29]

She went under a big tree that had shed the snow, and found that the singing was under a big log there. . . . She could hear the words of the song, which were: "Woman, come and take me. I am strong with Sun's power." . . . She conquered her fear, and, kneeling, lifted some bark that had slipped down from the log, and found under it, resting upon a mat of buffalo hair, a small reddish-colored stone that had the shape of a buffalo. . . . Mink Woman carried the buffalo stone concealed in her bosom, slept with it close under her pillow. . . . Then, on the fourth night, while she slept, the stone said to her: "Poor woman, I pity you and your poor starving people, and am going to help you. Now, listen carefully; I am going to tell you what you must do to save your people."

This revelation by the sun of the sacred buffalo stone is a spontaneous vision that establishes the origin of the winter buffalo-calling rites among the Blackfoot. Of equal significance, it also validates the spiritual significance of women as receivers of sacred revelation. In this way the social significance of women in roles of religious leadership is restructured and validated by the vision. As Boy Chief told James Schultz: "From that day, women had an ever-increasing share in sacred matters, until, finally they, and not the men, conducted the ceremonies of the building of the great [dance] lodge that was given to the Sun, every summer in the Berries Ripe moon [August]."[30] Similar foundation rites established by the spontaneous visions of women may be found among the Cheyenne and the Ponca.[31] More familial rites established by women may be found among the Gros Ventre.[32]

For the southern plains and the Great Basin area, the acquisition of power through spontaneous dreaming is well documented. The Ute, Paiute, and Shoshone frequently receive power in unsought dreams, and this is a recognized means for receiving and developing religious identity.[33] A similar attitude exists among the Apache, where an individual who sponsors a ceremony might hear a voice or have a direct visionary experience. The person does not fast or make any formal preparations for such an experience.[34] Among the Shoshone, remarkable power could be obtained in a spontaneous dream. Big Nez Perce, an outstanding Wind River Shoshone warrior, received such power that he was believed to be invulnerable to bullets. When hit, the bullets would knock him down and bruise him but never penetrate his body.[35] For the Kiowa, Parsons notes that the acquisition of power is frequently "accidental" and occurs without special ritual preparations.[36] The spontaneous quality of these dreams in no way diminishes their power or significance. Dreams and visions of the greatest power might be experienced spontaneously and without ritual preparation.

Many spontaneous vision experiences of children are also recorded, and they are frequently of remarkable power and complexity. The best-known example is the childhood vision of the Oglala Sioux holy man Black Elk, who, at the age of five (in 1869), while out playing with his new bow and arrows during a thunderstorm, received his first vision. His great vision came at the age of nine, during an apparent bout of illness.[37] A similar example was recorded by Clark Wissler for the foundation of the Sioux Medicine Bow society. A young boy, frightened by a thunderstorm and hiding among some trees, was given a white horse to ride with the thunder powers during a spontaneous vision experience in which he also received the Medicine Bow and its rites.[38] A remarkable story is told about a young Iowa boy named Lone Walker who, as a small child, followed his father during a buffalo hunt, weeping because he also wanted to participate:[39]

In the distance he saw them shoot a buffalo bull, a small one, and leave it lying there while they passed on. Just as he was passing the carcass, sobbing and crying, the bull spoke to him. "Ah, so it is you, Lone Walker? I'm glad you came, for I've recovered and am just about to get up again. Now I am going to tell you what to do from this time on." . . . Then the buffalo taught him the roots and herbs they used to heal the sick.

Such visionary experiences in early childhood are recorded as common among the great Plains shamans and healers. These early visionary encounters with mysterious, more-than-human beings manifest a potential capacity and sensitivity for visionary experience. Such knowledge is believed to be particularly common and normal in children. As an Oto woman expressed it when one of her young children told her that he had seen a bald-faced sorrel horse sitting by the moon, "There is nothing wrong. You are just going through that." Such experiences served to strengthen the belief in the reality and power of the visionary world, its accessibility, and the empowerment of the visionary state. Even though the Oto woman took no particular notice of her son's vision, he believed his wealth in horses was due to this experience.[40]

STRESS AND ILLNESS

One of the most common conditions under which a spontaneous vision can arise is that of extreme stress, illness, or anxiety—
although these states are not necessary preconditions for the
spontaneous vision. The relationship between conditions of illness, stress, or grief and the visionary experience has not been
explored outside the context of psychoanalytic theory. It would
be particularly inaccurate to posit a causal relationship between
stress or illness and visionary experience, because Native American thought with regard to illness and its causes is wholly different from current medical models.

Conditions of illness or emotional stress are most frequently
attributed, in the dream ethnography, to the actions of the sacred beings, either as a consequence of the infringement of social
or religious prohibitions or as a directing of negative or harmful
power through sorcery or other shamanistic practices. Alterna-
tively, an illness might be a sign of a particular psychic or shamanistic ability. Conditions of stress or emotional disturbance
might evoke the pity of the dream-spirits to give aid, particularly if the individual addresses them in a humble manner. In
every case, the state of being ill is commonly attributed to the
mysterious actions of the many beings that pervade the lived
world. From the phenomenological point of view, the visionary
experience is an enhancement of the psychic and spiritual condition of the sick person. The condition of vulnerability to the
dream-spirits, of being ill and thus under the power of those
spirits in a more direct and immediate way, could result in a
vision that subsequently led to a cure or to the resolution of
troublesome problems or other conditions of stress.

One frequent condition of extreme stress was to be separated
from the community during a severe storm and exposed to the
thunder powers. One young Absarokee warrior, fleeing from
the Sioux, managed to escape only to be caught in a thunderstorm:[41]

I watched the hailstorm coming and saw lightning quite close to
me. . . . I saw a big bird coming down among the clouds. His color
was white and he was large. . . . In descending to the ground he
made no noise. I saw him plainly. The lightning came from his

eyes. He sat on the ground. . . . The hailstorm did not come near but left a circle free around the bird and me. I watched the eagle going back up into the heavens. He said, "I am going to adopt you, that is why I came down. Whatever you ask for, we shall hear you." This was the first time I dreamt about him.

In a heightened state of watchfulness and anxiety, the young Absarokee beholds a manifestation that brings him into a direct, living relationship with the mythic reality of the visionary epistemé. The appearance of the Thunder Being is tangible evidence that the sacred beings can give aid and protection to the receptive individual. Furthermore, this individual notes that his experience must be framed in a visionary context: he says that even though awake, he "dreamt" about the Thunder Being. Thus he demonstrates that the experience is not simply literal or physical but visionary, which connotes religious contents and a particular state of awareness. This ability to distinguish the visionary encounter as a unique state of altered awareness is generally attributed to the active, causal presence of the manifestation, and it expresses a fundamental type of heightened religious awareness. The context of the experience also suggests that the visionary powers have a genuine concern and a caring attitude toward human beings, for this dream-spirit appears under circumstances of stress with promises of present and future aid.[42]

A Kiowa medicine woman called Pautsohain, who had escaped capture by the Pawnee, was caught in a thunderstorm while searching for her people. Exposed to lightning and large hailstones, she sought a place to hide:[43]

There was no place to hide. Then as a flash of lightning lighted up the prairie around me, I saw in the grass the dried-up carcass of a buffalo. The skin still covered the ribs, so I crawled inside to take refuge from the huge hailstones which were bruising me. After a while I dropped off to sleep. During the night the buffalo appeared to me in a vision. It spoke to me, saying, "I am going to give you a worthwhile present, valuable in time of war."

Subsequently, she is given knowledge of healing and the use of various sacred objects for wounds received in battle. This knowledge must be passed on to the male members of the buffalo society, each member of which will accompany a war party as doctor. This stress-related vision is interesting in that it shows clearly the multifaceted aspects of the visionary epistemé. Aid and protection is given by the buffalo. The storm is extremely threatening, emotion is heightened, and the buffalo preserves the woman. The strong symbolic connections among Plains people between women and buffalo may account for the predominance of the buffalo in this context. The warfare context is certainly congruent with the thunder power, and the conjunction of the two results in a visionary experience that unites both powers. The spontaneity of the gift seems directly related to the conditions of isolation and emotional stress. It also demonstrates clearly that women could receive visionary knowledge directed toward the establishment of male behavior. Finally, this spontaneous experience strongly contributed to Pautsohain's becoming a medicine woman. Women also had spontaneous visions that pertained to the safety of the entire tribe.[44]

Illness was a common, threatening aspect of Plains Indian life. Little White Man, a young Cheyenne father, became distressed over a serious, life-threatening illness that struck his infant son. Having decided to make a sacrifice for the healing of his child, he was unable to decide what form this sacrifice should take. He had a series of dreams showing him that he should allow himself to be pierced and hung from a sun pole.[45] It is interesting that the appropriate frame for interpreting this experience might be construed as a contest between the power that caused the illness and the sun, which would be associated with the form of sacrifice undertaken by the father. Part of the phenomenology of power lies in the conflictive structures embedded in the mythic world. Various beings are regarded as having more or less power in a shifting context of personal experience. In this case, the father undertakes a rigorous appeal to the sun in order to save the life of his child. Yet the child's illness is also a consequence of the actions of unknown powers. A series of spontaneous dreams directs the father's attention to a recognized, beneficent power that may give the gift of healing after he has demonstrated his willingness to suffer for his son's recovery.

Many narratives discuss the consequences of illness that lead to visionary experiences. A Cheyenne named Picking Bones Woman became ill and had the experience of floating out of her lodge and running above the earth into an entrance in the side of a big bluff.[46] There she conversed with a group of elders who gave her instructions to return an infant to her husband. She returned floating through the air to her lodge, where she saw her own body lying on a bed. This spontaneous experience demonstrates how the dream-spirits can act on individuals during an illness, when they are unusually receptive to the visionary state.[47] It also implies underlying tensions between husband and wife, a condition already noted as conducive to possible visionary experience.

When the Absarokee warrior Hunts to Die was wounded in battle with an arrow in the hip, he had a vision of a buffalo bull singing sacred songs and spraying water over him. As a result of this vision, he was healed and awoke just as he was being prepared for burial by his relatives.[48] The Sioux Black Elk also had a strange illness in which his arms, legs, and face became swollen and he was unable to walk. His parents were seriously afraid he would die because of his weakened condition. He also felt himself taken out of his body to a sky tipi where he received sacred instructions.[49]

These examples illustrate the range of circumstances in which illness may precipitate a visionary experience. Mostly, these illnesses are life-threatening, placing the individual in a condition of isolation and separation from the normal activities of daily life. The individual is under emotional stress and cut off from the normally supportive environment of the community. In this condition, he or she becomes receptive to the visionary manifestations implicit in the visionary episteme. As the reality of the visionary world begins to supersede the normal context of social existence, the individual enters into a heightened state where the enfolded order of the visionary world reveals its powerful, transformative contents. The illness of the individual becomes a bridge by which it is possible to enter directly into communication with more-than-human beings. Thus the condition of illness catalyzes a manifestation of power in the form of instruction and paradigmatic knowledge. The experience of the individual confirms the reality of the enfolded order, and the frequently rapid recovery and renewed health and ability of the individual dramatically demonstrate that reality to others.

DEATH AND MOURNING

Another critical period of liminality came during and after the death of a relative or mate. The emotional upheaval caused by death, the intensity of sorrow and mourning over the loss of a relative, was strongly felt. The unfortunate stereotype of the stoical, unfeeling "Indian" is not only a cultural misperception but also a denial of the powerful cathartic processes involved in loss and separation—a denial characteristic of modern, non-native cultures.[50] Rites of mourning and the intensity of feeling expressed frequently acted to create the appropriate conditions for visionary experience. The receptivity of individuals to the sacred powers was heightened as they made themselves pitiable through lamentation and tears. The mourning pattern frequently involved the individual in periods of separation and solitude. This condition of turning away from the social interactive world and toward the more liminal condition was fully recognized as a period of particular visionary significance.

The Nózhinzhon ritual of the Osage, previously mentioned, was also a supplicatory rite that could be undertaken during mourning:[51]

A man, having lost by death his wife, son, daughter, brother, or sister, takes the rite for a period of four days only, or he may continue it for a few months or even as long as two years.... At any time during the summer season the man who is stricken with sorrow by the loss of some beloved relative may take upon himself this rite and seek consolation from the Mysterious Power whose presence fills all space in the heavens and all things upon the earth.

This Osage search for consolation from Wakonda consisted of simply going off from the camp to wander alone or to stand weeping and mourning in prayer and sorrow to the Great Power. Such behavior during mourning, pervasive among Plains peoples, points to an underlying belief in the supportive, healing, responsive powers of the visionary world. To go out, away from society, to suffer, to be alone, and to be in sorrow and affliction evoked the pity of the dream-spirits. The mourning period could be as short as four days or as long as two years, depending on the emotional stress and sense of loss of the mourner. Furthermore, participation in mourning and in the seeking of spiritual renewal was wholly voluntary, particularly beyond the conventional four-day period.

A very expressive intensity of grief is characteristic of the Plains Indian female mourning pattern. As Boy told Cooper with regard to the Gros Ventre: "A woman does not ask for power. Power comes to her. When mourning for relatives and sleeping out [away from camp] and suffering without food, somebody might take pity on her and give her power without her asking."[52] Robert Lowie makes a similar comment with regard to practices among the Absarokee: "Young girls did not seek visions, but when older they might and did. Usually this happened when a relative had been killed or died a natural death."[53]

Generally, the visionary experiences of women arose in circumstances of spontaneity as a consequence of the intensity of their suffering over the loss of a close relationship. Mourning had a distinctive cultural sanction for the full expression of emotion by both women and men, who might also feel an acute sense of loss. Typically, a woman's hair would be cut off or unbraided and allowed to hang loose, her arms and legs would be gashed, she would wear old battered clothes, and other deprivations would be undertaken for an indeterminate period of time. These conditions, coupled with wandering in solitude and separation from the main camp, produced the appropriate circumstances for evoking the compassion of the dream-spirits.

An outstanding example of this type of experience is described by the Absarokee medicine woman Pretty Shield, who mourned for her infant daughter for more than two months, staying away from camp and wandering in the hills day after day:[54]

I had slept little, sometimes lying down alone in the hills at night, and always on hard places. I ate only enough to keep me alive, hoping for a medicine-dream, a vision, that would help me to live and to help others. One morning . . . I saw a woman ahead of me. She was walking fast . . . but suddenly she stopped and stood still, looking at the ground. I thought I knew her, thought that she was a woman who had died four years before. I felt afraid. I stopped, my heart beating fast. "Come here, daughter." Her words seemed to draw me toward her against my will.

Walking a few steps, I saw that she was not a real woman, but that she was a [sacred] Person, and that she was standing beside an ant hill. "Come here, daughter." Again I walked toward her when I did not wish to move. Stopping by her side, I did not try to look into her face. My heart was nearly choking me. "Rake up the side of this ant hill and ask for the things that you wish, daughter," the Person said, then she was gone.

Now in this medicine-dream, I entered a beautiful white lodge, with a war-eagle at the head. He did not speak to me, and yet I have often seen him since that day. And even now the ants help me. I listen to them always. They are my medicine, these busy, powerful little people, the ants.

It is interesting to note that Pretty Shield's solitude and suffering are directly connected to her desire for a vision that would help her and others. The search for power through visionary experience is often motivated by a desire to share the power received for the welfare of the community. The ghostly relative encountered here acts as an intermediary who brings Pretty Shield into a direct relationship with the dream-spirits, in this case the eagle and the ants. This encounter with the numinous is charged with the uncanny sense of potential relationship between the living and the dead, a condition normally enfolded into the visionary order. Here, as the vision unfolds, the encounter moves into progressively deeper strata of the mythic world. The dead help bring the living into a more direct experience of the visionary reality. And the powers revealed become part of an established relationship that lasts a lifetime, a relationship that becomes a counterpoint to the loss of relationship suffered through the infant's death. One of the functions of the dream-spirits is to redress the social imbalances created by loss and death.

A similar experience by Long, a young Absarokee warrior, was recorded by William Wildschut:[55]

Long . . . deeply mourned the death of his sister and stayed away from the camp a long time. He decided to fast. . . . He carried a gun with him. Before he went very far Long saw a deer . . . but before he could pull the trigger, the deer vanished. In its place stood a buffalo. He aimed at it and shot it. . . . As he drew near the buffalo rose and vanished. When Long arrived on the spot where the buffalo had been shot he found some buffalo grease and a stunted horn. He picked up these articles. But instead of continuing on, he returned to camp.

That night he had a dream in which the buffalo again appeared to him and gave him his medicine as represented in a bundle. Long was told that the privations he had endured during the winter [mourning his sister] had aroused the "Without Fires" pity for him. Therefore, they gave him this medicine without expecting him to fast.

Here, the young man is in sorrow and mourning for the entire winter, demonstrating his sincerity and humility. Adding to this, he decides to fast as a further expression of wanting to make himself pitiable to the visionary powers. But before he can fast, he has a mysterious encounter: his perceptions of the world begin to alter and take on a visionary quality as beings begin mysteriously to metamorphose. This metamorphic quality, as noted earlier, is an intermediary stage in moving ever more deeply into the visionary state. The whole experience is contextualized as a consequence of his behavior in mourning for his sister. Such a pattern reinforces the importance of kinship ties in a person's communicating with the sacred beings. The visionary experience is then recapitulated in a dream that communicates the full meaning of the experience.[56] Again there is a significant relationship between a female and the buffalo that grants power, another frequent symbolic conjunction.

Many examples of the power of death and illness to evoke a visionary state are given in the ethnography. Here is a remarkable visionary experience that the Sioux warrior White Bull had in old age:[57]

He was so ill . . . his soul left his body. He saw a man coming from the west all in white. The man said, "I came after you." White Bull rose and followed him. They halted and looked across Cherry Creek. There they saw four other men coming, four from the north. The man in white said, "Look, these men say they wish to befriend you." Soon they arrived. Immediately the skull and horns of a buffalo emerged from the ground. The skull moved, the earth cracked and trembled as the skeleton struggled to come forth. The hump and ribs emerged, the forefeet came out, and at last the whole skeleton heaved up and stood on the prairie. White Bull watched. Flesh covered the bones, hide covered the flesh, hair grew. The buffalo was alive.

The Buffalo said, "Behold me, I wish to be your friend, before we all go into the ground together. You have a good name, because you took it from our brother, the buffalo. I am strong and hearty, therefore they have appointed me to help you. Observe what I eat, I eat these. They make me strong. These four roots I eat. Do likewise." They all moved about over the prairie and found four plants growing. Then suddenly they vanished and White Bull found himself in his bed again. As soon as the spring was far enough advanced, the chief sent his wife out to look for these four plants, which he described. She found them. He ate them, and was cured.

The symbolism of rebirth is quite apparent here as part of the regenerative power of the visionary experience. To move into that reality through an altered awareness meant to be revitalized and renewed through the practical application of visionary knowledge. The four men become not only symbolic expressions of the world order and its sacred directionality, but also of the prescriptive herbs that heal the sick person. The power of names is also emphasized here; it is a buffalo bull who imparts the healing knowledge to honor the name of the sick person. Furthermore, the topological structure of the visionary world is reinforced, because a common belief among the Sioux was that buffalo were a chthonic power and lived beneath the earth. And all this occurs spontaneously as a consequence of White Bull's being in a near-death state, a condition that frequently invokes the visionary experience.

CHAPTER FIVE

Rites and Preparations

When I was a young man I wanted a dream through which I could know what to depend upon for help. Having this desire, I went to a medicine-man and told him about it. He instructed me what to do, and I followed his instruction in everything.

—Siyáka in Frances Densmore, *Sioux Music*

IN DISCUSSING the more formalized aspects of the vision quest, or dream fast, it is necessary to draw certain distinctions. The degree of formalization recorded in the dream ethnography is quite variable, ranging from very informal circumstances to highly formalized procedures that are carefully observed and directed by either relatives or religious elders. Two forms generally characterize the Plains vision quest. The first is the unsupervised pattern of dream fasting, which involves the individual in a search for a vision or dream as a self-determined quest, frequently undertaken without supervision or guidance. The individual might be either a neophyte or an experienced dream seeker. In either case, the individual proceeded to the fasting place without any guidance or assistance. The second type of dream fast is the supervised quest, usually carried out under the guidance of an experienced elder. The supervision could be highly or only minimally structured and given by a parent, another relative, or a recognized religious leader.

A close reading of the ethnography shows that the degree of formalization varies significantly within a single group. I interpret this as a function of the general informality of the quest within a particular community or as a consequence of limited traditional knowledge and supervision's having been passed on to the individual during a period of great cultural stress. Thus the dream fast pattern is highly complex and has many divergent forms both throughout the Plains area and within a particular Plains group. Nevertheless, this variability has several distinctive forms.

Among the late-nineteenth-century Lakota Sioux, whose vision quest practices are perhaps the best known, degrees of formalization were qualified according to the purpose of the dream fast. In 1896, the Lakota holy man George Sword told James Walker: "If the vision desired is concerning a matter of much importance, a shaman should supervise all the ceremony relative to it. If it is a small matter, there need be but little ceremony, but if it is of very great importance there should be much ceremony."[1] Such an attitude confirms a widespread recognition that the significance of a vision would be determined in part by the motivation of the individual—that is, in accordance with the actual intentions and goals of the faster. This motivation itself would be based on either individual concerns or more communally defined goals. The degree of ceremony indicates the seriousness of the intent or need. Among the Plains peoples, individuals frequently sought visionary experiences having to do with specific types of personal empowerment—war, healing, hunting, and so on.

Nevertheless, there are communally sanctioned times for seeking a vision that involve the entire group—for example, the Sun Dance or communal hunts. Among the more settled river-valley dwellers such as the Hidatsa, Mandan, Pawnee, and Dhegiha-speaking peoples, visions are recorded as adjuncts to communal ceremonial structures, and the motivation for undertaking a vision quest is frequently a communally defined goal. As recorded by Alfred Bowers, among the Hidatsa and Mandan, winter fasting for a vision had two distinctive patterns: the individual search for visionary instruction and the calling of the buffalo herds closer to the villages.[2] Of the two, the second was regarded as having greater importance, even though visions might be received by the individual. At such a time, restrictions were imposed on the entire community. If, during an individual fast, the buffalo herds arrived in the vicinity, it was considered a particularly good omen for the faster.

The most informal approach to visionary dream seeking is found in the Great Basin ethnography. In general, visions are recorded as coming to the individual without any formal questing. The acquisition of power through visionary experience is depicted as a spontaneous gift that could not be acquired except through unsolicited dreams or visions, although Willard Park notes that among the Paviotso, certain places such as caves were regarded as particularly favorable for inducing sacred dreams.[3] Edgar Siskin, whose work was done among the Washo in the late 1930s, notes that the attainment of power among the Ute, Washo, and Paiute peoples is through unsought dreams or visions.[4] Among the Shoshone, Robert Lowie records that the search for a sacred dream or vision was undertaken in a very informal manner.[5] Elsie Parsons mentions that among the Kiowa, "acquiring a 'familiar' or guardian spirit appeared to be a matter of accidental supernatural experience rather than a definite quest."[6] That so many Native American people received dreams of power or had visionary experiences in a free and spontaneous manner strongly suggests that visionary power came to certain individuals whether they fasted or not. In these cases, it came not as a result of stress or isolation but in a context of relaxation, and it was based on individual temperament and predisposition for the visionary experience.

In discussing the means by which power could be acquired among the Absarokee, Robert Lowie reported Grey Bull's belief that "some dreamt in their lodges. These usually became rich, acquiring plenty of horses."[7] These dreamers received visionary power through spontaneous means in the midst of their normal social milieu, without effort or trial. They were thought to be particularly lucky and blessed because they did not have to undergo the rigors of a more conscious search for visionary dreams. Grey Bull also remarked on those who were "usually poor people, [who] would fall asleep somewhere when very tired and get a vision." These individuals had visions but not in their lodges, signifying a displacement from the normative social milieu. In these spontaneous cases, the more the dreamer moved into the liminal world beyond the camp circle and away from the socially inherited symbols of cultural position and identity, the more ambivalent became the nature of the visionary experience. Individuals lacking strong social identity were regarded as unlikely to dream powerful dreams, although in practice anyone might have one. A general exception is that women often had spontaneous vision experiences in the home as well as away from camp.[8]

The significant point is that Plains peoples did not devalue in any way a dream or vision that was received spontaneously in an unstructured manner. The vision's power and validity were not determined by the quest per se but by its pragmatic results. A powerful dreamer was one who manifested visionary power in acts of a sacred and mysterious nature. There are many examples of vision seekers who suffered trying to attain visions and yet received no real empowerment. The central issue is not the manner of acquiring a dream or vision, but the ability to demonstrate a gift of power and thereby to validate the presence and reality of the visionary world. Among certain people such as the Mandan and Hidatsa, however, fasting itself was a means for increasing individual power, even if the individual received no vision.[9] For the Cheyenne, George Grinnell mentions that to practice wu-wun, or "starving," in the hills was a matter of sacrifice that benefited the faster regardless of his having received or failed to receive a vision.[10]

PURIFICATION AND PRAYER

Even in a very informal approach to the vision quest there is a certain degree of preparation, generally involving symbolic and purification activities meant to demonstrate the right-mindedness of the seeker. When an individual sets out to seek a vision, it means exposure to the mysterious and the unknown. This requires a certain degree of preparedness, a clarity of purpose, and a general knowledge of how such seeking should be undertaken. Among the Omaha, the traditional search for a vision was an informal and yet obligatory practice. The Nózhinzhon rite, as previously mentioned, was required of all young men shortly after puberty. The individual received little instruction. He was given a bow and some arrows for protection and told not to use them for the procurement of food. Clay was put on his head, symbolizing both humility before the powers and the primal matter of creation brought up from the ocean by the diving animals. Similar use of clay on the face or body of a faster is also mentioned for the Pawnee, the Kiowa, and the Plains Cree.[11]

The following is a description of the four day Nózhinzhon rite as normally undertaken by an Omaha youth. R. F. Fortune mentions that the youth would not have heard any recitation of previous vision experiences from his father or other relatives, because such a recitation would endanger the father's power and consequently his life:[12]

When going forth to fast, the youth went silently and unobserved. No one accosted him or gave him counsel or direction. He passed through his experience alone, and alone he returned to his father's lodge. No one asked him of his absence, or even mentioned the fact that he had been away. For four days he must rest, eat little, and speak little. After that period he might go to an old and worthy man who was known to have a similar vision. . . . Should he speak of his vision before the expiration of four days, it would be the same as lost to him.

A similar pattern of fasting with minimal instruction is found among the Oto, who made an interesting distinction between fasting for a vision with and without supervision:[13]

When a boy was about twelve years old he was sent out to fast and seek a vision. "You must fast if you want to be something. Especially this is true of boys. If you are a good boy and mind your teaching, you go off to fast alone. But if you are not, you are sent out to fast with a brave and a teacher, who is an old man. They make you fast so that you will be better. They make you ask for what you want."

The idea of "minding your teaching" means that the individual could voluntarily undertake the quest and seek power through a self-determined motivation. Such a motivation would be communally structured and reflect some degree of social expectation. Yet, the choice to go out into the mysterious world of

the visionary powers alone and unguided required inner fortitude and courage. Some individuals needed the supervision of
successful vision seekers in circumstances that were frequently
frightening and unnerving. A similar informal rite is recorded
for the Kansa, among whom both young men and women un-
dertook the fast for four days. Significantly, women frequently
dreamed of the accomplishments and powers of their brothers,
aptly illustrating the male-dominant structure of the Plains social order.[14]

A similar pattern of informal fasting for a dream is recorded
for the Pawnee. Even though the Pawnee account for all their
bundle rites and many other ceremonials as having originated
in visions, these visions most frequently occurred spontaneously
in circumstances of isolation or stress. Any individual could have
a vision experience and be taken to the underwater lodges of the
spirit-powers, even though the quest itself was not highly institutionalized. Being associated with the shamanic "doctor" tradition and not the "priestly" tradition of bundle ownership, the
vision was regarded as an expression of a spontaneous gift and
held a somewhat secondary position in relationship to inherited
bundle ownership. Nevertheless, there are numerous accounts
of Pawnee vision experiences. Young Bull received a dream that
he should "stand upon a hill to mourn," and having smeared his
face with clay, he stood on a hill near the village watching the
sun for seven days. On the eighth day he received a vision of a
bear that came out of the sun and blessed him.[15]

Among the upper Missouri River Hidatsa and the Mandan of
North Dakota, whose primary religious organizations revolve
around bundle ownership and associated rites, fasting for a vision was more formalized as a rite associated with the larger
cycles of communal ceremonies. From the age of fifteen or sixteen, young men were encouraged by their older "brothers" (a
more inclusive kinship term than consanguinity) to fast during
major ceremonials. Such fasting was believed to be a necessary
preliminary to receiving a personal vision. Frequently among
the Hidatsa, a young man's mother would "direct his efforts in
securing proper visions."[16] These rites, while having prescribed
times and conditions, were also supervised by ceremonial "fa-

thers" who were experienced warriors and not necessarily recognized holy men. Preparation was less formal than it was among the more nomadic peoples, and it was highly associated with war powers, having a strong emphasis on physical self-injury as a means of inducing visionary experience. The vision was regarded as an adjunct to the attainment of power through a tribal bundle rite, and not as an end in itself. Individuals who lacked long association with bundle rites found it difficult to have their visions recognized.[17]

The highest degree of formalization of the vision quest is found among the truly nomadic Plains people, for whom the quest is a central rite in establishing the religious identity of the individual. While a high degree of variability exists in the ethnography, dependent on the intention and motivation of the individual, certain features are fundamentally similar. One of the most elaborate rituals involving the vision quest is the transfer of medicine power among the Comanche. The Comanche healer and shaman, Sanapia, underwent four years of intensive training under the close supervision of her mother, a well-known holy woman. The transfer of power from mother to daughter culminated in a four-day dream fast after extensive preparations.[18] More usually, the quest begins with an approach to a known holy man or shaman who instructs the individual in a ritual sweat bath and guides him or her through the rites of the fast. It culminates in an interpretation of the dream or vision at the end of the final purification sweat. Among the Lakota Sioux, during the sweat bath the individual is purified for contact with the sacred and exhorted to pay close attention to the environment and to report honestly all experiences while fasting.[19]

Among the Absarokee and Gros Ventre, the faster bathes and then purifies his body by rubbing it with sweet-smelling sage.[20] Typically, among the nomadic groups, the hair is left unbraided as a sign of humility, and the only clothing worn—if any—is a breechcloth. Nakedness symbolizes the complete dependence of the vision seeker upon the visionary powers, and only a robe or blanket protects the faster from storms and cold weather.[21] Often a pipe and tobacco are carried to the site of the fast as a means of communicating, through prayer, with the dream-spirits. Prayer is an inevitable, central aspect of the vision quest and is regarded as such by all Plains and Prairie peoples.

No act of significance, such as the vision quest, would be undertaken without a direct appeal to the many mysterious beings. The method of prayer as direct address is widely shared by most indigenous communities throughout North America. By address I mean the spoken word directed to the visible and invisible beings (or being) that empower all the strata of the visionary world. This act is usually facilitated by correct gestures with the pipe.[22]

In an oral culture, where the integral relationship between speaking, hearing, and acting is raised to a fine art, the spoken prayer is part of the vital link between the individual and the living powers inherent in the natural world. The vital breath, which is regarded by many Plains peoples as a direct expression of the life force, is believed to be an intrinsic, spiritual power within all beings.[23] Every living being is animated by a principle directly associated with breath and thereby speech. To speak is itself a manifestation of the life principle; to speak in prayer means to address the life force, the "breath-soul," in others. To pray means speaking aloud, directly addressing the sacred beings, and establishing living relationships through honest, humble speech. The primary means for establishing the nature of the visionary intent, of demonstrating purpose and belief, is a sincere verbal appeal that demonstrates both humility and knowledge.

Even in the most informal settings, prayer is a vital aspect of the search for knowledge and visionary power. The appropriate manner of address—for example, by a younger individual to an older person, or between people who have kinship relations— permeates all Plains Indian social and religious interactions. To speak well means to understand the appropriate form of address in terms of the quality of relationship between speakers. In relationship to the dream-spirits, to whom specific kinship terms apply, the same or even greater respect must be shown through appropriate speech acts. In prayer this means a high degree of humility and a directness of appeal to the powers whose aid is being sought.

Among some dream societies, the appropriate prayers were

communally shaped; among others, they were individually determined. If the seeker were a young man, his prayers might express a traditional body of lore shared by all vision seekers. If older and more experienced, his prayers would reflect a more highly idiosyncratic content based largely on previous vision experience and oral traditions shared among other holy men or shamans. For example, among the Omaha, every youth was expected to learn the one prayer to be chanted by all during the fasting period: *"Wakonda!* Here in poverty he stands, and I am he!"[24]

HUNGER, THIRST, AND INJURY

In the ethnography, the most common place for seeking a vision is a hill, butte, or mountain. Certain buttes were recognized as particularly powerful and inhabited by dream-spirits willing to share their power and knowledge; each community had its own specifically recognized hills or buttes. The primary concept—to be up above the middle realm of normal human habitation—meant making oneself more visible to all the powers. Although these powers might be of any type, among many groups the power was conceived of as dwelling within the specific hill chosen by the seeker for the fast.[25] The symbolism of the hill or butte was deeply involved with the communally shared structures of thought and belief. Like the sacred earth lodges of performing shamans, the many buttes and prominent hills were thought to be populated by unusual or extraordinary beings.

The Kiowa and particularly the Pawnee recorded visionary experiences that occurred near certain river sites or, in a significant symbolic juxtaposition, on high buttes next to a river, thus uniting both the upper and lower strata of the religious topology.[26] Among both the Comanche and the Hidatsa, the grave of an outstanding warrior or medicine man could be chosen as the appropriate place to fast.[27] Another type of site that had widespread appeal was a place where ancient petroglyphs were carved into the rock.[28] Among the Plains Cree, the preferred site was a high hill, but fasting for a vision often took place in a tree, on a raft, or in a bear's den. Or the faster might choose to spend the entire period on horseback, hoping to receive a horse vision.[29]

The most common time of year for the vision quest, supervised or unsupervised, was springtime. Although this pattern was by no means rigidly adhered to, it was generally shared throughout the greater plains area. Springtime was considered to be a time of awakening of the visionary powers and of the revitalization of all living beings, both animals and plants, as well as such beings as thunder, who brings the spring rains. This was explained rather poetically by the Gros Ventre elder, Boy:[30]

The favorite time of the year for going out to seek war, wealth and doctor power was spring. . . . Bears were easy to get power from in spring. They were eager to give their power at this season. All nature is alive in spring. Grass, trees and leaves wake up. Hibernating animals used to sing before coming out of their winter dens. . . . The body of even a human being is sort of stationary in winter time. All we can do in winter time is to look after our bodies. But in spring the body feels good, and when we look around we see the grass and leaves and animals appearing. . . . They take advantage of the newness of all nature. Everything is in blossom. Most animals then have their young. It is the most "affectionate" season of the year.

Because springtime was a time of awakening, it was a time when the dream-spirits most willingly gave their gifts of power to a vision seeker. The springtime was that part of the temporal cycle expressive of the awakening of power, whereas, for example, midsummer was the time of collective tribal rites and, for many Plains people, a climatic time of communal power; the fall was the time of buffalo hunts, when the large summer communal groups broke into smaller winter encampments. In relationship to the sacred beings in the Plains worldview, time is a dynamic, existential condition that moves through periodic expressions of drama, nearness, and dynamic contact, reaching climactic, communal enactments and, in the winter, entering a period of withdrawal, distance, and subdued isolation. Here can be seen the recurrence of periodic manifestations of the sacred beings, reinforcing the cyclical pattern between the visionary and his or her sources of power. To seek a successful vision is to know the appropriate time for petitioning the sacred powers.[31]

In the formal quest it was frequently necessary for the faster to approach an experienced holy man for guidance and instruction. If, during the previous year, the individual had conceived the idea of fasting for a vision, then in the early spring (as well as at other times of the year) he would take a pipe to the appropriate person to supervise his quest. If this pipe was accepted by the holy man, then the faster was expected to submit completely to the guidance of the holy man. This was particularly true for the Sioux, the Blackfoot, and the Comanche.[32] Among the Gros Ventre, Arapaho, Cheyenne, Absarokee, Pawnee, and Kiowa, the faster could be assisted by a friend or relative who would help prepare the fasting place; or, the faster might seek a vision by going out alone. Among the Plains Cree and the Winnebago, the accompanying individual was an older relative, frequently a father or older brother. In the ethnography, these distinctions are partly determined by the age and experience of the faster: if the faster is younger and less experienced in the vision quest, he would be more likely to seek instruction. Older, more experienced men would frequently fast and seek visions on their own during raiding expeditions, or they might seek visions for remedies to an injury or sickness of a relative or friend. Outstanding healers and religious leaders were most likely to seek visions at times when they were prompted by their dreams and developing ability to increase and strengthen their spiritual power.

Having undergone the appropriate rites of preparation, the faster set out to find a place to fast, accompanied by an experienced elder or relative. The approach to the fasting place was often ritualized. Among the Comanche, a male faster was supposed to stop four times on his way to the fasting place, smoking and praying for assistance in his undertaking.[33] The site was prepared in the correct ritual manner for the fasting experience. An area might be cleared, creating a particularly purified spot where the faster would remain throughout the experience. An example of this procedure among the Lakota Sioux, given by Sword, demonstrates the care that was taken in preparing such a place:[34]

When he comes to the place where he is to stay while fasting, he should prepare a place about as long as a man and about half as wide. He should take from this place all vegetation of every kind and all bugs and worms and everything that lives. He should have four charms [tobacco bundles] made by a shaman and tied in little bundles about as big as the end of the finger. These should be fastened to the small ends of sprouts of the plum tree. These are spirit banners. He should put a banner, first at the west side of the place he has prepared; then one at the north side; then one at the east side; then one at the south side.

Another alternative in creating the fasting place is the building of various types of shelters: a pit dug in the earth, a stone shelter covered with brush, or a simple brush shelter. Among the Gros Ventre, such a sleeping place is recorded as a "call-for-power-lodge" or "nest."[35] A person might choose to fast in a communally recognized place of power, such as the tobacco garden among the Absarokee.[36] It should be remembered that a person could also choose to fast for a vision by simply wandering outside the encampment, moving from place to place. This is particularly true in the Absarokee and Pawnee sources, as well as for women in mourning. In such a cases, the individual wandered away from the protective encampment, making the whole of nature a potential arena for visionary experience.

Early sources suggest that traditional fasting often included a covered site in which the faster could rest, particularly the younger men. This seems true for the Assiniboine, Blackfoot, Plains Cree, and Sioux.[37] Even though Lame Deer, a Lakota holy man, speaks of a vision pit, earlier ethnography does not seem to mention such a structure. It may be a later development in the Sioux vision quest. Joseph Brown, in giving Black Elk's version of the vision quest, specifically mentions that the faster sleeps on the ground on a bed of sage.[38] It seems clear that there are several different means for setting up the site of the fast. An interesting alternative to the traditional fasting place is found in the story of the Gros Ventre Bull Lodge, who began at the age of twelve to fast by staying behind in the old camp circle after the people had moved. There he prayed over the alter where herbs were burnt in honor of the most revered object of the Gros Ventre, the Feathered Pipe. Eventually, he received a series of visions having to do with the pipe.[39]

In the place prepared, the individual would fast, neither eating nor drinking during a stay of many days and nights. Although the number four is a traditionally recognized sacred number, the actual length of the fast might range from a single day and night to as many as ten or more days and nights. The fast was a test of strength, endurance, and humility: the faster stayed until he received a vision or was too weak to continue. The idea of choosing a fixed number of days for the fast plays a very minor role in the ethnography. If the faster was sincere and fasted long enough, the powers would take pity on his suffering. Greater power could be obtained through longer fasts. On the other hand, if the fasting was tied to ceremonial cycles, as it was among the Mandan and Hidatsa, the fast would last only as many days as the ceremony. Going without food or water made the faster "poor" and pitiable to the spirit powers. In all cases, fasting for a vision among Plains peoples involved the voluntary abandonment of the comforts of food, drink, and normal shelter. Further, the seekers placed themselves in a liminal condition devoid of normal social relationships in the hope of establishing more powerful kinship relations with the dream-spirits.

The renunciation of food and water is a form of sacrifice intended to evoke a compassionate response. Because the dream-spirits are regarded as more empowered than human beings, they are thought of as willing to share a surplus of their power with those less fortunate, just as the wealthy and powerful within the human community are supposed to share their wealth with their "poor" relatives. This phenomenon of giving and sharing power is a central feature of the Native American social and religious structure. The social norms of sharing and reciprocity express the greater reciprocity believed to exist between humans and all the beings of the sacred world. In general, the Plains peoples emphasize that the correct approach to the dream-spirits involves expressing feelings of being poor and dependent; human beings depend upon the visible and invisible powers of the world to sustain their existence.

To heighten this dependence and make themselves truly poor, many individuals practiced various forms of self-injury. The general forms of mortification, motivated by a deep desire to demonstrate intensity and commitment to the task at hand, were widely shared among the Plains people. Most commonly, strips of skin were cut from the body and held up as offerings. Another typical practice was to cut off a finger or, more commonly, the last joint of the little finger. Both men and women resorted to this practice in times of great stress or sorrow. A rather remarkable example of this practice was described by the Mandan woman Scattercorn when she told about the fasting of the famous Mandan shaman Big Coat:[40]

He began to cut off his fingers and offer them to the Sun, Moon, and big birds of the sky. He cut off three fingers of each hand, leaving only the thumb and middle finger of each hand which he needed to use the bow and arrow. He cut gashes in his legs and arms. He even cut off flesh and offered it to the Holy Women. Before he stopped fasting he had nearly everything as a guardian. He was always successful when leading war parties.

The general relationship between power and suffering is that the greater the suffering and sacrifice of the individual, the greater is the possible gift of power to the individual. Big Coat accomplished the rare task of gaining multiple powers over an extended period of youthful fasting by making an extreme number of sacrifices. Such powers were also gained by others without any sacrifice; consequently, the quality or degree of power cannot not be evaluated simply by the means of its obtainment. The means reflect the temperament of the individual more than the degree or quality of empowerment. Significantly, Big Coat's power was primarily war power and not, for example, the power of healing. Suffering did not guarantee the gift of power. There are a number of accounts about individuals sacrificing fingers but not receiving visions.[41] Nevertheless, among the Gros Ventre, Absarokee, Assiniboine, Cheyenne, Mandan, Hidatsa, and Sioux, such self-mortification was common, particularly in rites related to the sun dance, during which individuals were pierced with eagle-claws through the chest or back muscles and sometimes suspended from rawhide thongs attached to skewers thrust through the cuts. This type of mortification is still practiced. Other forms of sacrifice included dragging buffalo skulls or leading a horse with thongs attached to skewers driven through the skin.[42]

HEIGHTENED AWARENESS

Although the places and times of fasting are subject to innumerable variations, the intentions of the faster are highly congruent throughout the Plains and Prairie ethnography. Whether the individual chose to be pierced through the back and drag a heavy buffalo skull over the hills, or to be pierced through the chest and hung from a tree limb, or to go wandering alone through the hills offering a finger, or to choose a specific site and remain there many days without food or water, his emotional and mental attitudes were recorded as quite similar to those of other fasters. The intent of the faster was regarded as the most significant and important feature of the fast. This is best illustrated by the general teaching that throughout the fasting experience, the individual is expected to pray constantly and observe carefully every movement and appearance around the fasting place. The appropriate attitude involved concentrating exclusively on the spirits being addressed in prayer and making oneself pitiable. This was accomplished through weeping, starving, and praying in isolation.

Clark Wissler describes the beseeching cry of the Blackfoot vision faster as "a mournful wail almost like a song, the words being composed at will."[43] This intention to cry is also epitomized by the Lakota Sioux, among whom the fasting experience is called *Hanblecheyapi*, or "crying (*cheya*) for a vision (*hanble*)." The term "crying" is taken in its most descriptive sense, for the faster is supposed to stand weeping, tears flowing while praying constantly for a vision.[44] Similarly, among the Kiowa, the faster cries out "*Honde da'kya!*" ("Help me!") when addressing the sacred beings.[45] Among the Hidatsa and the Mandan, young men were "taught how to cry."[46] As mentioned, the Omaha prayer used during the vision fast was the same for all young seekers.[47] A similar practice of crying for a vision is recorded for the Absarokee, Arapaho, Gros Ventre, and Cheyenne.[48]

Arriving at the site selected for the fast, the individual would immediately offer an appropriate prayer to all powers demonstrating his dependence on them and his need for their help. Humbling himself before the powers, he would make his prayer with the pipe that accompanied him throughout the ritual fasting period. The use of prayers and gestures with the pipe was an intrinsic feature of Plains and Prairie religious practice. A typical use of the pipe within the fasting circle was expressed by Sword:[49]

He should have a pipe and plenty of *cansasa* [a special bark] and tobacco mixed. He should then light his pipe and point the mouthpiece first toward the west . . . north . . . east . . . and then south. Then he should point it toward the sky and then toward the earth and then toward the sun. He should have some sweet grass and very often he should burn some of this and some sage. If he does these things in the right way, he will surely receive a vision.

The pipe was frequently used to establish peaceful relations between opposing parties in times of war or during kinship conflicts. In the context of fasting, it can be seen as symbolic means of establishing peaceful relations with and good intention toward with the spirit powers. The pipe is offered so the powers will come and join the faster and help him fulfill his vows of seeking spiritual guidance. It is significant to consider to whom these prayers are addressed. In a general sense, all the powers are addressed (individually or collectively as one great power), but particularly those with whom the faster wishes to establish a personal relationship. Praying to particular powers did not, however, guarantee that it would be those powers who appeared to the faster. For example, a Comanche would in general pray to the power who would be a benefit to both himself and his people.[50] Among the Omaha, prayer was addressed to the highest power only. The elders explained the rite as follows:[51]

In the *Nózhinzhon* the appeal was to *Wakonda*, the great power. There were other powers—the sun, the stars, the moon, the earth—but these were lesser; the prayer was not to them. The appeal was for help throughout life. As the youth goes forth to fast he thinks of a happy life, good health, success in hunting; in war he desires to secure spoils and escape the enemy; if he should be attacked that the weapons of his adversaries might fail to injure him. Such were the thoughts and hopes of the youth when he entered upon this fast, although he was forbidden to ask for any special favor.

That the youth is forbidden to ask for any special favor indicates the underlying religious conception of a complete surrender of the individual to the highest power, who would reveal, through the dream-spirits, that which would be of most help to him. Such a conception reveals a sophistication in human psychology, for the experienced members of the community were fully aware that the individual could not, through conscious intention, actually determine the outcome of the vision fast. The mysterious nature of the vision experience—its variability and unpredictability—precludes a consciously predetermined attitude that might seriously impair or obscure the spontaneous arising of the vision experience. Even though a particular power might be addressed or sought, the actual form of empowerment frequently took an altogether different character. As depth psychology has fully recognized, mental concentration on non-rational, imagistic contents requires a state of receptivity free from rational preoccupations.[52]

A significant counterpoint to prayers addressed to the highest spiritual powers was recorded by James Walker for the Sioux:[53]

You may invoke the spirits [while seeking a vision] in words or songs and you must always address them in a reverential manner. First, you should make an offering of the smoke of the *cansasa*. Offer it first to the Spirit of the East. . . . If this spirit does not send a vision, then call upon [each of the other spirits of the directions]. . . . If these spirits do not send a vision to you, then offer smoke to the Spirit of the Earth and call upon it. If no vision is sent you by this spirit, then you may call upon the spirit of heaven, the Great Spirit. But do not offer smoke to the Great Spirit until after you are sure that the other spirits will not send a vision to you.

Here, the highest power is regarded as so powerful and encompassing that it can only be approached in the most solemn manner after addressing all lesser powers. Such an approach to prayer corresponds to the Lakota belief that dreams and visions could be no greater than the capacity or maturity of the individual dreamer. Frances Densmore recorded a Sioux elder's saying: "A young man would not be great in mind so his dreams would not be like that of a chief; it would be ordinary in kind, yet he would have to do whatever the dream directed him to do."[54] The guiding religious conception is that the individual must address the powers in a ritual manner to allow them to respond in accordance with the maturity and preparedness of the seeker. The degree of ritualization of prayer often corresponds to the experience of the faster: the more experienced seekers tend to use a more ritualized approach to prayer because of the instructions they have already received from dream-spirits.

Another point of view on which power should be addressed is illustrated by the Gros Ventre. The faster is to direct his prayers to the highest power, Behä'tixtch, the Leader of All, "so that the one to whom he went, the one who owned or lived in the hill would be forced or commanded to grant the power that was being requested".[55] Here, the idea of a hierarchy of power is expressed and made accessible to the faster at the highest level. An appropriate appeal to the highest power would cause a lesser power to be sent. Rarely, if ever, would the highest power appear to the faster. The manifestation of sacred power, as I have mentioned, is always through a specific agency identified with a particular being. Among the Blackfoot and other Plains communities, any power could be appealed to, the sun being most commonly addressed, particularly at dawn and dusk.[56] Among many Plains peoples, the relatives of the fasting individual also pray for success during the fast, an act that is believed to strengthen the possibility of receiving a good vision.[57]

An attentive state of mind, heightened through constant prayer and fasting, is directed toward every nuance of activity and change in the environment. The faster constantly seeks a visionary appearance, even in the most minute activity. If the visionary was in a distracted state and "thinking about his wife or about other affairs, he would get nothing."[58] The intention of the faster must be focused exclusively on the vision quest experience and to any possible appearance of the spirit powers. Engaged in constant prayer, frequently moving about in a ritual manner, slowly and with great concentration the seeker studied every nuance of his environment. Among the Sioux, this focus is called *wacinksapa*, "attentive understanding."[59] As mentioned by Joseph Brown, this quality of attentiveness is a pervasive feature of Sioux religious life and is especially important during the vision quest. As Black Elk stated with regard to the vision faster:

"He must always be careful lest distracting thoughts come to him, yet he must be alert to recognize any messenger which the Great Spirit may send to him, for these people often come in the form of an animal, even one as small and as seemingly insignificant as a little ant."[60]

Continuing to walk slowly about the prepared area, perhaps making flesh offerings, praying with complete attentiveness, fasting from food and water, with tears flowing, constantly beseeching the sacred powers, naked and exposed to the elements, the individual frequently entered a state of heightened awareness. In this state, the sacred powers began to manifest the visionary quality of the enfolded order.

Often the individual experienced a tremendously enhanced sensory acuity. Hearing, for example, might be remarkably increased. The Sioux Thomas Tyon gave the following narrative about a vision faster who lay on the ground praying for a vision:[61]

With his arms very properly uplifted in prayer, now as he lies there, he hears something stamp the ground behind him, coming towards him, creeping up stealthily, little by little. He is very excited. So perhaps, all of a sudden, he thinks to raise up his head as it goes by, they say. And he looks at the thing that comes stamping the earth. And then it is very little even though he heard the sound of its breath, it is said. It was only a grasshopper walking although it came stamping the ground, they say.

Speaking in a traditional narrative style, the narrator relates how this enhancement of sound frightened the vision quester. The experience is not the vision itself but rather a preliminary heightening of awareness that often precedes the actual vision experience.[62] Animals can speak to the visionary in an equally preliminary fashion, warning him about some inappropriate action he may have unwittingly committed. For example, the Cheyenne Brave Wolf was told by a swift-hawk that he was fasting too high up on Bear Butte and was too close to the power.[63] Or the faster might, as in a Gros Ventre example, be told to go to another place to receive the power that was requested.[64] In summary, a number of events might precede the actual visionary encounter—events that presuppose a heightened state of awareness. These threshold experiences set the stage for a direct encounter, heightening the perceptions of the visionary and preparing him for a fuller and more powerful manifestation.

CHAPTER SIX

The Mystery of Presence

The man whom the gods helped and visited in dreams, was said to have mystery power; and one that had much mystery power, we call a mystery man, or medicine man. Almost everyone received dreams from the spirits at some time; but a medicine man received them more often than others.

—Edward Goodbird, Goodbird the Indian:
His Story Told to G. L. Wilson

THE BASIC INTENTIONAL STRUCTURE of the vision quest involves a direct experience of the enfolded order through an encounter with one of the many beings empowering the religious topology. In the context of this encounter, the individual receives various instructions, objects, and one or more songs, all of which are meant to evoke the specific power given to the visionary. The visionary's consciousness is directed toward a particular kind of religiously perceived "object"—a visionary manifestation—and toward a specific result—enhanced ability or empowerment. This manifestation of the numinous, of the sacred character of the visionary world, is expressed as a dramatic encounter with the powers that infuse the natural world. The reality of the manifestation, like the reality of a dream, is accepted in the dream ethnography as a fundamentally viable, meaningful expression of contact with sacred beings. The meaning of the encounter as an expression of empowerment is sought through continuing reflection and dialogue with experienced elders. The visionary epistemé, an implicit order of potential empowerment, is unfolded in substantive forms, images, symbols, and actions. Its inherent potency, taking on the specific attributes of individual experience, is then shared with others through unusual and often remarkable demonstrations. The sacred quality infusing both the visionary and the objects he or she has made according to the templates of the vision is widely recognized as emanating either from the dream-spirits or from a more mysterious and comprehensive source. The unfolding power of the individual is stimulated by deep, moving, and pervasive forces. The experience of the holy is identified with both a variety of causal sources and its specific manifestations.

To facilitate the encounter in the structured quest, various ritual actions are formulated that recreate the circumstances of the spontaneous vision experience. The concept of recreation is not meant to imply that spontaneous vision experiences preceded, in a historical sense, the ritualization of the vision quest.[1] The fundamental conditions of the spontaneous vision experience, however—isolation, lack of food and water, injury, the petitioning of the sacred powers for aid, and the natural disposition for visionary experience—are exactly the conditions of the successful ritual vision fast. Mourning rituals with slashing of arms and legs often resulted in a visionary encounter. Self-inflicted wounds and weeping and crying are recognized practices for inducing visionary experiences. For the individual to turn to the spirit powers when lost or injured is an essential feature of many Native American religious practices. The goal of the ritual fast is to heighten these liminal experiences and bring them into fully conscious awareness. Careful observation of the conditions surrounding the spontaneous vision, coupled with normative patterns of ritual behavior, would certainly contribute to a formal shaping of the structured quest.

Under whatever conditions the vision experience might arise, the encounter with the sacred is charged with power, mystery, and transformation. In all cases, the phenomenology of the visionary experience involves crossing a critical threshold from the explicit world of the everyday to the implicit reality of the visionary world. That such a threshold is recognized is evidenced by the attentive preparations and concentration of thought necessary for an actual encounter. When such concentration is coupled with fasting, restrictive movement, and possibly bodily mortifications, a powerful, dramatic condition is created for crossing the threshold. For the neophyte, this would be a supreme challenge; for the experienced shaman, a matter of training and practice.

That a threshold experience can be posited is demonstrated by the nature of the visionary narratives, their continuity and consistency. The vision is expressed in every case as having a discernible beginning that is consciously recognized by the seeker. There is a distinctive but subtle change in awareness to a new order of experience that is holistically organized as a "flow" moving through a definite beginning–middle–end pattern. A point in the distance, a barely heard voice singing, a shadowy form—all become clear, moving into more cosmologically complex realms of visionary experience and through a period of instruction and gift giving. Then the visionary returns (frequently in reverse order) to the original condition and place of fasting, withdrawing from the altered, implicit condition to the transformed explicit, communal realm.

Shifting out of the dynamic equilibrium of everyday, ordinary awareness, crossing the critical threshold, means breaking the symmetries of daily perception and action—thereby inducing a potentially higher sense of order, process, and empowerment. The visionary realm is always perceived as the more potent, more comprehensive, reality. Entry into the visionary experience reveals an unfolding of potentiality and affirms the sacred character of the natural world. Social equilibrium—that is, the ideas, beliefs, and behaviors of a socially congruent and communally similar group—gives an internal cohesion to the experience through the means of powerfully enforced collective sanctions. Such a normative process of fundamental social cohesion, of dynamic, interactive mutuality of belief and action, of continuous reconstitution of the past as present in the vision experience leads to a highly developed autopoiesis.[2] Yet interaction with the greater potentiality of the visionary realm could also introduce change, randomness, uncertainty, and empowerment that broke the symmetries of normal social existence and opened social structures to emergent possibility and transformation. I do not mean to suggest that such a break was necessarily radical, but rather that it was a continual process of variation and moderation through which social transformation could be validated.[3]

Once a person is across the visionary threshold, experience unfolds in an unbreakable series of events: it goes forward to completion; the experience is not interrupted. All the dreams and visions recorded in the ethnography represent complete cycles of experience. The vision never seems to break off randomly at some unfinished point. It has a holistic structure that moves through visionary space-time from present moment to present moment and from place to place in an unbroken flow.

This unilinear flow of experience is a primary quality of all visionary experiences recorded in the ethnography and is a phenomenological constant. The critical issue is the ability of the visionary to initiate or catalyze this deep flow of experience. Once catalyzed, the vision unfolds through a meaningful pattern of events and is completed in a manner generally significant and memorable to the visionary. The self-consistency of the visionary experience—that is, the fact that obtrusive, unrelated events never break into or distract the visionary from the continuity of the experience—is another aspect of its continuity. Regardless of how complex the contents of the vision are, they have a recognizable consistency, a coherent order, that tends to culminate in a series of dramatic incidents through which the visionary receives personal instructions and, often, remarkable power.[4] Yet another significant characteristic of the experience is its affective component. The experience is a powerful emotional encounter in which the individual confronts the mysterious reality, the awe-inspiring presence of powerful, sacred beings.

The impact of the vision experience on the visionary is transformative: the individual has a direct experience not only of the viability and reality of the religious world but also of power. This experience in the unmediated visionary state, in the face to face encounter, epitomizes the Plains religious vision. The religious experience is always an interactive encounter that imbues the visionary with a greater sense of personal identity because of the intimate link formed with the sacred beings. The power of the vision is a gift to the visionary by the dream-spirits, whose reality has become experientially actual and present. The transformative quality of the vision experience is a consequence of actually interacting with the powers that sustain the world. The consequence of this interaction is the empowerment of the individual if he or she retains the ability to evoke the gift of power in a context of everyday need and thus to reestablish the interactive relationship. To attain this power also requires courage and stamina, for such an encounter can be overwhelmingly frightening and dangerous.

FEAR, AWE, AND AMAZEMENT

Having found the appropriate place for fasting, often a southern slope on a high hill or bluff where the faster could observe the rising and setting sun, he smoked, wept, and prayed for the powers to hear his plea and announce themselves in some visible way. Having made the appropriate sacrifices and kept his mind intent and focused on the immediacy of the experience, as night came on the faster would lie down covered with a buffalo robe, waiting for the vision. Throughout the night, the he might rise and pray frequently; at daybreak, the he greeted the sun with prayers and continued crying for a vision. Such a pattern would be continued day after day, unbrokenly, without food or water, until a vision occurred or the faster felt he could not go on.

The exact form the vision might take was wholly unknown to the faster. As Sword explained to James Walker:[5]

Hanble (a vision) is a communication from the *Wakan-Tanka* or a spirit to one of mankind. It may come at any time or in any manner to anyone. It may be relative to the one that receives it, or to another. It may be communicated in Lakota, or *hanbloglaka* (language of the spirits). Or it may be only by sights and sounds not of a language. It may come directly from the one giving it, or it may be sent by an *akicita* (messenger). It may come unsought or it may come by seeking it.

As previously mentioned, the vision faster would rarely have heard of the vision experiences of others, because power received in visions was only discussed at ritually appropriate times and rarely, if ever, in public or in a family setting. If the faster was a neophyte, the first vision he heard about might be in the context of the preparatory sweat lodge where, at least among the Sioux, he could hear the vision experience of the shaman who prepared him.[6]

Contact with the sacred powers is widely regarded as dangerous because the powers could manifest in uncanny and frightening ways.[7] This is particularly true, as I have mentioned, if the vision seeker is wide awake when the vision experience occurs. Little comment is made in the ethnography about being awake or asleep. Significance is expressed in the demonstration of power, not in the state of the visionary. The visionary epistemé is constituted out of a wide range of experiences such that the waking-sleeping distinction is rarely mentioned. Nevertheless, the distinction is noted.[8]

The heightened awareness, or threshold condition, that precedes the actual vision encounter makes a profound impact on the faster. In this condition, fear and anxiety are common. As this threshold condition begins to manifest itself, the visionary experiences an increased acuity and openness to the mysterious conditions of the visionary world. Clark Wissler writes concerning the Blackfoot: "It is said that the majority of young men fail in this ordeal as an unreasonable fear comes down upon them the first night, causing them to abandon their post. Even old experienced men often find the trial more than they can bear."[9] The increased intensity and the arising of the uncanny aspects of the vision experience, coupled with isolation and exposure, drives many to abandon the quest, often on the very threshold of its manifestation. John Cooper records one such experience of a Gros Ventre adult who ran away saying only, "I could not stand that kind of thing!"[10] In the Sioux sweat lodge preceding the vision fast, the faster is told: "My friend, perhaps something frightening comes to you and you want to run away; stand with a strong heart! In this way you will become *wakan*."[11]

In the threshold condition, the first appearance is often that of a messenger sent to communicate a preliminary message or lead the visionary to a sacred place where the vision can manifest in all its detail and complexity. The most common messenger is either a crow or a raven, which appears in its natural form and speaks to the visionary, or which appears as a human being wearing black feathers or clothing to indicate its identity.[12] Such an encounter was experienced by a Blackfoot medicine man during his fast away from camp: "I stayed there seven days and seven nights and at last had a dream. I saw a Raven flying toward me and heard him sing. This was in the daytime but I was asleep. Then a person appeared and said, 'There is a hill down by the river and a man invites you.' Now the Raven was a messenger."[13]

Other messengers might appear simply as a human being who invites the visionary to follow him or her, as among the Assiniboine,[14] or as a young boy who asks the visionary to accompany him to his father's lodge.[15] The figure of a young man or a boy as messenger is quite frequent; it reflects a normal aspect of Plains social life, for the role of messenger was often assigned to young men. Among the Teton Sioux, the *akicita*, or messenger, was a recognized part of both the social and the visionary world, and it might take the form of any sacred being.[16] Black Elk's vision illustrates this when the two men descend from the clouds to lead him up to the flaming rainbow tipi.[17] Among the Plains Cree, the messenger could be a stone in human form.[18]

The messenger often announced the coming of a second, more powerful being who intended to give the visionary a gift of power. An Absarokee shaman named Sees the Living Bull related his vision experience to Two Leggings before passing on some medicine to him:[19]

A person rose above the horizon until I saw his entire body. As he walked toward me, fires burst out where he stepped. At last he stood next to me and delivered the message that Bird Going Up was coming to me. He was wearing strange moccasins, the left upper made from a silver fox's head, the right from a coyote's head. . . . The man wore a beautiful war shirt trimmed with scalp locks along the arms. . . . A little rain woke me and my dream became a real vision. My dream person was standing next to me.

He carried a coup stick with a raven sitting on it. This raven tried to teach me the language of the birds but the man stopped it. Suddenly I heard a loud thunderclap. I seemed to be picked up and dropped. . . . I saw a bird's big tail and large claws, but could not see the body. Red streaks of lightning shot from each claw. . . . My dream person told that this bird [Bird Going Up] was great, that the noise from its throat sounded like thunder.

The raven returned to its perch on the coup stick and my dream person told me that Bird Going Up had told him not to let the raven teach me the language of the birds. Instead, he would teach me some of his medicine songs [sings seven songs]. Pointing west he asked if I saw a burning mountain. I saw it but did not understand its meaning. My dream person told me never to go to the Flathead or Shoshoni country.

Here is a close association between the messenger and the raven that perches on the coup stick he holds. The raven has the power to teach the visionary the language of the animals but is forbidden to do so by the messenger. Sees the Living Bull then encounters the awesome presence of the Thunder Being with red lightning shooting from its claws. This encounter has a profound impact on the visionary, who says he felt as though he was "picked up and dropped." After receiving the medicine songs, he is given a warning to stay away from Shoshone and Flathead country, for he might be killed there. In this narrative, the mythic reality of the celestial Thunder Being takes on immediacy as a living being, which confirms its actuality. After three unsuccessful attempts, the visionary receives his medicine songs and establishes a direct, immediate relationship with the power.

Sometimes the initial appearance in the vision is not that of a messenger but of some frightening spirit sent to test the courage of the faster. Gilbert McAllister recorded such an encounter in the 1930s, when the stepson of the famous Kiowa shaman Dävéko told how his stepfather fasted in the mountains to find a cure for his own illness:[20]

The third night after the sun set he lay down. He heard a noise coming toward him, as if someone were dragging a stiff dried buffalo hide. . . . He could hear what he thought was an owl talking to him. He could almost understand what was being said. Maybe it was an owl trying to frighten him; but he lay still, not moving a muscle. The noise diminished. The owl seem to turn into a man, and he told *Dävéko* to look at him. *Dävéko* did but he saw only a pile of bones. When he looked again the man was there and the bones were gone. Then the owl retreated and the noise stopped. It was quiet. *Dävéko* got up and filled his pipe and prayed again.

It was a belief among the Kiowa, as well as among other southern Plains people, that a dangerous or threatening spirit might come to try and drive the visionary away. The owl frequently had associations among many Plains and Prairie people with death and with mysterious night power.[21] Here the owl has distinctive associations with the dead (the bones) and therefore with ghosts, which were greatly feared by the Kiowa, Comanche, and other southern plains and Great Basin groups.[22] This aspect of fear at the threshold condition is part of the uncanny experience of entering the visionary world. As the visionary encounter begins to reveal its contents, ambiguous images of a threatening nature manifest themselves. They generally reflect shared beliefs and images that embody deep ambiguity and uncertainty—in this case, the association of owls with the dead.

Another example of the mysterious nature of the visionary experience comes from among the Omaha, where owl dreamers and visionaries formed a society called Wanoxe ithaethe, "those to whom the ghost has shown compassion."[23] It was believed that these visionaries could foretell a person's approaching death. R.F. Fortune recorded the following Omaha vision:[24]

He came to the hilltop. He swept clean the fireplace. He scooped a bedding place in a bank of soft earth to sleep in. He slept by day and watched by nights, and cried to *Wakonda* at sun up.... The fourth day the sun came up with a thick fog so he could not see. As he stood crying to *Wakonda* he heard a human voice crying back on one side of him, then another on the other side, then others behind, before, above and all about him. A big thing like a bird swished by him close but its voice was human. Then the fog lifted for a moment and he saw through it a figure as large as a man standing but looking like an owl, and lots of small owls of common size flying over its head. A wind of fog whirled over him and covered him like smoke. His body felt as if it was being turned inside out ... leaving it clean like.

This vision encounter leaves the visionary feeling purged, purified, and transformed through the mysterious encounter with the owl power. The images of owl and man are fused together into a single startling manifestation. The threshold experience is initiated by the sound of voices coming from all directions, plunging the visionary into an unfolding plurality of appearances.

The owl-man appears mysteriously and initiates the visionary into the sacred world of owl dreamers. The vision establishes the necessary link with the inherent powers of the sacred world. The identity of owl and man becomes the identity of the visionary as he too acquires the owl power and learns to foresee, as the owl does, the coming of death. However, the encounter with a ghost could have a paralyzing affect on the individual, sometimes called "ghost-sickness." R. F. Fortune recorded a spontaneous vision that occurred to an Omaha boy named Small Fangs:[25]

When he was about ten years old he woke in the middle of the night seeing a ghost with a red cloth folded over its forehead, and a blanket slanting from left shoulder to right hip, with every facial feature clear. As he saw the ghost a numbness crept up his legs and his arms until they were quite benumbed so that he could not rise. The ghost retreated slowly, facing him, out of the door. After a few minutes of complete numbness Small Fangs rushed to the door— only the moonlight was there—and slammed it. Next morning he described the ghost to his father who identified it as Badger, a sacred man who had died when Small Fangs was yet on the cradle board. His father told him to tell no one.

PSYCHIC TRANSFORMATIONS

Another significant characteristic of the successful visionary experience is its apodictic quality: the quality by which the experience appears to be self-evidently and unquestionably real. This clarity and vividness was described by the Lakota Sioux John Fire (Lame Deer): "The real vision . . . is not a dream; it is very real. It hits you sharp and clear like an electric shock. You are wide awake and, suddenly, there is a person standing next to you who you know can't be there at all . . . yet you are not dreaming; your eyes are open. You have to work for this, empty your mind for it."[26]

This kind of encounter is not something that can be easily attained; it requires a complete effort and commitment on the part of the seeker. Exposure to the powers, in a vulnerable state of receptivity and concentration, results in an intensity of experience that is rarely questioned. The true vision experience is primarily characterized by this sense of its intensity and self-evident reality. Such an apodictic quality strengthens the communally shared belief in the reality of the dream-spirit as a distinctive and autonomous entity inhabiting mythically accessible worlds of personal empowerment.[27]

In 1918, when John Fire was about sixteen, he underwent his first vision quest, probably as a consequence of the death of his mother.[28] His experience is very expressive of the emotional characteristics of the vision encounter, in terms of both his fear and his sense of empowerment. It left an indelible impression on him—a certainty of its self-evident reality. Left alone on a hill with only a pipe, a rattle, some tobacco, and a blanket, he had the following experience one night while huddled in a vision pit:[29]

Darkness had fallen upon the hill. . . . Sounds came to me through the darkness: the cries of the wind, the whisper of the trees, the voices of nature, animal sounds, the hooting of an owl. Suddenly I felt an overwhelming presence. Down there with me in my cramped hole was a big bird. The pit was only as wide as myself, and I was a skinny boy, but that huge bird was flying around me as if he had the whole sky to himself. I could hear his cries, sometimes near and sometimes far, far away. I felt feathers or a wing touching my back and head. This feeling was so overwhelming that it was just too much for me. I trembled and my bones turned to ice.

I shook the rattle and it made a soothing sound, like rain falling on rock. It was talking to me, but it did not calm my fears. I took the sacred pipe in my other hand and began to sing and pray: "*Tunkashila*, grandfather spirit, help me." I don't know what got into me, but I was no longer myself. I started to cry. Crying, even my voice was different. I sounded like an older man, I couldn't even recognize this strange voice. I used long-ago words in my prayer, words no longer used nowadays.

Slowly, I perceived that a voice was trying to tell me something. It was a bird cry, but I tell you, I began to understand some of it. . . . I heard a human voice too, strange and high-pitched, a voice which could not come from an ordinary, living being. All at once, I was way up there with the birds. The hill with the vision pit was way above everything. I could look down even on the stars, the moon was close to my left side. It seemed as though the earth and the stars were moving below me. A voice said, "You are sacrificing yourself here to be a medicine man. In time you will be one. You will teach other medicine men. We are the winged ones, the eagles and the owls. We are a nation and you shall be our brother. You will never harm or kill any one of us. You are going to understand us whenever you come to seek a vision here on this hill. You will learn about herbs and roots, and you will heal people. You will ask them for nothing in return. A man's life is short, make yours a worthy one." I felt that these voices were good, and slowly my fear left me. I had lost all sense of time. I did not know whether it was day of night. I was asleep yet wide awake.

After this, Fire's grandfather, Tahca Ushte, or Lame Deer, a Mineconjou chief who had been killed by white soldiers long before, appeared to him and gave him his name, after which Fire said, "Then I felt the power surging through me like a flood. I cannot describe it, but it filled all of me."[30] This remarkable description delineates many of the most significant features of the vision experience.

The primary consequence of the encounter is the transformation of the visionary—his immediate sense of empowerment. This experiential sense of transformation is characteristic of the apodictic vision. There is an unquestioned energetic charge to the experience that leaves the visionary feeling that the gift of power has transformed him in a profound and lasting way. Before attaining that power, the visionary undergoes a number of emotional reactions. The threshold experience is described as a sudden feeling of an overwhelming, often frightening presence that tells to the visionary he is no longer alone. The quality of this presence, its *wakan* nature, is that of mystery, power, and the unknown. It is a sacred manifestation in the deepest sense because it represents the initiation of the visionary into the immediacy of the visionary world. Spatial and temporal awareness are transformed. The vision pit is experienced as if it were enlarged to include the entire sky. Time stops, and a sense of timelessness ensues. Simultaneously, there is an immediacy of contact transmitted through physical sensation—the feathers or wings touching the back or head of the visionary. This touch is part of the symbolic transfer of power, which is frequently accompanied by physical sensation. Among the Plains people, the symbolic use of an eagle wing to transmit healing power or "blessing" is common.[31]

The young visionary experiences such intense fear, awe, and amazement in the presence of the sacred power that he fears being overwhelmed. He then moves into an experience of self-transformation as he takes up the pipe and begins to pray for assistance. He no longer recognizes himself: he has become like an older man and speaks in an unusual way using archaic words. Like Black Elk seeing himself as the sixth grandfather, and like many other visionaries, Fire experiences himself as older and more knowledgeable. This shift in personal identity represents an actualization of potential in a dramatic and memorable form: the visionary experiences himself as he might become. Transformed, he moves even more deeply into the visionary realm, where he begins to understand the language of the dream-spirits and beholds the world from a celestial point of view. Then comes the instruction from the eagles and the owls, who foretell his future as a medicine man. Further instruction is promised in other visionary experiences, and he is warned not to harm either owls or eagles, whose language he will come to understand. He is also instructed to ask for no payment in carrying out his healing of the sick. He is reassured by these instructions, and his fear leaves him. Finally, he is given a new name, which is meant to symbolize the entire experience and denote a new potential identity.

Significantly, the fulfillment of what is demonstrated in potential requires other visionary experiences to actualize the potential. This potential quality of the vision experience is another phenomenological characteristic. While most visions give the visionary some specific power or ability, the full actualization of that power is frequently part of an ongoing stream of dream and visionary experiences that are only fully realized in the later maturation of the visionary. Only after a great deal of training and a whole series of initiation experiences was Sanapia, the Comanche shaman, able fully to actualize her gifts of power. When invoked, this power made a dramatic and dynamic appearance that overpowered her normal perceptions of the world. Her power, given to her by her mother as a result of visionary experience, was eagle power that would come to her when she practiced healing:[32]

Sanapia reports that her Medicine eagle looks like eagles she has seen in the wild except that it is much larger. She can feel her eagle's presence before she sees it. . . . When the eagle came to her, everything around her disappeared with the resultant image of an eagle against a murky gray background. . . . While the eagle was present, Sanapia trembled violently and perspired freely. She states that her heart beat very rapidly and she felt as if she was going to faint.

It is this type of presence that the mature shaman can invoke when performing some demonstration of visionary power. It is, however, a power that in most cases requires many years of effort and further visionary experience to actualize fully. The initiating dream or vision experience may require many subsequent dreams and visions to enhance the understanding and effectiveness of the inherent power of the original vision.

Not all vision quests were successful, even though the individual might have a vision experience. The vision might lack the apodictic quality so essential to the successful vision quest, by which the individual remains unshakably convinced of the validity and significance of the encounter. Less successful dreamers and visionaries might experience a far higher degree of ambiguity in the visionary state. Ambiguity and uncertainty characterize a minor portion of the Plains and Prairie ethnographic dream record, but these cases give some indication of what the unsuccessful or perhaps youthful vision quest was like. The vision experience of the Absarokee warrior Two Leggings demonstrates this point quite well. Two Leggings made numerous attempts to acquire power through the vision fast. He met with many difficulties, though he eventually acquired a successful vision. The following is an early vision experience of the young warrior's while he fasted in a prairie-dog town:[33]

For three days and nights I lay in that dog town, without eating or drinking. . . . [He cuts off the end of a finger as an offering.] I heard a voice calling from somewhere. . . . I heard the words of my first medicine song. . . . I saw the face of the man who was singing and shaking a buffalo-hide rattle. I also heard a woman's voice but could see only her eyes and the beautiful hair on top of her head. . . . Many people seemed to be coming and I became confused. . . . The singing grew faster and I fell back as if drunk. . . . When he shook his rattle I saw a face painted on it. . . . A face opened in a painted face on the rattle, and I began to faint. . . . The woman kept telling me that what I was wishing for had come true. . . . I did not think my dream was powerful, but at least I had some medicine songs I had dreamt myself.

Here the potential order of the visionary realm overpowers the young visionary. The enfolded structure of the vision is well expressed in the series of faces that appear, first as the singers, then on the rattle, then from within the face on the rattle. Each successive manifestation challenges the visionary to retain his consciousness; unable to do so, he becomes confused and faints, losing the clarity of his vision. In the end he retains only the song, with no clear knowledge of the rich contents of the vision. He realizes that his experience is not powerful, that he has been unable to sustain the full impact of the visionary state. This sense of ambiguity and of being overwhelmed frequently characterized the unsuccessful vision and might leave the visionary confused and uncertain about the use or nature of the power manifested.

BETWEEN THE WORLDS

Another common characteristic of the vision experience is a remarkable "lightness" of being. The sense of embodiment, of being bound by the conditions of physical existence, gravity, and muscular limitation, is shed for an unbounded sense of lightness and freedom from bodily restraints. The Absarokee warrior Plenty Coups mentioned how, during his vision, his feet "touched nothing at all. . . . I walked in the [dream] Person's tracks as though the mountains were as smooth as the plains."[34] The Cheyenne Picking Bones Woman mentioned how, in her vision experience, "she was running but her feet did not touch the ground—they seemed to move a little way above it."[35] The young Black Elk experienced flying up into the clouds to receive his great vision. The experience of flying in the clouds is quite common, particularly for thunder dreamers.[36] An Arapaho man told Alfred Kroeber about his experience *after* the conclusion of his vision fast: "When the informant had fasted seven days, he returned. As he ran it seemed to him that he was not touching the ground, but he saw that his feet were on the earth."[37]

The experience of flying or of a lightness of being is a condition that reflects a significantly altered state of awareness. In this altered condition, the visionary experiences an expansive and freer movement through the various strata of the world cosmology. The interconnectedness of this cosmology becomes more immediately accessible to the visionary. The diversity and strata of the sacred world are unified through the visionary's journey. The lightness of being expresses the freedom of the individual to move through the mythic world in contact with beings of the various sacred strata. The inhabitants of those worlds become accessible to the visionary, and the visionary realm is experienced as a single, unified extension, an unbounded totality, of the natural world.

As the last-mentioned example shows, this condition is not confined to the ritual period of the fast, but can extend far beyond that period or occur spontaneously in other contexts. The usual religious explanation for this phenomenon is that the "soul" is able to act separately from the body. According to the ethnographic record, however, a distinction between the body of the visionary and a conscious experience of a soul is rarely made. The unifying journey of the visionary is presented as an altered state of awareness and not as an experience of a particular metaphysical "aspect" of the person.

Vision experiences involving flying can take a somewhat comical turn, as one did for a Blackfoot visionary. His account also demonstrates the necessity of distinguishing between literal and symbolic, or shamanistic, interpretation of the vision experience:[38]

The male hawk came and put me to sleep right where I was. This hawk immediately turned into a man, wearing a buffalo robe who addressed me, "My son, leave my children alone. I will give you my body that you may live long. Look at me. I am never sick. So you will never have any sickness. I will give you power to fly. You see that ridge (about a mile away) well, I will give you power to fly there." On awakening ... I took off my clothes, and with a buffalo robe went back some distance from the edge of the river. Then I took a run and springing from the edge of the cliff, spread out my arms with the blanket for wings. I seemed to be going all right for a moment, but soon lost control and fell. I was stunned by the fall and was drawn under a rock by the current where I went round and round, striking my head. ... This is one time in which I was fooled in my dreams.

The gift of power, embedded in a visionary world actualized through altered states, was rarely interpreted in such a literal, physical manner. The invocation of the visionary power might allow the visionary to fly to the hills—but not necessarily in physical form. The literal interpretation here is a consequence of a disjunction between the gift of power and its correct use. The successful visionary learned, through experience and further instruction, the exact means of invoking and using the power given. The foolishness of the sorcerer's apprentice is his mistaken use of rudimentary ability and his failing to distinguish between correct invocation of visionary power and its brute expression in the physical world.

An interesting alternative to the experience of flight is an Arapaho explanation recorded by Alfred Kroeber. After a three-day vision fast near the Cimarron River, the visionary heard footsteps approaching:[39]

A man called to him to come to his tent. He thought someone was trying to deceive him, and he paid no attention. The person continued to call him. The fourth time he said, "Hurry and come. Other people are waiting for you." Then the informant consented. He went in his thoughts, but he himself did not get up from the ground. He went downward from where he was lying, into the ground. He followed the man who had called him, and entered a tent.

Here the visionary is conscious that he is able to leave his body lying on the ground and, in an altered condition, to travel beneath the earth in "thoughts." He does not speak of a soul but of a mental awareness or personal transformation that carries him into the below realm. Again, this is an altered awareness that enables the visionary to distinguish between various types of perception and action. He is aware not through his bodily senses but through a projection of his self-awareness into the psychic world of the below powers. There is a recognizable continuity of perception in an altered and heightened condition of awareness. His attention becomes completely focused on the unfolding of the dramatic events of the vision, without distraction or interruption. The visionary realm unfolds its latent potential by drawing the visionary into the uncanny manifestations of its contents through a vivid and dramatic alteration in awareness.

Conversely, the visionary's perception of the natural world itself may be radically transformed. In a Woodlands example, the Potawatami Shanapo fasted for a vision for eight days until he had the following experience:[40]

On the eighth night he dreamed that one . . . who lived in the falls appeared and told him, "Look yonder and you will see something laced there as your reward for fasting," indicating a rock in the center of the falls. The whole earth looked transparent and he went to the rock island, going over ice. When he got there he discovered a sacred kettle which was as bright as fire. It was a bear kettle from the underneath god to feed from when a sacrifice was given.

The transparency of the world and Shanapo's radical alteration of perception reflect the intensification of perception that frequently accompanies the vision. The world becomes imbued with presence and seems metamorphosed through the manifestation of inherent power. The earth's transparency expresses cogently a symbolic aspect of the experience: the world is now open to new depths of significance, and the forms of nature are only manifestations of the underlying power or presence. The world is illumined in such a way as to manifest dramatically an inherently sacred quality, a luminous presence, profoundly affecting the awareness of the visionary. The bear power is expressed in the sacrificial kettle that shines brightly, manifesting its centrality to the visionary scene. Later, this kettle will become the object most representative of the vision, and its use will be a constant link to an altered perception.

Another condition that may be experienced by the visionary is a profound sense of disorientation, which may be a threshold condition preceding a spontaneous vision experience. Among the Canadian Sioux, it was believed that if people became lost or confused about finding their way home, it was because the dream-spirits wished to communicate with them. The Canadian Sioux Two Women went hunting but could not find his way back to camp. After marking trees and going in what he believed was a straight line, he found himself back where he had started. Finally, he made camp at this place, and later in the evening, as he sat at his campfire, he was approached by a messenger of the *wakan* beings:[41]

The person declared that the man had a weak mind and had forgotten that the *wakan* beings had told him certain things. He was continually getting lost because the *wakan* beings were angry; he intended, without their knowledge, to tell the man. . . . After he [Two Women] was born he had received instructions in dreams; but as soon as he awoke he had forgotten them. . . . The spirit had instructed the man before he was born but he had forgotten.

Only by recalling his former existence would Two Women be able to overcome his sense of disorientation. His vision is a means for recovering prenatal memories of a life among the spirits. Failure to do so leads to a twilight condition of separation and an inescapable encounter with the mysterious powers. The danger of forgetting dreams is also emphasized. Dream knowledge is considered essential to understanding the deeper strata of personal existence. Failure to attend to dreaming can lead to profound disorientation and may catalyze a dramatic encounter with the unknown powers. Belief in reincarnation is common in the Siouan ethnography; knowledge of previous existence is considered to be particularly evident among certain children and is frequently communicated in dreams and visions.[42]

Among the Pawnee, the unusual vision experience of a well-known holy man helped to established the belief that visions had their own independent preexistence. They were believed to inhabit a stratum of the celestial realm that existed just below the realm of the lesser sky powers:[43]

Katasha, the place where the visions dwell, is near the dwelling place of the lesser powers, so they can summon any vision they wish to send to us. When a vision is sent by the powers, it descends and goes to the person designated who sees the vision and hears what it has to say; then, as day approaches, the vision ascends to its dwelling place, *Katasha*, and there it lies at rest until it is called again.

A holy man who lived long ago, had a dream. He was taken up to the place where all visions dwell, those that belong to *Kawas*, the brown eagle, and those that belong to the white eagle, the male. While he was there the day began to dawn and he saw the visions that had been sent down come climbing up, and he recognized among them some of the visions that had visited him in the past. Then he knew in truth that all visions of every kind dwell above in

Katasha, and that they descend to us in night and that as day dawns they ascend, returning to rest in their dwelling place.

Here the autonomy of the vision as preexisting, ontologically distinct, and under the control of other sacred beings exemplifies the distinction that is often made between the dream-spirits and the actual vision. This distinction, which is given its most expressive form among the Pawnee, represents a clear demarcation between the powers that inhabit the various strata of the world cosmology and the visionary means by which power is communicated to an individual. The vision is regarded as a communicative medium and not as an end in itself. The powers communicate through the vision, but the real existence of those powers is intrinsic to the very nature and enfolded order of the religious world. Consequently, the mysterious beings are not identical with the visionary means by which power is communicated. This is why the vision is never regarded as proof of individual power. The vision communicates the gift and message of the sacred beings, but it is not equivalent to those beings, nor does the vision necessarily mean that the individual is fully empowered by those beings. Always, the power is greater than the medium of the vision. This is an intrinsic feature of the Plains religious worldview.

Finally, not all visions are of a strictly individual nature. Some examples exist of collective visions. These visions might manifest themselves in such a way as to take on a very real existence, thereby confirming the interpenetrating relationship between the sacred realm and the life of the people. A Gros Ventre hunting party seeking food during a time of great need and hunger had this experience: "They all looked and saw a herd of buffalo coming from the sky. The herd dropped close by. When people see anything like that they say it is a holy thing. The men chased these buffalo and killed one. It was bigger and fatter than the real kind and that is how they knew. They talked about this a whole lot."[44]

In this example, absolutely no distinction is made between the visionary appearance and the actual experience of the hunters. The buffalo is real; its coming from the sky is remarkable but acceptable within the context of normal religious belief. That the visionary animal turns into an actual buffalo that can be hunted and eaten is wholly consistent with the metamorphic nature of the sacred realm. The intentional structure of hunting the buffalo catalyzes a mysterious event that in turn strengthens belief in the sacred nature of the world. All the men report seeing this mysterious event. The normal boundaries between the actual and the possible dissolve into a unified, visionary reality in which the human participants encounter a self-evident manifestation of unquestionable power.[45]

CHAPTER SEVEN

The Transfer
of Power

The being conferring power is not content with saying that it shall be, but formally transfers it to the recipient with appropriate ceremonies. This is regarded as a compact between the recipient and the being then manifest, and each is expected to fulfill faithfully his own obligations.

—Clark Wissler, "Ceremonial Bundles of the Blackfoot Indians"

THE PRIMARY VISIONARY EXPERIENCE is a direct encounter with the dream-spirits, who give the dreamer instructions meant to enhance his or her knowledge, ability, and success. The dream-spirits' motive is believed to be their compassion or pity for the suffering of the individual. In crying for a vision, the visionary fasted, offered bits of flesh, and wept to evoke this compassionate response.

Fasting for a vision is recorded as one of the most highly charged emotional circumstances of Native American Plains life. Men, who rarely expressed extreme emotions of need or sorrow (other than in war or upon the death of a relative), found in this context a prescription to invoke such feelings. Making oneself pitiable before the sacred powers stands in sharp contrast to being fearless, detached, and resistant in the face of pain, injury, or suffering. Even the most fearless warrior is required to make himself pitiable if he wishes to evoke the compassion of the spirit powers. The vision seeker's lamentations and emotional expression are cathartic of deep feelings of dependence and conditionality. The structured nature of the ritual fast provides a sanctioned means for emotional release in the context of religious action. That this expression should occur in isolation and commonly in times of crisis suggests the potentially dangerous and disruptive effect of such expressions.

The general Plains and Prairie concept of the compassion or pity of the mysterious powers, as recorded in the ethnography, is summarized by James Dorsey for the Dhegiha-speaking peoples as follows:[1]

Icha'eche, literally, "to pity him on account of it, granting him certain power." Its primary reference is to the mysterious animal, but it is transferred to the person having the vision, hence, it means "to receive mysterious things from an animal, as in a vision after fasting; to see as in a vision, face to face (not in a dream); to see when awake, and in a mysterious manner having a conversation with the animals about mysterious things."

Inevitably the gift of power is given as a response to a period of suffering or trial for the visionary. The reciprocity established between the visionary and the dream-spirit is based on the dependence of human beings and the generosity of the powers aroused by human suffering. In speaking of the same concept, Alice Fletcher and Francis La Flesche note that the visionary form that appeared was impelled by the emotional appeal: "The form, animate or inanimate, which appeared to the man [in a vision] was drawn toward him, it was believed, by the feeling of pity. The term used to express this impelling of the form to the man was *I'thaethe*, meaning 'to have compassion on.'"[2]

This impelling of the manifestation is not, however, unconditional. Individuals must lament and suffer if they truly wish to receive a vision. Those who fasted for a vision must be willing to express fully their feelings of dependence on the powers through an emotional and dramatic appeal. In the context of religious belief, this dependence is not regarded as weakness but rather as demonstrating a submissive will to the sacred beings, as well as expressing an intrinsic recognition of human limitation.

The unstructured vision experience usually associated with women, particularly during times of emotional stress or during seclusion in the menstrual lodge, also reflects aspects of religious belief. The social context for emotional expression is recorded as more flexible for women than for men. From the religious point of view, because women are more expressive of emotion and intense feelings, the spirit powers are more likely to respond to them regardless of their ritual preparedness. Vision fasting rites apply most distinctly to men and encode a male need for a structured context to facilitate the necessary emotional conditions for a submissive appeal to the powers. That the sacred beings were likely to take pity spontaneously on the suffering of women was a commonly shared belief. Significantly, while most women experienced either animal powers or some female presence, many men also had visionary experiences of female beings, strongly suggesting temperamental differences among visionaries. Furthermore, female sacred beings tended to be associated with gifts of healing and medicine rather than with war power.

The temperamental differences of visionaries—their predisposition toward certain types of behavior—were sanctioned through dreams and visions. Some women did have visions commending them to participate in male activities such as war parties and horse raiding. The following is a Pawnee example collected by John Murie:[3]

Woman Who Goes as a Warrior . . . dreamed of a man with a bundle on his back. [The man shows her a bundle and the rites that accompany it.] Then he addressed the woman as follows: "Woman, I am the one who gave you the idea of going on the warpath with the men. I made them successful. I gave you the skin and the rope [which she had captured, with horses, on two different raids]. You found the rope on a mare. You will get the [magnifying] glass and the pipe. You will make the pipe yourself. You must do as I have done. If the clear thing lights the pipe, it will be a sign of success; if not, it will mean ill luck. These things are given to you by the sun, so it will be the only one to receive smoke. I am going." The woman awoke.

The pipe and buffalo-hair rope formed part of an individual bundle that expressed the woman's triumph both as a visionary and as a warrior. She is specifically instructed by the dream-spirit to take up the ways of men until she has constructed her bundle. The man in the dream is a manifestation of the sun power, to whom she must make exclusive offerings of smoke. This unique synthesis of the woman, the male sun and the bundle legitimately validaties her predisposition to join the male war parties.[4] As in the case of male moon dreamers, such dreams sanctioned a person's behaving according to opposite gender roles.

A good example of the symbolic significance of female dream-spirits granting gifts and instructions to male visionaries was recorded by Edward Curtis for the Cheyenne warrior White Bull:[5]

On the second night a woman came bringing a pipe in one hand and a spear in another. I hated women at that time, and would not look at her. I thought she came from Thunder because she was carrying the spear. "I have brought you this pipe," she said. "Whenever you go to war, you will overcome the enemy if you have this pipe. Take this lance and no man will be able to shoot you, but if a woman shoots you, you may fall." ... Just behind her sat many spirits with horns on their heads. They looked like human beings, but afterwards they turned into horned owls and flew away, the woman following them. From a little distance she made a great noise like thunder and I knew she was from Thunder.

In this instance, the temperament of the individual is such that his vulnerability (and anxiety) about women and female power is obvious. Only a woman can possibly kill him in battle. Moreover, the dream-spirit is an image of the Thunder Being—a female image, even though thunder is generally a male warrior power, as symbolized by the spear. Such symbolic inversions demonstrate the intimate relationship between individual psychology and the mutability of visionary manifestations. The powers, representing the stable features of the mythic world, can manifest in various forms in accordance with the predispositions of the individual and thereby reorder the individual's actions and behaviors in the social world.

Another example of female power given to a male visionary is that of the Absarokee healer Fringe:[6]

We came to a great painted lodge that was red and black in stripes. ... I saw many horses near. ... An Otter was on one side and on the other was a White Bear. Both were angry because I was there and spoke crossly to me; but the Person said: "Be quite! This is my son."

We entered the striped lodge.... I saw his woman sitting. She was strangely handsome and tall. When she smiled at me, I knew she was very kind, that her heart was good.... The [male] Person said, "This is all, my son." ... the woman asked, "Why do you not give this son of yours something he may use to help his people, some power for good, if used by a good man?"

He picked up a strip of Otter skin and a picket pin and gave them into my hand. "Take these, my son," he said in a voice so kindly that I was not certain if it was his own.... The woman [said], "Will you tell him nothing?" The Person smiled. I saw his face change greatly. "Women are kind," he said, and took me by the hand. "I will tell him that this water will heal the sick among his people." All his life Fringe was a quiet, gentle man; and if he ever caused even the enemy any suffering, no one ever heard about it.

The mediating influence of the feminine is clearly at work in this vision. The gifts of power given to Fringe are an otter skin, frequently associated with healing, and a picket pin, which had both male (for staking a horse) and female (for staking down a tipi) associations. The woman is portrayed as kind, and she intercedes for the benefit of the visionary. Characteristically, a female dream-spirit symbolically reflects the gentle character of the visionary. Female figures might also be manifestations of religious figures that are part of the mythic lore—for example, Mother Moon among the Pawnee.[7] In considering the kinds of instructions given in a vision, it is essential also to consider the various forms the powers take as expressive of both unique individual predispositions and communally shared symbols.

WORDS AND SONGS

The intentional center of the visionary encounter is the set of instructions, songs, and gifts given to the visionary. The unfolding of the vision experience culminates in these instructions. In keeping with the normal patterns of the transmission of knowledge in many oral cultures, the primary instructions are given in the form of actions that must be imitated. The visionary is instructed to observe carefully the behavior and appearance of the dream-spirits and then to emulate that behavior and appearance in the appropriate setting. Such an imitative pattern reflects a socially recognized context for learning. Although certain speech acts might be foregrounded in the transmission of power, it is the background of correct action based on imitation that provides the salient context for those speech acts. In general, what is communicated is the knowledge of how to use or manifest personal power. This knowledge is not a verbal knowledge but a demonstrative knowledge that produces a visible result. Success in war, healing, or hunting were direct manifestations of such knowledge. Verbal articulation is a far more esoteric concern and is generally limited to advanced visionaries and elders who had considerable experience in handling power.

Among the speech acts involved in the communication of power, three primary patterns may be identified: dialogical interactions, commands or instructions, and sacred songs or chants. Each is an exceedingly brief and condensed form of communication; lengthy explanations given during a vision experience simply do not exist in the Plains and Prairie ethnography. Instead, verbal exchanges are minimized in favor of the active, visual presentation of significant behaviors and symbols, in keeping with the imagistic orientation common to an eidetic, right-hemispheric cultural orientation.

A fourth type of speech act, less common, is the mysterious or unrecognizable one—the sacred talk of the shaman. It was particularly developed among the Lakota Sioux, as mentioned by Sword: "If one has a vision . . . it may speak to him or it may not speak. If it speaks to him, it may speak so that he will understand what it says, but maybe it will speak as the shamans speak. Maybe it will make only a noise. He should remember what it says and how it speaks. Maybe it will speak without his having a vision."[8] This mystery speech represents an esoteric side to the vision experience insofar as it is basically incomprehensible to the visionary. Such a speech act necessitated an exegesis by an experienced visionary, which strongly suggests that the verbal component of visionary experience was itself often liminal. It could range from "noise" through an incomprehensible use of recognizable language to coherent speech. All these expressions are regarded as potentially significant and laden with meaning.

Dialogical interactions frequently occur at the initial moment of encounter between the visionary and the dream-spirit. The visionary first sees the dream-spirit, who then engages him or her in a brief exchange oriented toward discovering the purpose or intent of the visionary. The Lakota Shoots at the Mark gave an example of this type of exchange to Clark Wissler:[9]

The second day of this ordeal [of fasting with piercing], the young man heard something above him say, "Young man, what do you wish that you torture yourself in this way?" The young man looked up. He saw a man, barely visible. The man looked old, and his hair was white. Again the young man heard the words, "Do you want something?" "Yes," said the young man. "I want many women, many horses, and to kill one enemy. I have suffered much because of my poverty, now I want something." "Very well," said the man, as he gave him a thick red stick in sage grass. "Now go home."

Shoots at the Mark was given instructions for the use of the Elk Flute ("red stick"), which was believed to exert a powerful influence over women. After the initial brief exchange of questions and answers, the vision shifted into an unfolding of actions and behaviors that must be imitated.

The brief dialogue in this example summarizes the intentional, motivational structure of the vision. The primary questions asked are why the individual has undertaken to suffer and what it is he desires. Such a summary is typical of the dialogical exchange. Indeed, this exchange in many ways summarizes the entire vision experience *as communicated to the ethnographer*. Perhaps it is the retelling of the vision itself that leads to this emphasis on dialogical exchange, because the exchange encapsulates the experience in an intelligible frame that reveals intention without necessarily revealing the specifics of the visionary contents. It would be a fundamental error to assume that such a narrative represents the full visionary experience. Many visionaries were simply not willing to talk in detail about their experience, for to do so was tantamount to giving away their power.

Commonly, the intent of the faster is more general, as the following Kiowa-Apache vision narrative suggests:[10]

A fellow was out seeking a vision. He stayed out three or four days. Then Owl spoke to him: "What are you looking for? What do you want?" He said: "The other people have medicine and that is why I am here. I want to learn something." Owl said: "I can give you something. Tie some sinew around each finger. Put up a tipi and sit on the west side. Hang a cloth down in front of you from above.

Have a pipe there. Sing this song that I will teach you. Then I will do anything you want." Owl taught him this song. Then Owl said: "Go back to your camp. I will talk to you in your sleep."

Direct address in the form of commands or instructions is a normative aspect of many vision experiences—particularly instructions received from various animals that speak to the visionary. The dialogical component of the preceding example is very brief, and it is quickly followed by specific, descriptive instructions: a didactic communication of appropriate behavior and actions. Given as a gift, these instructions are meant to facilitate the visionary's ability to communicate with the owl spirit, which would then assist him. The speech pattern is nondiscursive, persuasive, and authoritative. No reply is called for, only an attentive concentration. Its persuasiveness lies in the very specific nature of the instructions: if the visionary does as instructed, all will be well. The "if-then" structure is part of the imperative mood of the communication. Such a mood is supported by a collective affirmation of the efficacy of actions performed according to instructions received during a vision experience. Dream-spirits speak in an authoritative manner because they have a superior knowledge of the use of power.

Another example of this imperative mood may be seen in a vision or dream sent simply to warn about impending danger, as happened to the Absarokee woman Little Face: "Being tired after the long move, Little Face laid down on her robe . . . and she slept. 'My friend! My friend!' Somebody was whispering in her ear. 'In four days your people will be attacked by the Lakota.' The woman, sitting up now, saw the woman mouse on her robe. 'Get up. Go out, and do something quickly.'"[11]

Another aspect of the authoritative structure of communication is its isomorphic relationship to normal social instruction. In a power-conferring situation, the visionary might receive guidance from a concerned elder, as in the vision of Shoots at the Mark. Such an exchange has strong social connotations requiring a marked attitude of respect and obedience. Such an exchange is guided by kinship interaction and social patterns of learning. Anyone seeking the guidance or assistance of an elder would certainly be expected to attend carefully to all instructions and to carry them out in a respectful manner. Visionary encounters reflect the normal interactive patterns between knowledgeable elders and those with whom they share their knowledge.[12]

The visionary figure could appear as an elder brother, a beautiful woman, a handsome man, a particular animal, a mother or father, or even a child. In all cases, however, the dream-spirits have an authoritative presence and speak didactically.[13] At the same time, their expressed motivation for giving instruction is that of compassionate concern elicited by the suffering of the visionary. The following Pawnee example illustrates the fundamental social and kinship relations exemplified in many visions, as well as the instructive tone:[14]

One night in a dream, Young Bull's father saw a buffalo bull standing alone pawing the ground and throwing dust over its back. This buffalo . . . said, "My son, I am your father; my spirit is with you. Now look yonder and you will see your brothers in rows. They also watch over you. When in battle be not afraid; we will be near you and protect you.". . . He woke up and began to sing. And this was the way he got these two songs.

The dream or vision song, usually a short, repetitive chant with a relatively brief melodic line, clearly expresses the generative transfer of power to the visionary. As a condensed symbolic medium of oral culture, it elicits power through repetition and intense concentration. The structure of the vision song or chant is one of phrases sung over and over to call the power or elicit the results promised by that power. This repetition and concentration is a ritual means to induce the appropriate state of mind in the visionary, a state of identification with the dream-spirit. The chant-song actualizes the present in terms of the generative power of the vision, unfolding the visionary epistemé to reveal its hidden contents.

As noted by Clark Wissler, the Blackfoot regard the vision song as the most important aspect of the transfer of bundles derived from vision experiences.[15] This belief in the centrality of the song is reflected in the use of dream songs throughout much of Plains and Prairie Indian ceremonial life. A crucial feature of all ceremonial behavior is the singing of songs to invoke the sacred beings of the rites. To have or own a song given by a power in a vision is perfectly congruent with the more generally held religious attitude that song is a primary medium of communication with those powers. In this sense, vision songs should be regarded as similar to prayers in that they call upon the aid of the visionary powers.

The song and its power can also catalyze a visionary experience. Many examples are given of individuals who, when alone or separated from others, hear singing off in the distance. Following this sound frequently leads to a visionary encounter. The following Pawnee example was told about Roaming Chief and the visionary origins of two songs used in the bear dance.[16] After becoming lost and wandering for many days without food, Roaming Chief entered some wooded hill country and heard a woman's voice singing:

The singing came from a certain tree, which he approached and in the shadow of it he saw a woman standing facing the sun and singing. . . . She had upon her head a young cedar sprout and carried in her left hand a small limb of a cedar tree. The man watched her for he thought that she was a woman, but when he looked where she was standing, she disappeared; and now the singing came from the tree. It made him feel good. His spirit was glad. . . . At last he was in some kind of spirit [sic] that enabled him to understand what was going on. It was the tree, the spirit of the tree, and in this spirit he was guided through the land.

In this vision, Roaming Chief encounters Mother Cedar, who teaches him through subsequent dreams the appropriate songs to sing to invoke her power and presence, as well as that of the bear with which the cedar was closely associated in Pawnee religion. The song also induces a heightened state of awareness in the visionary, by which he is able fully to comprehend the significance of what he is hearing. The axis of the visionary encounter turns on the singing and the songs given to Roaming Chief and points to the central significance of the song as an instructive medium of power.

The vision songs heard by Roaming Chief were later incorporated into the Pitahawirata bear dance. During a performance of the ceremony, Roaming Chief goes with the members of the bear society to bring in a cedar tree. Having painted his face and tied a small cedar branch in his hair, he proceeds to sing the vision songs he heard. The following is an example of one of the songs:[17]

Hear, he speaks.
There she stands. As he tells of the vision.

[Response]
There she stands. There she stands.
She who stands in the shadow of the tree.
Now I do see her here.
There she stands. There she stands.
She who stands in the shadow of the tree.

I tell of it.
A valley extending. [Response]

Oh how frightened I became,
That woman when I heard her. [Response]

And well I do now,
That woman, her singing. [Response]

Now let it stop,
That woman who is different. [Response]

This song exemplifies the ways in which the experience is narrated in the context of singing while simultaneously invoking the sacred presence of Mother Cedar. The song is sung in a ceremonial context of reverence and respect. A sense of awe is central to the song, as is expressed by the fear experienced in the vision. The visionary expresses the feeling of the immediacy of awe while singing. Mother Cedar is present, and the singer sees her once again standing before him in the form of an actual tree planted in the center of the ceremonial lodge. The tree becomes imbued with the powerful presence of the vision through the medium of the song. The visionary epistemé unfolds its mysterious contents and recreates the original visionary encounter, thereby sanctifying the ceremonial gathering with the mystery of presence. Repetition plays a key role by focusing attention and acting as a musical and rhythmic means for inducing the altered awareness. Eventually Roaming Chief became a leader of the bear ceremony because of the power of the beautiful songs he had received from the vision.[18]

The vision song is a communicative medium whose primary function is to enhance reciprocity between the visionary and the dream-spirit. The song originates with the dream-spirit; the individual does not create it, but only hears or receives it. The origin of the song is always outside the individual. This is in accord with the basic auditory-oral orientation of peoples who are not dependent on written language. That which is spoken (oral) and that which is heard (aural) represent the most viable media for the communication of meaning. The dream-spirit as an authoritative figure, speaking in an imperative mood to the receptive and retentive visionary, parallels the formal patterns of traditional oral instruction. To hear well and to remember accurately is a hallmark of maturity and intelligence.

Structurally, the vision or dream song is a bridge between normal speech patterns and the visionary encounter. Its highly condensed, rhythmic form is expressive of its symbolic contents. Many vision accounts contain as a central element the giving of one or more songs to the visionary as a primary means for communication with the spirit power. As in the songs of Roaming Chief, the visionary establishes contact with the power through the ceremonial use of the songs. It should be clearly recognized, however, that many vision accounts do not contain a song, and the entire vision may unfold without a single word's being spoken. The dominant feature of the vision is its visual contents, whereas the verbal content is frequently minimal or even completely absent.[19]

THE DANGER OF POWER

In order to discuss the danger of power, it is first necessary to summarize its general nature as conceived by the Plains and Prairie peoples.[20] A primary concern of this work has been to articulate the processes of personal, individual empowerment and its manifestation, particularly as it relates to religious action and thought. The many aspects of power as related to leadership roles, social organization, and political and economic success cannot be meaningfully understood in a strictly religious context.[21] My concern is the meaning of empowerment as it relates to the Native American religious worldview and specifically to the visionary encounter. In this sense, empowerment has a twofold definition: first, as it refers to the dynamics of a general mythic and religious worldview (power as intrinsic to the visionary episteme); and second, as it refers to the direct experience of the individual (empowerment per se).

As intrinsic to the Plains religious worldview, power is constituted as a plurality of presences that sustain and infuse a unitary perception of both the visible and invisible worlds. It is embodied in specific manifestations of the extraordinary, and it communicates viable means for enhancing and sustaining human life. The presences are dynamic and moving sources of creative inspiration. They generate transformation and metamorphosis and are conceived of as world creating and directive. All powers must be approached with reverence and regarded with great respect, and they manifest themselves as gifts given to those who make themselves pitiable. In a unitive sense, power is mysterious, sacred, and all pervasive. Simultaneously, it can manifest itself as dangerous, destructive, and ill disposed toward human beings. From the point of view of the individual, empowerment is knowledge of specialized behavior that invokes exceptional results and, generally, heightens social identity. Power is synonymous with knowledge, maturity, and capability.

Congruent with both perspectives are the phenomenal qualities of the exceptional, the extraordinary, the mysterious, the outstanding, and the remarkable. These qualities epitomize the unitary nature of power as intrinsic to the visionary episteme. The mark of empowerment is the ability to accomplish anything beyond the ordinary, including continual success in everyday tasks. This ability is inevitably attributed to gifts received in dreams and visions or sometimes through inheritance or the ownership of sacred objects that have been purchased but whose origins lie in visionary experience. In this sense, the emphasis falls on the spiritual or psychic nature of empowerment, rather than on its social or institutional concomitants. From the religious point of view, power is conferred through a spiritual encounter, through entry into the visionary epistemé and the direct experience of the vision. The whole concept of power is validated through the transmission of the extraordinary or the mysterious for the benefit of the individual or the community. While it is true that an individual might accrue wealth, for example, through the ability to heal, that accrual would inevitably be attributed to the dream-spirits that had conferred specific ability and benefits on the individual and not to the individual alone.

Empowerment took its primary social manifestation in the various religious societies that an individual could join after having a certain type of visionary experience. Dreamers and visionaries tended to form societies (or sodalities) revolving around a visionary encounter with a specific dream-spirit; there were buffalo dreamers, elk dreamers, bear dreamers, and so on. Membership in these societies might enhance individual social identity and confer religious status on the dreamer.

On the other hand, individuals having visionary ability might be regarded with suspicion and distrust, depending on how they chose to use their abilities. Being identified as a witch or sorcerer—that is, someone who used power for destructive ends, particularly within his or her own community—was a highly ambiguous social position that could result in persecution and death. This status reflected the fundamentally ambiguous nature of personal empowerment. Powers could be used to enhance and promote human welfare or to destroy and seduce, depending largely on the specific nature or type of power bestowed on the individual. Negative dream-spirits did inhabit all strata of the world cosmology—especially the chthonic realm—and could bestow destructive power. The ability to cause illness, seduce women, kill a fellow member of the community, or cause harm and disorder was attributed to many visionaries. Nevertheless, the primary emphasis and the pervasive nature of power was expressed as beneficial and protective for the individual. Most dream-spirits were personified as compassionate and caring, desiring to promote social welfare and enhance human life.

Another social aspect of power is its strong association with age. Elder visionaries in the community are generally respected for their knowledge. Personal empowerment in this sense is often equivalent with knowledge attained through years of experience. This knowledge is, however, a specialized type of knowledge: it refers to the various ways of evoking, seeking, or acquiring empowerment. It is also knowledge of how to communicate power and how to handle the objects associated with it. If the power sought, for example, is success in war, it would be necessary to gain access to the dream-spirits of war. Only those who had already achieved such success could truly guide the seeker; he would need the knowledge of a war shaman or religious specialist who understood the requirements and procedures that must be followed. Inevitably this would be an elder member of the community. Many religious societies, like those among the Arapaho, were age graded, thereby strengthening the association between age and knowledge.[22]

Knowledge as power is an intrinsic feature of the Plains religious worldview and is differentiated according to the degree and type of power received. It is made explicit through the number and types of power that the individual could invoke. The correct handling of many different types of power would mark an outstanding visionary as both knowledgeable and capable of many extraordinary acts. A powerful elder might be regarded with ambiguity, however, because of the general belief in the danger of having an overabundance of power.

It is the ambiguous qualities of power in terms of its source and usage that most often result in its being regarded as dangerous. Ambiguity is most frequently found in the personal or individual aspect of power. From the religious or cosmological point of view, power is dynamic, all pervasive, beneficial, and positive.[23] This is demonstrated by the substantially documented fact that a majority of Plains and Prairie men and women who seek empowerment are subsequently regarded with respect and admiration, not fear. Many such individuals become recognized holy men or holy women whose aid is sought by all members of the community. Those who are feared might use their power in ambiguous ways and for socially marginal ends. The nature of power is relative to its use; its negative influence is almost always attributed to particular individuals, and to the type of power they might attract.[24] Individuals who receive empowerment from chthonic beings do not necessarily engage in sorcery, while some who receive positive gifts might practice sorcery. Thus, the ambiguous quality of power—for example, among the Nez Perce—is essentially tied to personal use, since any power might be used for negative ends.[25] Another aspect of this ambiguity is that any powerful shaman might use his powers to defeat a potential rival. Conjuring contests in which shamans pitted their visionary abilities against one another are quite common in the Plains and Prairie dreaming ethnography.[26]

The gift of power is not always given freely by a dream-spirit. Many examples exist in the ethnography of the visionary's being repeatedly tested by the dream-spirit before being given power. As previously mentioned, the Kiowa-Apache believed that the courage and fortitude of the individual were tested during a vision quest by the appearance of frightening events or beings.[27] Elsie Parsons recorded a similar testing by a dream-spirit who told a Kiowa visionary to leave the mountain where he was fasting. He refused to follow this injunction, realizing that it was "only a test."[28] Morris Opler mentions the Apache belief that the most severe test comes when the visionary is taken to the home of the dream-spirit:[29]

The first trip to the holy home is the means, often, by which the power tests the faith of the novice and determines whether he is the kind of individual through whom it should work. Frightful animals guard the portals through which the candidate is conducted; insecure bridges, steep inclines, and forbidding elders challenge his way. But, if desire for a ceremony is strong enough, he reaches the very center of the power's abode and gains the knowledge for which he has come.

In discussing the vision experience of the Lakota Plenty Wolf, William Powers mentions that a visionary was tempted by two seductive deer spirits but shielded himself with his pipe.[30] Such testing reinforces the ambiguous nature of power and challenges the visionary's capacity to discriminate between the various spirits that appear. This discernment of spirits is an essential feature through which the visionary is judged fit to receive the real gift of power. It also suggests that empowerment could only be handled correctly by those with the necessary inner strength and determination.[31]

While the majority of visionary experiences are positive and retained as essential to the development and capabilities of the individual, in a minority of cases empowerment is rejected. On occasion it is thought to be too dangerous or demanding. There is also a correlation between the rejection of power and the spontaneous vision. Most individuals who set out on the vision fast desire a vision and are generally, though not always, willing to accept the power offered. In the case of a spontaneous vision, the visionary might more readily reject the power offered. In the ethnography, this is true among the Arapaho and particularly the Gros Ventre. An Arapaho woman rejected bear power that came to her spontaneously because she did not wish to become a bear healer, something she regarded as too dangerous.[32] Among the Gros Ventre, it is said that power would shorten the life span of the individual; and such ideas were propagated through exhortations given by the village criers.[33] John Cooper mentions many such examples, several of which are of women who received spontaneous visions but rejected the power. The elder known as Boy rejected spontaneous power when it was offered, even though he was threatened by the power with the loss of his prosperity.[34]

Another reason for the rejection of power had to do with the type of empowerment offered. When a Kiowa visionary was presented with a variety of powers, as the result of a prolonged fast, he rejected the ability to cure smallpox because of the horrifying, scabby appearance of the spirit that offered it to him.[35] A Winnebago account also records the rejection of a visionary war power in the form of a remarkable serpent because it was too powerful for the individual to handle.[36] A dream-spirit might appear that is altogether too strange and bizarre to accept. Edward Curtis recorded such a Cheyenne example of rejecting power:[37]

The fourth night I heard singing below at the foot of the mountain. I went down crying and saw an animal at the spring. It was blue, with spots of white and had horns. It said, "This water is mine. It is different. In the summer it is cooler and in the winter warmer than any other water. Whenever I breathe I cause a fog. What do you wish?" I did not speak to that animal, but returned to the top of the hill.

The power might be rejected because the individual did not wish to become a doctor or to perform ceremonies. Among the Washo, a shaman would be paid to drive the solicitous dream-spirit away.[38] An Apache example shows how the visionary might respond to the power so as to avoid receiving such responsibilities: "I might reply to the power when it comes, 'I am a poor fellow, and there are many other people here good enough for that. Let me alone. I don't want your ceremony.'. . . They claim it is more dangerous to take it than to refuse it sometimes. They say some power might help you nicely for several years and then begin a lot of trouble.[39] Significantly, the context here is that of an unsolicited dream that comes spontaneously to the dreamer. An often cited reason for the rejection of power is that the gift is accompanied by too many restrictions and prohibitions. The visionary frequently has to observe various restrictions in behavior for the empowerment fully to manifest its potential. Power is often rejected because the visionary does not wish to observe these restrictions.[40]

To reject power offered spontaneously or in a sought vision could be extremely dangerous. This is particularly true for thunder dreams. Any individual who refused such an offer of power would be in danger of being struck by lightning. Wilson Wallis, writing about the Canadian Sioux, mentions several examples of thunder dreamers who ignored their calling to become Heyoka and who were subsequently killed by lightning. One thirty-year-old woman, who had received many thunder dreams and refused to become a Heyoka, was struck while sitting in her tipi and killed instantly. Her husband, who was also in the tipi, was completely uninjured.[41] Robert Lowie mentions that a horse that appeared in a vision to a Sioux warrior warned him that if he did not perform a horse dance "he would either die soon or suffer all his life for it."[42] Other dire predictions are given in the ethnography, all of which basically assert that the dream-spirits could retaliate if power was refused. Among the Oto, power might be rejected because of the temptation in old age to use it against others.[43] In all these cases, the obligations of power are to use it correctly and with maturity; otherwise, destructive results could be expected. The correct use of power is clearly given in the vision, and to deny or ignore these obligations could be disastrous.[44]

A NEW MATURITY

The gift of personal empowerment is often accompanied by certain restrictions and prohibitions that act to pattern the behavior of the visionary. This patterning is unique to each visionary and expresses the qualifying sanctions that must be observed for the successful manifestation of power. It is useful, therefore, to distinguish between prescriptions and proscriptions given in the ethnography. Most vision narratives contain definite instructions for calling upon and manifesting the gift of power. The making of sacred objects, special paint or dress, ritual actions and behavior, the singing of sacred songs—all these constitute the prescriptive aspects of the vision. Less emphasized, but clearly present in the ethnography, are the prohibitions that restrict the general interactive behavior of the individual. These proscriptions generally apply to everyday individual actions or interactions outside the context of invoking or using power objects, which are be handled in the carefully prescribed manner. The individual is proscribed in daily life from actions that could weaken or dissipate power. Such proscriptions, or socially restricted behaviors, kept the visionary constantly mindful of the obligations of empowerment and the need to act with respect and caution. The religious nature of visionary power, its mythic and cosmological dimensions, require both sobriety and concentration for handling it effectively.

The general nature of proscriptive behavior involves a clear emphasis on self-discipline and self-control. The imposition of these behavioral guidelines tended to strengthen the visionary's awareness of his or her relationship to the mysterious power. Frequently, these restrictions emphasized relationships of respect between the visionary and a particular dream-spirit. Robert Lowie recorded the following Assiniboine examples:[45]

If a person dreamt of an animal, he was not supposed to kill it or eat its flesh. A Stoney woman dreamt of a bear. Thereafter she made it a rule not to eat bear-meat. On one occasion she tasted some; in consequence, she came near being transformed into a bear herself. . . . The mother of the woman who abstained from bear-meat also dreamt of a bear. She requested her husband to bring her a cub. She nursed it together with her own child, one at each breast.

When grown, the bear remained in camp. . . . Men dreaming of buffalo sometimes dreamt its age as well; in this case, they would spare animals of that age, but could kill all others.

A distinct sense of self-restraint based on respect for the animal is illustrated here. Significantly, the danger is that in ignoring the prohibition associated with the animal, dreamers might become so closely assimilated by the power that they would be in danger of losing their human identity. This is particularly true of bear power. This type of spirit possession is not uncommon, especially during ritual dances and ceremonies.[46] Accepting bear power meant accepting an intense psychic connection with a dream-spirit that could protect but also overwhelm the individual. The proscription against eating or killing the animal functions to maintain a relationship of respect and distance from the source of empowerment, protecting the individual from the overabundance of its manifestation. Many other such prohibitions against eating visionary animals or parts of their bodies are given in the ethnography.[47] The mother's breastfeeding of the bear cub is a dramatic demonstration of the close affinity that could exist between dreamers and their power, and it illustrates the intense kinship relations that were formed through the agency of dream-spirits.

Frequently, the gift of power is accompanied by a warning that the visionary, while strengthening his or her capacities in one way, will simultaneously become vulnerable in another way. Such vulnerability demonstrates that power is not given in a unilateral sense but is strictly relative to the normal limitations of human interactions. Dream-spirits can help strengthen and focus the capacity and ability of the individual, but their aid is conditional and relative to particular circumstances. In this sense, power carries a dynamic charge: it can be lost, violated, diminished, enhanced, or transferred. It is not a static quantity but a dynamic quality that reflects the mythic and all-pervasive, implicit structures of the cosmos.

As such, power is limited in its human manifestations. When the Kiowa shaman Dävéko received hunting ability from the thunder eagle, he was given a warning: "This spirit told him, 'Don't let anyone point an arrow at you or pull a bow string in your direction. That is dangerous for you. It will kill you, and an iron spike will come out of your mouth.'"[48] The symbolism is that when the hunter points his arrows at an animal, he intends to kill; but this pointing makes him vulnerable to similar behavior from other Kiowa. The intentional structure of the power given to the visionary often reflects a reciprocal symbolism that reveals a structural similarity between the gift of power and its limitations. The hunter is made conscious of his enhanced power to kill by simultaneously experiencing a heightened vulnerability to symbolic actions connected with hunting or the handling of weapons. The focused intent of the hunter and his success makes him vulnerable to mimetic acts on the part of others. Such symbolism is consistent with the sacred nature of power. The act of hunting and all associated actions become charged with a potency that is dangerous to both the hunted and the hunter unless handled correctly. Power is multifaceted and interactive; acting with power means being vulnerable to power—such is its dynamic character.

Prescriptive behaviors are legion in the visionary ethnography. Almost every vision includes prescriptions that must be followed when handling sacred objects or invoking dream-spirits. An important aspect of every vision is the precise way in which various objects are to be made, handled, and used when invoking specific results. Certain of these objects had profound religious associations and represented commonly held attitudes of reverence and respect. The pipe was one such object. The Lakota Plenty Wolf received visionary instructions for its use and handling:[49]

As I prayed, someone seemed to be coming, making loud growling noises. But I didn't see anything. Then all of a sudden I saw that it was a spirit. I couldn't budge the pipe, and I didn't know what was happening. But I was clearheaded, and I got down and walked on my knees. Then I stopped and prayed. A voice from behind me said, "That was your grandfather talking to you. Did you understand?" No, I said. Then the voice continued: "You will have a ceremony. This pipe belongs to the people. Walk with them with this pipe. Be wise. Don't be with your wife during her menses. Don't slip and fall with the pipe. Don't fall asleep with it. Don't turn your back on it. If you do there will be hardships. Always

walk straight with knowledge. The people now depend on you."
"Hau," I said. "Hau." Then I saw that it was a bird, a dove. There
were two doves talking to me.

The instructions given by the doves in this vision correspond
to the general religious use of the pipe in all Plains Indian ceremonies. This correspondence is typical of many prescribed behaviors—they have continuity with a generally shared repertoire of religious practices. The significance for the visionary is
in the specific instructions of his personal dream-spirits. The
vision validates the religious symbolism and significance of the
pipe for the visionary. The use of power is generally consistent
with existing religious symbolism and belief, although visions
could act as means for validating new usages. The visionary
context reinforces the sacredness and care with which all such
religious symbols must be treated. Because the object is imbued
with power, it must be handled with attentive concentration and
respect, and never casually or indifferently. There is always a
distinct, prescriptive context for its use.[50]

Although the vision experience conferred on the visionary possibility and potential, the actualization of that potential might
take many years. Powerful visions are often followed by other
dreams and visions, all of which combine to guide the visionary
to the full maturation of his or her ability. For the master dreamers, or shamans, this meant an entire lifetime of dedication and
devotion to the fulfillment of all the requirements of visionary
experience. While power could be sought as a means to an explicitly and socially conceived end, the shaman's calling is most
frequently associated with the search for knowledge. A recognition of the reality and profound significance of the sacred character of the religious world, the inner impulses of a questioning
mind, and the determination to delve ever more deeply into the
mystery and meaning of life are intrinsic to the shaman's search.
The initial vision catalyzes new behaviors and attitudes that must
be explored over an extended period of time. This search culminates in the attainment and development of knowledge. There is
very little evidence in the ethnography that the vision resulted
in an immediate transformation of the individual. To be a person of knowledge is the goal of the successful shaman. Such a

transformation takes many years and requires constant instruction, practice, and determination, as well as humility and a concern for the well-being of others.

Both the prescriptive and proscriptive aspects of the vision encounter require maturity and patience if the vision is to be actualized. In the case of the Sioux Black Elk, his great vision did not begin to actualize itself until nine years had passed, during which time he mentioned his experience to no one.[51] An even more cogent example was recorded for the Absarokee Sitting Elk. At the age of six, he took part in a sham fight among other boys and was injured: "[He] fell asleep and dreamed. . . . A man with a lance decorated with hawk-feathers stood forth and sang three songs and charged the enemy. . . . He reappeared without a scratch on his body. . . . At forty [Sitting Elk] began to feel certain that it had been a real vision from the spirits, and thereafter used the songs and made his medicine known."[52] Thirty-four years passed before the vision began to exert its influence on the Sitting Elk. Only then did he feel ready to engage the vision as expressive of his actual power and ability. A period of time during which a vision lay fallow was not uncommon. Plains visionaries were well aware of the responsibilities and dangers of using visionary power. Because of the strong religious aura that imbued all vision experience, it was clearly recognized that power must be handled correctly or dire results could occur.

The search for equilibrium between the push-and-pull structures of social expectation, familial obligation, and personal responsibility had to be balanced against the demands and obligations of the visionary encounter. To do so required maturity and frequently the help of more experienced elders. To become a master dreamer, or shaman, to follow a more structured involvement with the sacred powers, required intensive training and numerous visionary encounters. While the vision experience frequently marked the end of youth, it did not immediately confer a new religious identity. Power had to be demonstrated—manifested within the context of recognizable patterns of behavior. The new structures and obligations were modeled on existing "right relations" between the various members of the community, both in terms of recognizable social identity, such as affiliation with a specific group of dreamers, and in terms of overall kinship patterns. As Irving Hallowell has clearly pointed out, the relationship between a visionary and his or her power involved reciprocity patterned on recognized social interactions.[53] The individual character of the experience was retained in a social context of religious belief and ritual behavior, which involved the visionary in an interpretive search for the correct balance between individual experience and social milieu. The visionary must come down off the mountain and return to the life of the people.

CHAPTER EIGHT

Sharing the Dream

The recent event transformed into imagery is the bridge into the dream, just as the pictorial narrative transformed into a verbal report is the bridge out of it. The moment we learn to walk the bridge, our lives can come full circle.

—Jon Tolaas, "Transformatory Framework: Pictorial to Verbal"

IN ORDER TO APPRECIATE the problems of sharing and re-telling dreams and visions, it is necessary briefly to retrace a central line of analysis. The mystery of presence with its frightening and awesome aspects eventually gives way in the successful vision quest to a vivid realization of a discreet manifestation. This manifestation has a recognizable (often human) form and communicates specific instructions. It is a direct encounter with the dream-spirits that inhabit the world strata. Such an encounter acts as an important catalyst to personalize the complexity and diversity of the mythic world, giving it a valued, individualized form. The primordial contents of the mythic world, with its plurality of forms and visionary appearances, are an unbound unity of powers whose discreet manifestations are subject to continual metamorphosis and transformation. It is this unbound quality of the mythic world that must be kept in mind. The visionary encounter reveals a continuous variation in both qualitative experience and specific contents. Like pearls on a string, the visionary experiences of the individual collectively encompass the unique encounters and abilities that lead to personal adornment, power, and knowledge. Those experiences manifest a unique history of religious development in symbols and actions that validate the richness and plurality of the religious world.

Yet the unique psychic history of the individual also contributes a memorable testimony to the collective identity of a people. It is this dialogue between the contribution of the individual and his or her social existence within the broader community that constitutes the general interpretive history of the vision. The unbound quality of that history, its openness to individual experience, reflects the character of the Plains religious world. The binding guidelines of tradition and memory shape the primary means by which the visionary transparency of personal experience takes actual form and becomes embodied in the artifacts of culture, behavior, and social identity. The shared structures of social life provide a malleable context for the gradual transformation of the collective as a result of the visionary encounter. The ongoing activities of interpretation and integration provide the instrumentation for such change. The direction of these activities is generally the assimilation of the unknown into the known, but there is a significant factor that underlies the continuity of cultural assimilation: a deeply shared belief in the continuous guidance, manifestation, and assistance of the sacred powers—powers whose actions cannot be wholly predicted or understood. The long history of visionary lore, the record of continuous communication with dream-spirits through generations of vision experience, results in an abiding context of reverence and respect for the emergent quality of the vision experience.

The variability of the dream encounter is reflected in the difficult task of translating the dream into a communicable form. Perhaps the most significant social feature of the vision experience is its communicable elements. Something is revealed or shown to the dreamer that participates in a variety of communicable genres. However, what is communicated is frequently not understood or immediately grasped. This is an important aspect of dream sharing: the communication is veiled. Meaning is concealed in the often dramatic and awesome experience of the dream encounter. Dreaming is mysterious. It participates in an enfolded totality of human social and mythic experiences and frequently takes years, if not an entire lifetime, to become clear and explicit. This difficulty in dream interpretation gives rise to the problem of communicative efficacy. What is the effect of the dream on both the dreamer and the community? What is communicated? Why is the dream veiled and difficult to interpret? Who is the authoritative interpreter? All these questions are an essential part of the phenomenological structure of the dream communication. Dream sharing is problematic and participates in the even deeper problems of the unbound nature of the religious, mythic world. The dreamer is faced with the dilemma of finding a way to understand the vision or dream in terms of traditional, shared meanings while simultaneously striving to perfect and develop its individual significance.

The communicative experience is by no means a strictly verbal instruction; it is more often a complex mix of ritual, symbolic gesture, and words spoken or sung. The epitome of the verbal situation, embodied in the dream song, is a highly idiosyncratic communication. As in many other religious traditions, these songs are gifts that require only use, not interpretation. Words given by the dream-spirits are regarded as decisive for preparing the individual to meet the demands of personal existence. Furthermore, they are used to invoke the powers so that a visionary can strengthen his or her communicative link with the dream-spirits. Unlike the tendentious "Word" in the Judeo-Christian–Islamic tradition, these dream songs are of a private revelatory nature; words of power are not to be discussed or debated, only *used* to invoke their sources. Communicative efficacy refers to finding the appropriate means for sharing the vision experience. The most salient means is to sing the dream song and to demonstrate the gift of power. In the ethnography, verbal interpretation is entirely secondary, playing little or no functional social role and integral only to more speculative discourses between visionaries, usually in a context of secrecy.

Telling the dream does not equal the experience of the dream. This is a function of the inadequacy of language with regard to visionary experience. One of the functions of language is to symbolize experience—that is, to condense and code the complexity of thought, feeling, action, and awareness into communicable forms. But to insist that verbal communication fully expresses the dream experience is a gross oversimplification. The dream telling cannot ontologically reproduce the event; it only encodes the experience in recognizable verbal form. Language determines only one means by which the experience is communicated. Language supplies an encoded, semantic, communally shaped basis for articulating and discussing various aspects of experience It does not, in itself, predetermine the experience.[1] This does not mean that language has no formative power in its intrinsic structural coherence. It only means that the potency of language lies in its continuity with other types of expression and similar (but not identical) experiences—in the structural conventions by which experience is shaped in communication. The vision encounter expresses the primary reality, the sacred contents of which are then shaped and reshaped through a variety of symbolic enactments and socially significant constructions. The visual contents of the experience are translated into mimetic acts that communicate the reality of power. The verbal character of the dream report is a secondary concern.

There are a number of reasons why the spoken report of the vision experience is of secondary importance. First, the translation of dream imagery into verbal description is highly challenging. Contemporary research in imagery has developed around the various dual coding models involved in this very problem of the relationship between visual and verbal processing.[2] The general theoretical consensus is that the translation of primary imagery into verbal expression involves the ability to access and relate distinctive modes of cognition, emphasizing brain-hemispheric conditioning. Second, in the Plains visionary ethnography, the tendency is always to enact the dream contents as a means of manifesting the power conveyed in the vision experience. This enactment is combined with the making of physical icons or visionary objects and with the recreation of visual imagery and actions. The translation of the experience into verbal form is done rarely and cautiously, if at all. The sacred quality of the vision, along with the primordial character of the encounter in a highly imagistic culture, reinforces the idea that verbalizing the dream or vision is tantamount to abandoning its power. This is because the image, whether mental or physical, is believed to be charged with a sacred content that must be treated with care and respect. Those seeking interpretation would, of course, relate their dreams, but only to particular elders in circumstances of privacy.[3]

The processing of the vision, both in memory and through interpretive acts, is a matter of integrating highly condensed imagery, with its multiple, diverse associations and mythic connections, into the serial processes of articulate thought and expressive action. Such a synergistic activity requires a combination of bodily, mental, and emotional expression in a context of religious experience to produce an act of power by which the vision can be socially validated.[4] Such validation can rarely be accomplished through verbal report, except in the case of precognitive or prophetic dreams. These prophetic dreams represent a special case in which knowledge (usually seeing, not hearing) is transmitted to the visionary and is then verbalized to the concerned parties. It should be noted, however, that prophetic dreams and visions are part of the repertoire of advanced visionaries who are highly experienced in this type of dreaming. In the vision quest of most seekers, such an ability would be rare or the consequence of a shamanistic calling. Furthermore, the report of such a dream is concerned with the result of the precognitive experience and not with a detailed account of the dream itself.

Those most likely to excel at verbalizing dreams would be those most frequently involved with dreaming experiences. Consequently, it is among the religious specialists that the best examples of both dream articulation and interpretation are found.[5]

DIALOGIC PATTERNS

There are, nevertheless, a large number of dream narratives that have been collected by ethnographers over the last hundred years. If it is assumed, on the basis of contemporary research, that nightly dreaming is part of the mental life of every human community, then the ethnographic record represents only a small fraction of the dream life of the Plains and Prairie peoples. It is important to consider that the entire dream and vision ethnography is actually less than the total number of dreams in the life of a single individual. Qualitatively, however, the ethnographic record is excellent, and it records the outstanding visionary experiences of many of the most remarkable visionaries and religious specialists. On a more modest level, every ethnographic example is selective: visionaries choose, from the richness of their dream life, the most salient and significant experiences. These are then communicated to the ethnographer in what can be described as a culturally unique situation. The sharing of dreams in the ethnographic context was not only unprecedented but also largely the consequence of an oppressive cultural domination. The suppression of Plains Indian life and religious practice resulted in the sharing of cultural experiences that were themselves seriously threatened.

Because there was no context in oral traditions for the transformation of the dream or vision into a written text, such texts were new, intercultural artifacts. Furthermore, there was no context for sharing dream experiences with people who were not members of the dreamer's community. The ethnographic practice of eliciting and recording dreams was unique to both the visionary and the ethnographer, for few fieldworkers ever recorded their own dreams. Consequently, the ethnography of dreams is scattered piecemeal throughout the more general anthropological record.[6]

The symbolic and affective nature of the dream experience cannot be easily or adequately conveyed in a text; therefore, the dream should not be thought to equal the text. The text is a frozen and filtered record of a highly dynamic, religious encounter.[7] To appreciate the significance, power, and meaning of the dream, it is necessary constantly to work back into the primordial nature of the religious experience and forward into its dynamic social enactment. The text captures only part of the visionary encounter and requires a religious context to be fully appreciated. This recontextualization of the dream is essential for any in-depth understanding of Native American religions.

Recognizing the unique artifactual nature of the dream text, there is nevertheless a pattern of dialogical exchange that is intrinsic to the vision encounter as well as to the shared religious context. This pattern of dialogical exchange begins when the neophyte seeks instruction or guidance from an elder shaman, and is elaborated in the vision encounter when he receives further instructions from a dream-spirit. Returning from the vision encounter, the successful visionary could choose to tell the experience and receive an often tentative interpretation. The cycle then completes itself in later retelling of the dream under ceremonial circumstances, such as among members of a dream society or for the instruction of other neophytes by a recognized visionary.

Dialogic patterning permeates the entire process—insofar as dreams were told at all. Many did not tell their dreams or ever discuss their visions. This was particularly true of elder dreamers and religious specialists. The majority of interpretations in the ethnography refer to the dreams and visions of younger dream seekers. Such a dialogical pattern can be described as an interactive relationship between a knowledgeable elder (or dream-spirit) and a less knowledgeable youth. The experienced shaman or elder provides a cultural context for the interpretation of the experience. Among elder dreamers, this context is fully active, and explication by others is far less common in the ethnography. It is not the telling of the dream that expresses its significance, but its enactment and the subsequent manifestation of power.

Insofar as the dream or vision might be discussed, its visionary contents could be subjected to any number of verbal, visual, or symbolic influences. This diversity of expressions reflects the dialogical structure of the social and religious world. By "dialogical" I mean a community of interactive speakers, each of whom gives expression to a variety of perspectives, speaking in his or her own voice. Among the Plains peoples, this dialogue is further structured by kinship relations, age, and gender. Yet there is no overriding dogma that necessitates a rigid symbolic interpretation. Every image, story, enactment, prohibition, or performance communicates possible nuances of meaning for the understanding of the vision. This living quality of the community, its existential circumstance and multifaceted contents, creates an interactive milieu in which every visionary participates.

Dialogical interaction is highly contextual. It contains many nuances and paralinguistic features that contribute to its overall contents. Meaning and significance cannot be separated from this interactive social context without a tremendous loss in richness and complexity. On a more abstract level, the comparative analysis of the various texts, both within a single community and between communities, helps to restore something of the richness of many voices speaking together.[8] The associated meanings are not strictly verbal but also have to do with the various images, symbols, structures of movement, and songs, all of which serve to enhance the understanding of any specific item or of the overall significance of the vision. For the Plains Indian visionary, dialogical interaction is a dynamic process of the negotiation and sharing of meaning in a context of communal religious belief.

Nevertheless, within the general dialogical pattern, there lies a more problematic issue. It has to do with the entelechy of the visionary encounter. The Native American concept of the sacred as mysterious, unusual, and strange—as well as powerful, awesome, and omnipresent—also reveals that the human being who receives dreams and visions participates in this mystery. If the human condition is veiled, concealed in mystery, then the dream encounter can be continuously unpacked as new experiences and insights develop. The master dreamer's path is one of a continuing series of visions and dreams, all of which contribute to unfolding maturity and knowledge. The vision is never strictly self-referential but includes both familial and social dimensions— thus establishing interactive relationships that also contribute to the overall understanding and significance of the dream experience. Success in war, hunting, or healing through visionary means involves relationships with others.

Furthermore, continuous visionary encounters serve to deepen the power and understanding of the individual. The dream cannot be interpreted or understood in any "finished" way; it is part of an ongoing process of interaction, dialogue, reflection, and insight unfolding over the years. This is why the Lakota John Fire could say, referring to his great vision, "It took me a lifetime to find out."[9] The entelechy of the dream is its potential nature, its capacity to facilitate future growth, interpretations, and development.[10]

The interpretive context for developing maturity lies embedded in the existential problem of the human condition as self-concealed. Meaning and potential are latent within the emerging structures of human experience and are intrinsic to the dialogical relationship between informed and uninformed members the community. Visions and dreams have a definite ontological content insofar as they express enhanced power and meaning. The veiled contents of the vision symbolize the potential condition—they speak of the possibility, the as-yet-unrecognized capacity of the visionary. In the mature visionary, this potential has come fully into play and is expressed in recognizable acts of power.

Understanding the dream involves the integration of both personal and social existence. Dreaming facilitates this process of integration by unfolding an expansive range of experience and opening the dreamer's mind to more actualized contents of the visionary epistemé. Functionally, the vision opens the eyes of the visionary to manifestations of the sacred and to the structures of the religious world. It also reveals potential for action and understanding. Before the vision, this possibility of experience lies concealed in the general fabric of shared beliefs. After the vision, it becomes a more integral aspect of personal existence. But this does not mean that the vision is fully understood. The successive layers of meaning and potential that inhere in the vision come to be unfolded only in relationship to the maturity and development of the individual. The mature visionary is the one who has understood, who has unpacked successfully, the visionary content through religious action and self-expression.

This kind of understanding requires a successful translation of the reality of the vision into a meaningful pattern of shared social relations. The dialogical structure of the search for meaning and understanding of the vision is part of a larger field of shared, generative meanings—the semiotic web of related words, images, acts, relationships, objects, and artifacts that work together to contribute to the specific expression of individual understanding. The visionary's challenge is to provide a perspective compounded of feeling, intuition, perception, thought, imagination, and action. This interactive expression is itself embedded in a highly charged religious topology that continually manifests potential through a directed solicitation of mythic powers and beings. This complex structure of interrelated and incorporated meanings is unified through the pervasive presence of *wakan*, mysterious reality. The dialogical context for the expression of personal meaning is part of a reciprocal process involving the full range of semiotic relations that exist in the richly imagistic social fabric of Plains and Prairie culture. Verbal expression is assimilated to the imagery and drama of ritual enactment. The discussion of a dream or vision takes place only in appropriate, often ritual, circumstances. Sharing the dream involves finding the appropriate setting to express a mystery that is not fully comprehended, given by the dream-spirits, and participant in the ongoing dynamic processes of religious maturation.

PRIVACY AND SILENCE

The vision, a powerful, private revelation, is spoken of only under the most guarded circumstances—if at all. The appropriate context for understanding this guardedness lies in the patterns of oral transmission of religious knowledge in Native American culture. Knowledge is transferred through actions and words spoken under conditions of secrecy. Speaking of a dream or vision means sharing the knowledge and empowerment contained in the vision. Such a sharing could mean the loss of that power or knowledge. To remain silent about the vision is the most certain means of retaining the gift. Consequently, there is a problematic relationship between silence and the need to speak. The religious context of the vision, its sacred sources, and the prohibitions surrounding it give rise to an implicit tension that made silence a prerequisite for the maintenance of power. Yet in certain circumstances, the individual must speak of the vision to validate the power. This tension pervades the ethnographic literature and reflects an existential feature of the dialogical circumstance. Speaking must be guarded, yet it is often surrounded by conditions that validate such speaking. The existential concern around which this tension develops is not speaking per se but speaking as a means for the manifestation of power. This kind of tension is a common feature in sacred discourse.[11]

Dream telling is carried out in ritually prescribed circumstances and only with select members of the community; dreams are rarely spoken of to anyone outside these prescribed relationships. To speak, particularly in a context not sanctioned by the community, is very dangerous. The Lakota holy man Black Elk told John Neihardt that in narrating his great vision he was "giving his power away" and felt he would die very soon afterward.[12] It is important to note that the context for Black Elk's telling his vision was not a culturally sanctioned situation where such a telling might be acceptable. Told in the appropriate context—in a medicine lodge with other visionaries—such a telling might not endanger the speaker or diffuse the power. The ethnographic context is a nebulous in-between that lacks the appropriate cultural sanctions for such speaking. As such, it was a liminal situation and could have no integrative function. Frances Densmore captured the essence of this situation during her recording of dream songs: "An aged man once recorded his dream song for the writer, then bowed his head and said tremulously that he thought he would not live long as he had parted with his most precious possession."[13]

While most dreamers and visionaries were reluctant to speak of their experiences, in some cases there was a strong cultural prohibition against it. Alanson Skinner, working among the Plains Cree, noted the "strict taboo against telling these dreams which prevailed."[14] Consequently, he collected no dream texts.[15] David Mandelbaum noted that a Plains Cree would tell his dream or vision as a way of explaining his participation in a curing or his leading of a ceremony, but this might be many years after the vision experience.[16] Before that, no one knew of the visionary's experience. A similar, if less rigid, prohibition existed among the Gros Ventre.[17] If a dreamer wished to speak of a dream or vision, he or she might be prohibited by ritual sanctions. Among the Omaha, the visionary was forbidden to speak of the experience before the passing of four days: "For four days he must rest, eat little, and speak little. After that period he might go to an old and worthy man who was known to have a similar vision. . . . Should he speak of his vision before the expiration of four days, it would be the same as lost to him."[18]

The danger of speaking, of giving away the power through insubstantial talk, dissipates the generative potential of speech.

Silence is enjoined on the visionary so that he or she can learn through private discussions with knowledgeable elders the appropriate context and use of language. Talk of dreams and visions is a generative phenomenon—an expressive verbal act that communicates a power capable of acting on others and effecting transformation in communal perceptions of the world. The whole process of communicating dream contents is evocative. The structural "grammar" of the communication is strongly nonverbal (iconographic, imagistic, object oriented) and kinesthetic. Speaking is not about the phenomenon but is an actual manifestation of the phenomenon, not "information" but manifestation. As such, it is secret knowledge and an essential part of the religious life of the community.

An Omaha thunder dreamer might keep silent about his dream for some time and only speak of it if he was with a war party that needed the help of the sacred beings.[19] Among the Comanche, visionaries were prohibited from speaking about the nature of their power unless commanded to do so by their dream-spirits. The Comanche also believed that if a bad dream was not told during the four days following the dream, no bad luck would occur.[20] For the Plains peoples generally, even though the membership of a society might be public knowledge through performances of various types, the actual knowledge possessed by its members was open only to those who were eventually permitted to join the society.

Secret knowledge was that given to a visionary for the enactment of rites that manifested positive results in the context of shared practice among like-minded dreamers. A distinction was made among the Dhegiha-speaking peoples between social and secret societies. The first were made up of individuals who could perform the acts required for membership:[21]

To this class belonged the warrior societies as well as those for social purposes only. The secret societies dealt with mysteries and membership was generally attained by virtue of a dream or vision. Some of these secret societies had knowledge of medicines, roots, and plants used in healing; others were noted for their occult and shamanistic proceedings and furnished the only examples of such practices in the tribe.

The secret nature of this knowledge was such as to preclude casual or discursive talk. Discussion was carried on only among members of the society to which the visionary belonged. I found no record of any such discussions between members of the different societies. The religious conception underlying this guarded concern was the belief, reinforced through direct experience, that the powers who gave such knowledge gave it only to specific individuals for specific uses. Because knowledge was practical, not theoretical, the visionary had a very specific context for the use of power. The power was discussed only with other like-minded dreamers in a context of privacy. The very nature of such a proscribed group limited discussion to that group alone.

Another reason for keeping silent about such knowledge had to do with the exact nature of the power. If the power was negative or destructive, the recipient would not be likely to discuss it with anyone. The practice of witchcraft was highly dangerous and could arouse hostility among other members of the visionary's community. Edward Curtis recorded the following as practiced among the Assiniboine:[22]

Another heritage from their long association with the Cree was the practice of the *Waéchonsa,* who for a price would engage to bring disease or death upon the enemy of him who sought their service. This power was obtained through dreams, which must be kept secret, and whose commands it was essential to obey implicitly. The *Waéchonsa* in his conjuration made an image of birchbark (or rawhide), punched four holes through the vital parts, and buried it in a freshly raised mound on a hilltop. These things were of course done secretly.

Such conjuring was done among other Plains and Prairie groups, as well as among the Plateau peoples, as a consequence of having dreamed of certain chthonic spirits such as rattlesnake or badger. It was explained among the Nez Perce as a consequence of the faster's having a "hostile, jealous, or customarily irascible" nature.[23] Such knowledge was kept as secret as possible and rarely shared with anyone. Of all secret traditions, the practice of witchcraft was perhaps the most guarded because of the hostility it could arouse.

The secret nature of visionary knowledge was also strongly

associated with the developed shamans. The more visionary experience the individual had, the less likely he or she was to talk to uninitiated members of the community. Knowledge of this sort was esoteric in the sense that it was compounded out of the direct visionary experiences of the individual in discussion with other such visionaries. The lived world of everyday existence was charged with a plurality of visionary, mythic forms through which the religious contents of experience could be conveyed. Visions participated in the shared mythic structures of religious discourse by adding individual contents to the overall pattern of mythic relations. Yet the Plains and Prairie ethnographic record does not present visions and dreams as subordinate to a general mythic tradition. Mythic structures of inherited oral narratives provide a background against which the individual vision history develops.[24] A group of like-minded dreamers provided the necessary social context for assimilating visionary experience without forcing that experience into a rigid mythic pattern. The unbound nature of the visionary experience and its emergent qualities were woven into the larger patterns of the inherited mythic discourse to form the specific contents of shared belief. That such contents had a more esoteric form within the context of a particular group of dreamer-shamans seems likely.[25]

Another dialogical context, besides the recognized visionary society, is the sharing of power between husband and wife. Many shamans shared their power with their wives, who became helpers during ceremonial rites and might inherit the full use of the power upon the death of the husband. George Grinnell recorded the following for the Cheyenne: "A man cannot become a doctor by himself; when he receives the power, his wife—who afterwards is his assistant—must also be taught and receive certain secrets. . . . A man may become a doctor through a dream, thus receiving spiritual power directly from above, but even in this case he must have a woman to help him."[26] It is significant to note the use of the imperative here: the man *must* have the assistance of a woman. This sharing of knowledge by the husband and the necessary assistance of the wife reflect the recognition on the part of many Native American peoples of the uniqueness of female power as distinct from male power.

In relationship to male power, female power is highly charged and dangerous, particularly during menstruation, and it could neutralize the effectiveness of male rites. An example of this kind of difference between male and female power is discussed by Ray DeMallie for the Sioux: "According to Deloria, the menstrual blood gave a kind of temporary power to a woman, a *wakan* quality. This was not thought of as polluting but rather as at odds with the *wakan* power of men; woman's menstrual power clashed with a medicine man's power. The clash was characterized by the word *ohakaya*, 'to cause to be blocked or tangled.'"[27]

The combination of male and female power could enhance the efficacy of the power at work. Among certain Plains groups, there is a commonly shared belief that husband and wife could work together. This is particularly true among the Cheyenne, Blackfoot, Comanche, Gros Ventre, and Absarokee. The frequency with which dream-spirits appear as a couple is very high throughout the ethnography. Many visionaries are taken to a place of power where they are received by a man and woman, both of whom give the visionary a gift of power. The dual symbolism of this shared power is expressed in a context of intimacy between husband and wife, strengthening the spiritual bonds between them. The knowledge might not be shared with any others. The use of the power thus emulates the dream-spirits, who also appear as husband and wife.[28]

THE DREAM TELLING

Perhaps the most fundamental problem of any dream sharing is that of disclosure. Sharing a dream means disclosing deeper aspects of personal empowerment, generally expressed in a dramatic way symbolizing the specific nature of personal aspiration, intention, and identity. Thus the form and content of the disclosure—made even more problematic through the translation of the vision into a verbal report—are often difficult to understand. To disclose the dream means to share its visionary contents as they refer to a specific unfolding of individual potential. Some individuals are simply not willing (or able) to make such a disclosure—particularly those older and more experienced in such matters. The circumstances for such a disclosure are highly structured because of the sacredness of the dream's contents and because such a disclosure frequently deals with secret knowledge. The dreamer's inner life is not revealed casually. Disclosure is a socially potent act because it is tantamount to the evocation of the powers in a context of shared responsibility. The telling of dreams and visions is regarded as a serious religious matter, and to lie or exaggerate in any way may subject the visionary to punishment by the dream-spirits.

As I mentioned earlier, the neophyte's first introduction to the ceremonial sharing of dreams occurs in the context of preparing for the first vision fast. During this preparation, the youth might hear of a vision experience from a relative or a shaman.[29] Young women might hear of such visions during their first time in the menstrual lodge.[30] Thus one form of dream telling involves establishing a precedent by which the teller relates the importance of dreams and visions through reference to personal vision experiences. The Absarokee Two Leggings was told of the vision experience of White Bear Child as a precedent for his own dream experience.[31] The shaman might tell of his vision to establish a precedent for the neophyte, providing a context for the manifestation of the mysterious and uncanny. The telling of other visions is done only in relationship to historically well-known dreams and visions, thereby establishing the visionary priority of those retained by oral tradition. This telling of the vision experiences of others helps give some context for both the vision experience and its later narration. Historically remembered vision narratives are used (very selectively) by some groups to establish a context for the vision experiences of the present generation. This sense of precedent might be the only context with which the young dreamer was familiar.

Having returned from the fasting place, the successful visionary would undergo various forms of purification, most commonly a sweat lodge with sage incense. In those few places in the ethnography where visions are discussed, such as among the Lakota, the directing shaman and other elder men would participate in the sweat lodge and listen to the visionary recitation. The visionary would be expected to give a serious and detailed account of all that had occurred to him. The Lakota Tyon mentions the exhortation that was given to the young faster: "'Listen, without jesting, tell about your vision! In a *wakan* manner you arrived home,' he said, it is said. 'Yes,' the vision quester said, 'in this manner, I dreamed something,' he said, and all those sitting in the lodge said in chorus, 'Haye,' it is said."[32] The narrator here is reporting a tradition of interactive discourse, a dialogical pattern in which the elder men would respond to each aspect of the dream telling with a collective "Haye," meaning that they had heard clearly the important thing he had said.[33] The "it is said" is an example of narrative verbal art and as such is framed in a way that marks it as something traditionally known.[34]

The pipe that the visionary carried is treated with care and respect as a witness of all that happened. The following exhortation was given by the Lakota Black Elk to a visionary about the importance of telling the truth: "You have brought back to us the pipe which you offered; it is finished! And since you are about to put the pipe in your mouth, you should tell us nothing but the truth. The pipe is wakan and knows all things; you cannot fool it. If you lie, Wakinyan-Tanka, who guards the pipe, will punish you!"[35]

The context for such an exhortation involved the deeply sanctioned belief that the dream-spirits were aware of the actions and speech of everyone. The purified rocks of the sweat lodge could hear the speech of the visionary. If the powers that granted the vision heard a lie, they would become ill disposed toward the visionary.[36] Thus the sanction against lying or exaggeration had its basis in religious experience and in events regarded as punishments having actually been witnessed—for example, injury, being struck by lightning, or other misfortune. If the visionary was reluctant to speak about his vision, as many were, the shaman might demonstrate his clairvoyant ability by telling the visionary what he had experienced before he spoke.[37]

If the visionary was an experienced man and had received a powerful religious vision, he might require some special ceremonial preparations before telling his dream. The famous Absarokee shaman Fringe required, as a result of one of his vision experiences, that the elder shamans of the village build four sweat lodges, each facing west, with medicine trails connecting them, the first lodge being made of a hundred willows.[38] Only after using each of them did he tell his experience. Such elaborate preparation would be in keeping with the specific instructions given in the vision. With the elder men gathered in the sweat lodge, the visionary would tell of the experience in detail. It would then be discussed by those gathered there according to their own experiences and to symbolic interpretations worked out collectively. Fringe's vision experience was interpreted as follows:[39]

The striped lodge, painted red and black, meant that he would heal wounds, become a great Wise One among them. They said the picket pin showed that he would possess many horses, gifts from the men and women he had healed; and that the Otter and the White Bear would be his Helpers throughout his life on the world. They told him, too, that the Otter was his medicine, but said he would never become a chief, that he was too kindly to become even a great warrior. "You are like the Person who led you beneath the Medicine Water," they said.

Such symbolic interpretation is quite common and very widespread. Visions are usually regarded as having rich symbolic associations in a cultural milieu that is strongly visual and imagistic. The vision has an overall significance: Fringe would become a great shaman and healer, not a warrior or chief. It also contains explicit symbolism: the striped lodge, referring to wounds (not internal problems or other types of illness), and the picket pin, meaning horses given in return for healing (not stolen in war). Furthermore, the personal identity of the visionary is declared to be similar to that of the Person who gave the powers. This is a revelation of the inner character of the visionary as disclosed through the symbolic actions of the vision. Subject to the gentle influence of women, with a nonviolent character, he would be compassionate and helpful. Both of his powers are chthonic but are positive sources of healing. The inherent symbolism is given a personal meaning in the context of collective discourse. The appearance of painted lodges or picket pins in the visions of others might be given entirely different interpretations based on the overall contents of the experience. This flexibility in interpretation is part of the unbound nature of the vision encounter—every vision has to be interpreted individually.[40]

Often the vision is difficult to fathom or interpret. Among the Lakota, such a case would require deliberation and thought over an extended period. James Walker recorded the following:[41]

If the vision is plain and easily understood, they advise him as they see fit. But if the vision is vague, they go again into the sweat house and meditate upon the proper interpretation of it. If they soon agree upon this, they expound it to the candidate or it may be that they require some time to agree upon a proper interpretation, in which case they leave the sweat house and each goes to his home. They meet either with or without the candidate and discuss the matter at will until they come to an agreement, when they notify the candidate that they have agreed. Then they meet with him and expound his vision and give him advice according to their interpretation of it.

It should be noted that the visionary is under no compulsion to follow the advice of these advisers. Only if the advice is related to membership in a society would he have to follow it, perhaps terminating his attempts to join if the vision is interpreted as unfavorable to such membership.[42]

In this way, interpretation could be used to exert social control by determining membership in various societies. This would depend, however, primarily on the content of the vision and on a collective decision. Furthermore, the interpretation might remain vague or uncertain and require additional visions and dreams for clarity. This could take many years. A widespread practice required waiting for further dreams to clarify a vision that was poorly understood. Another practice was to confer with other dreamers who shared the same power. In all cases some consensus was sought, even if only between the dreamer and one other individual. The task of interpretation was generally a shared task—if the dream or vision was discussed at all.[43]

There are many other contexts for dream telling. Among the Dhegiha people, as among many Southwestern groups, bad dreams must be told immediately. This is particularly true of dream or vision experiences involving the dead or ghosts. After the dreamer tells about such an experience, members of the ghost society are called and the visionary is subjected to ritual purification.[44] Among the Pawnee, dreams and visions about various ceremonies must be related because they indicate that the dreamer should assume sponsorship for the appropriate ceremony. This telling of the dream or vision was done in the context of the relevant society meeting:[45]

At a recent meeting of the [Bear] medicine society, when the ceremony had ended, a woman named Yellow Corn Woman arose and said, "I had a vision. I saw Bear Chief wearing the bear robe over his shoulders and the bearclaw neckpiece around his neck. . . . He said, "My sister, Father (Bear) and Mother (Cedar Tree) have not had any smoke for many years. We (dead people) are watching for our people to have the ceremony. The people think the ceremony is lost. It is not, for one of the Bear men who knows the secret ceremony is still with you. I ask that you tell the people so they can have the ceremony, for it is time."

"I woke up and the last few days I have been crying to think that I should be the one to tell you. I have a cow which you can have so you can have the ceremony." Then she began to cry.

Here, a renewal of the ceremony comes through a female society member who would normally have no leadership role. The unbound nature of the vision experience, however, marks her as a messenger for the dream-spirits and as a sponsor (she gives a cow). Subsequently, a man named Big Star told the leaders of the ceremony that he knew how it should be performed, and the Pawnee bear dance was reinitiated in 1910. Another alternative for dream telling might occur years after a vision experience, when the visionary was prompted by other dreams to hold a ceremony and announce his dream to the appropriate society.[46]

The most common situation for dream telling among both Plains and Prairie peoples was during healing ceremonies. The shaman would recite the dream or vision experience as a means of validating the powers upon which he or she called in an attempt to cure the sick.[47] Densmore collected a very interesting Teton Sioux narrative that combines both dream telling and a visionary affirmation on the part of the sick person and others of the reality of the shaman's power:[48]

I sent for a medicine-man to treat me. . . . Beating the drum rapidly with the rattle, he said, "Young man, try to remember what I tell you. You shall see the power from which I have the right to cure sicknesses, and the power shall be used on you this day." Then he told the dream by which he received his power as a medicine-man.

He was still telling his dream and singing, but when he paused for an instant I could hear the sound of a red hawk; some who were there even said they could see the head of a red hawk coming out of his mouth. He bent over me and I expected that he would suck the poison from my body with his mouth, but instead I felt the beak of a bird over the place where the pain was.

This example of seeing the power of the shaman during healing is quite typical. As I have mentioned, sickness is a liminal condition that is itself conducive to visionary experiences. Under such circumstances, narrating the dream is thought to invoke the dream-spirit and thereby to heighten the altered condition of both the shaman and the sick person. This is another example of the collective vision experience. A related situation for dream telling might arise during the opening of a bundle containing the necessary objects for healing, or during bundle renewal ceremonies.[49]

Another circumstance for dream telling is during the transfer of dream powers to others. This is a highly significant process by which the original dreamer gives away the dream power simply by telling the dream to another in the appropriate ritual context. It demonstrates how power could be transferred through a speech act. This was a distinct practice among the Absarokee. Two Leggings, for example, was told that he might expect to receive certain dreams from others who wished him well as a shaman's assistant to Sees the Living Bull. A special sweat-lodge meeting was held, during which dreams were given to him as he assisted at the meeting:[50]

As Neck Bone stooped to enter he told me had seen a vision of horses. He called me his child and gave me those horses. Small Face had dreamt of the new grass. . . . he wished I would live until then [spring]. Burns Himself . . . said his vision of a successful war party was now mine. The fourth man . . . said his vision had shown him several scalps and in the coming season, he hoped I would take them. . . . A person can only receive four visions at a time so the other guests sat down without speaking.

It should be noted that the gifts given did not include songs, which implies that certain aspects of power were retained by the donors. A similar practice was recorded by Alfred Bowers for the Hidatsa, when Poor Wolf gave away a roan horse he had been promised in a vision.[51]

A similar context for dream telling arises when important dreams or visions are purchased by others. This was practiced among the Omaha, Ponca, Blackfoot, Absarokee, Mandan, and Hidatsa.[52] An Omaha example is given:[53]

The telling of visions merely to satisfy curiosity was not done in Omaha [society]. Such action would have led to *nonka* [sacred punishment]. If a father possessed a power from revelation he would tell a son only the details in return for a heavy payment from the son, and only in giving over the power to his son and so denuding himself of it . . . it was well believed that the father in deeding over the power to the child, signed his death warrant.

All such examples illustrate the generally shared belief that to speak of the dream is dangerous and creates a situation in which the dreamer might lose the power. Speaking of dreams is done only under highly circumscribed conditions for specific ends. More generally, dreams are spoken about in one-to-one relationships between friends and relatives. The evidence for this is simply the widespread knowledge of the great dreams of well-known individuals. The actual contents of these dreams, however, are often not remembered (or not shared). Instead, what circulates is the story that the dreamer had received extraordinary power— as in the case of the famous Sioux Crazy Horse, whose dream of the dancing horse was well known, even if its precise contents were not.

CHAPTER NINE

Mythic Discourse

A man in whom the people had confidence sought a vision and in the vision was instructed in the forms and ceremonies for establishing an association, and what the duties of such as association were. He would instruct others in these matters and associate them for the purposes of the organization in compliance with his vision."

—James R. Walker, *Lakota Belief and Ritual*

MYTHIC DISCOURSE involves the processes of interpersonal communication, or dialogical interaction, based in an inherited religious worldview and structured by a variety of communicative genres. This discourse is framed as religious knowledge and contextualized in terms of a communally shared social and topological orientation. By framing I mean the process by which verbal, imagistic, mimetic, and symbolic interactions give coherent form and meaning to the lived world. For the Plains peoples, this process involves the dramatic presentation of inherited communicative patterns through voice, image, and action. Its religious consequence is to denote the sacred contents and origins of the lived world. It is the process of elaborating the coherence between topological structures of the world and dramatizing their social and sacred significance. More formally, mythic discourse is the use of narrative, music, poetry, and performance to recreate memorable, foundational events in a context of social solidarity for the purpose of explicating similar or related events.

The language of mythic discourse is highly imagistic and concrete, relying on shared symbolic forms and conventional styles of expression. The characteristic expression is the well-told story or a dramatic enactment. Behavior is constantly being articulated in terms of communally shared narrative structures. Various forms of dress and paint, the ritual handling of certain objects, and different types of stylized behavior all contribute to mythic discourse. All talk of dreams, visions, and related objects or actions is intrinsic to such discourse. Such discourse contributes to a shared understanding of what is sacred and how the sacred must be approached or handled. Mythic discourse includes dramatic demonstrations of personal empowerment and ability as testimony to the truthfulness of its religious content.

Mythic discourse, then, is an expression of the visionary epistemé. The means by which mythic discourse proceeds, in the Plains Indian ethnography, are not analytical in the philosophical sense, nor are they based in the rational affirmation of a preconceived theory, as in the modern psychological sense.[1] Rather, mythic discourse is a process of elaboration and demonstration intrinsic to social needs and pragmatic circumstances that are powerfully influenced by the unique contents of a specific visionary history. This history is both an individually and a communally defined history informed by an ongoing process of interpretation and ritual action. Mythic discourse articulates religious thought in the form of stories and events that culminate in a sacred praxis—for example, in the extensive use of visionary objects—and it is given expression in a wide spectrum of dramatic presentations that deeply affect the participants. Cultural identity is strengthened through this enactment, and individual symbolization of dream and visionary contents contributes an emergent quality to this identity. The relationship between the shared contents of mythic discourse and the personal vision is dialogical. Every visionary who enacts a vision, who dresses in accordance with the vision, who sings visionary songs or manifests visionary power contributes to the general contents of mythic discourse. The enactment of the visionary epistemé, sanctioned by the deepest religious beliefs, is a powerful influence on the contents of that discourse.[2]

The powerful dynamic quality of the vision experience is central to the general structure of mythic discourse because it provides a dramatic, existential encounter that validates more general ideas and practices. Among the Plains peoples, this discourse is not determined by overt authority but, as I have shown, is frequently negotiated according to collective experience and a context-specific wisdom. The mythic structures of thought and experience are not best represented by a textual corpus, but rather by a fluid, dynamic field of interactive events and meanings embedded in a sacred topos. This field is constituted by its coherence and integration with the visual and tactile world. Yet it embodies a totality of visible and invisible beings, places, signs, and symbols. Thus the field is not enclosed by a particular property of narration or thought but is constituted as a totality of potential encounters and revelations that are made explicit through visionary enactments. The social milieu of the religious world is an indefinite, heterogeneous set of complex relationships given coherence by the recognizable structures of mythic discourse, belief, and action. Its temporal continuity is maintained through the "teaching of the elders," through ritually enacted events, and by the tangible markers of the religious topology. Discourse is part of an ongoing process of interpretation largely communicated through ritual action.

In contradistinction to non-native religious discourse, which in the modern context is strongly demythologized, mythic discourse emphasizes the embedded nature of its contents in a shared context of interactive social processes. Rudolph Bultman's contention that the truth of religion can only be uncovered by stripping it of its mythological framework has had a profound impact on Western religious discourse.[3] The rational, ascetic prejudice against myth and mythic worlds that is part of such abstract and rational discourse requires, as its counterpoint a new emphasis on the inseparability of myth from the living fabric of religious action or symbolization. Intellectually framed dogma that imbues demythologized analysis with its own brand of validity has little to offer in the contextual study of religious cultures and their rich imagistic, symbolic, and ritually enacted plurality of mythically embedded meanings and associations. The processes of mythic discourse are inseparable from sacred action and the multiple nuances of cultural symbolization. Religious discourse in a context of demythologization cannot contribute to the understanding of the mythic unless it can articulate an understanding that fully expresses the richness and pervasiveness of mythic processes. This cannot be accomplished through an approach that discards all mythic contents as obscuring the message of the text. The understanding of the mythic requires an extratextual strategy that involves the full spectrum of human experience and cultural symbolization.[4]

It is necessary, first, to discard the idea that "myth" refers to a fixed, inviolable content upon which all members of a community agree. The text is not the context. Second, it is necessary to discard the idea that there is a particular authoritative or autocratic social group that can impose an unquestioned interpretation on a particular experience. Instead, the content is variable and individual. Third, it is important to recognize that both the content and the interpretation are part of a semiotic interaction of verbal and nonverbal expressions. Simply put, mythic discourse refers to a complex process of ongoing interactions and not to a specific type of content. The "text" in this case is not simply a written document but the narrative context in all its complex relatedness to the entire field of religious action and behavior.

The structures of mythic discourse are found in fluid patterns of communication and are transformed over time through individual and collective experience. In the Native American setting, discourse allows for variation and multifaceted symbolic expression. Mythic contents are understood differently by different members of the community. Social consensus as part of a process of interpretation among concerned individuals and specific social (and religious) groups often reflects varying degrees of marginality and emphasis. While mythic referents (which must include objects and actions) may have a broadly shared identity, their use in the discussion of a particular vision experience is highly variable because of the variable nature of the vision itself. The marginality of the vision experience often lasts many years, if not a lifetime, before the vision becomes socially integrated into the collective life of the people. Yet such marginality might contribute significantly to cultural transformation.

The content of the vision and its unbound quality bring a constant stream of communication from the dream-spirits that demands serious attention and consideration. The vision might also reveal new cultural influences leading to social transformation, which in turn can have a direct impact on other aspects of shared discourse. The stable features of such discourse are those reproduced over the generations—symbolic events and sacred beings that come to embody the unique history of a specific community. Yet the centrality of the vision experience to the Plains peoples is one of the primary sources of religious innovation. The openness of the topological boundaries and the diversity of the visionary experience allow for a constant influence from what is constituted mythically as the highest sources of religious knowledge. When a dreamer brings a unique experience into the general discourse, it might have many or few immediate symbolic correlates. Nevertheless, it participates in a shared symbolic system that is given heightened meaning through both the general mythic discourse and the shared ceremonial practices adaptable to the individual vision. Or the dream or vision experience might contain its own unique form of symbolic expression that is unrecognized by the community at large. This is particularly true in the vision origins of the various societies that were established throughout the plains as a result of the experience of one or more individuals.[5]

Thus dreaming has a determinative power both individually and socially and is an active and dynamic force in the shaping and elaboration of the general mythic discourse. This is the creative aspect of dreams and visions. Every shared dream or vision enters into the general stream of mythic discourse and helps shape the religious worldview of the community.[6] One of the primary theses of this study is that among Plains and Prairie peoples, dreams and visions are a fundamental means for social and cultural transformation. Because of the unbound nature of dream and visionary experience, and because of the religious sanctions surrounding the vision encounter, the results of the vision can act as a source for an ongoing transformation of religious thought and behavior. The conventional attitude that dreams and visions are "stereotyped" experiences strictly reflecting cultural norms is not supported by the ethnography. The innovative and creative aspects of the visionary experience provide a context for new interpretation and understanding that is generally congruent with existing social patterns. Yet they also provide a means for more individualized interpretations that come to have highly personal and idiosyncratic meanings. It is this dialogical relationship between the social form and the visionary content that provides a context for collective transformations.[7]

The dynamic quality of Native American mythic discourse, grounded in shifting, perspectival views, expresses an epistemé of considerable depth and antiquity. The visionary basis of such an epistemé cannot be grasped within a single conceptual frame as having an identifiable history and documentation. Only the bare remains of protohistorical tradition are visible; the great mass of shared experience over the generations is hidden in the shards and pieces of archaeological investigation. Yet there is something very cogent in the dreaming process, something remarkably powerful in its imagery and depth, something directly part of the human experience and embedded in the dreaming aspects of all cultures, ancient and modern. Consequently, mythic discourse expresses itself through the highly complex structures of strongly held religious ideas and actions, subject to reflection and interpretation in terms of a knowledge that is both archaic and other. The reality of the sacred as a mysterious, awesome, and inexhaustible source of inspiration communicated through the variable forms of visionary experience is apt testimony to its essential and indecipherable history. The innovative quality of dreams and visions must be seen as intrinsic to a long, complex tradition of changes and transformations. As such, visions and dreams do not necessarily represent dramatic or revolutionary transformations, but ongoing processes of continual adaptation and development in the face of the encounter with mystery and power.

At the heart of this ancient epistemé, richly informed by actual dreams and visions, is a reflective, dialogical interaction fully convinced of the reality and potency of the sacred. In general, dreams are absorbed into the mythic structure as fully expressive symbols of sacred power and as vehicles of transformation and self-actualization. Mythic discourse and complementary ritual actions have helped create a recognition of the sacred quality of dreaming over uncounted generations of experience.

In such an archaic historical context, dreaming is seen as a primary source of knowledge. Dreaming as a sacred activity gained a credence and significance among the Plains peoples that made it an essential, central element in all aspects of human experience.[8] Dreams and visions are part of an ontological process through which human life is enhanced and explored. As an epistemic base, the power and authority of the vision impact the community through the successful demonstration of its potency. Action in imitation of dreaming is revealed, in Plains culture, as a manifestation of the reality of sacred symbols and beings that aid and support human life in the search for an enhanced quality of existence. It is also a demonstration of knowledge that may exceed the culturally recognized realm of the known.[9]

"IT IS SAID"

Dreaming is a creative basis for what might be called higher knowledge in the Native American context. For the Plains peoples it is a primary means of revelation for many activities and concerns. Dreams and visions constantly revealed new applications of many types, such as: inventive technologies, hunting methods, warfare strategies, healing practices, and herbal formulations, along with other innovations in culture. It is widely stated in the ethnography that much of the essential cultural practice and technology of everyday life originated in dreams. For example, the origin of fire making was attributed to visionary experience by the Lakota, according to the holy man Black Elk:[10]

In one of the seven bands was a chief named Moves Walking. He claimed that he had a vision of the sun, which is heat. He told them that he could make fire from the sun, somehow. Moves Walking took the soap weed, the bottom part which is like cotton. The root when dry is soft as hair and almost like cotton. He took a bunch of that and set it down. The stick coming from the soapweed is dry. He took that and made it into a square; at the point he made it sharp. Then he put the cotton on a piece of wood; he put the sharp stick down to the wood through the cotton. Then he spun the stick; it got hot and made fire. Moves Walking had been taught all this, so he taught the people.

The origin of fire in this example is not conceived of as an individual discovery, nor is it for the benefit of the individual. The sun reveals secret knowledge to Moves Walking through a vision, thus establishing a direct relationship between the sun, as a living being, and the community. The vision itself establishes the mythic origins of fire through religious experience. That fire can be produced in this way is the pragmatic demonstration of the reality of the vision. Thus sun, fire, technology, and the vision are woven into the basic fabric of mythic discourse, reinforced by imagery, color, and action.

Another example is the discovery of the use of flint as an essential tool. The Blackfoot Rain Cloud received instructions through a vision for the use of flint:[11]

One night, Rain Cloud had a vision, in which his sacred helper appeared to him and told him to do certain things. Accordingly, the next morning he went out and searched for and found a small piece of flint stone. . . . Rain Cloud put the piece of flint into the fire, where it soon split into small slivers of rock. Taking one of these, and working it with a slender stick that he had pointed by rubbing it upon a rough rock, he made of the flint a very good one-edged knife.

The context for this vision is presented as a time when such tools did not exist among the Blackfoot and when there was no known technology for the shaping of the stone. The visionary source of this technique is accepted by the community and, as a consequence, imbues stoneworking and flint tools with a sacred quality and origin.[12]

Hunting techniques were also received in visions. Indeed, the name Blackfoot itself is attributed to such an experience. An ancient tradition mentions a time when the Blackfoot first came upon the plains and encountered the buffalo:[13]

Then, in accordance with a vision that the old father had, he made a black-colored medicine, rubbed some of it upon his eldest son's feet, and it enabled him to run so swiftly that he easily overtook and killed some of the strange animals. Whereupon the old father said that Blackfeet should thereafter be his name.

When the buffalo proved difficult to hunt on foot, the visionary Mink Woman received instructions from the buffalo for establishing the *piskan*, or "buffalo surround," with its accompanying techniques for drawing the buffalo into it.[14] Consequently, the people had an abundance of food and basic materials to improve their way of life.

The vision, then, serves as a primary religious means for cultural innovations of the most essential type. This function not only strengthens the centrality of the vision in the religious life of the people, but it also helps give definition to the religious topology. Each vision experience contributes its contents to the totality of the mythic discourse and helps give form and substance to religious thought and action.

The visionary origins of cultural technologies are essential to the healing and medicinal practices of all Plains peoples. It would be no exaggeration to say that the majority of healing techniques are received in visions and dreams. One of the gifts most commonly given in a vision encounter is that of specific healing or hunting rites and techniques. These would be displayed during the appropriate times, adding their contents, through both enactment and imagery, to the shared contents of the collective discourse.

The majority of ceremonial societies are also derived from visionary experience, as I have mentioned previously.[15] The visionary origins of religious and ceremonial societies are fundamental to Plains life. The earliest ethnographic records contain references to the dream origins of various types of social organization. It is not unlikely that the dream and vision origins of many technologies and types of organization can be traced back to the most archaic periods, for the earliest ethnographic record shows patterns that were already highly developed. This is not to say that all cultural innovation occurred in dreams and visions, but only to point out the pervasive belief in such origins. Obviously many factors contribute to cultural transformation. Sacred power, however, as revealed through visionary dreams, is one of the most fundamental, authoritative sources for such innovation. The actual ethnography of dreams fully supports this observation.[16]

Many of the recorded visions and dreams also contribute to the shared contents of mythic discourse. The religious experience of the vision constantly acts to strengthen consensual ideas about the sacred because dream-spirits repeatedly appear to the visionaries. These appearances are often understood as manifestations of the various mythic beings that inhabit the religious world. Some of these appearances, beyond those of either animal or human form, are regarded as those of mythic beings of the most powerful type. Direct visionary encounters with the Thunder Being, for example, are recorded throughout the ethnography. Water Monster appears to many of the Dhegiha-speaking peoples.[17] Pawnee visionaries saw Mother Cedar, as well as representations of the sun.[18] Visionary encounters with the sun were actually very widespread, as exemplified in this Winnebago vision narrative:[19]

His entire body was painted red and he wore an eagle feather on his head and garters around his legs. When he came near to me, he said, "Human I bless you. You may now go home and eat. Everyday I will bring the blessing of life to you. If you think of me when you are in any difficulty, you will pass through it safely. The sick you will be able to heal through the blessing I give you. I am the Sun, even if a day is cloudy, then know that I am keeping life for you beyond the clouds.

Here, the sun gives the visionary a blessing that is meant to sustain him throughout his life. It is a promise that the sun will care for him on clear days as well as stormy ones if he will think of that power (generally through prayer). He will be able to help the sick as an agent of the sun's healing strength. The entire content of the vision contributes to the mythic structure of belief and legitimizes the topological structure of the discourse by providing a witness who feels he has actually spoken with the sun at particular fasting site. The powers are in communication with human beings for their benefit. Through such experiences the mythic contents of belief are sustained and developed.

Among the Blackfoot, the appearance of an old man and old woman in a vision are traditionally taken to be manifestations of sun and moon.[20] Such appearances, however, might be given other interpretations instead, all contributing to mythic variability. One Blackfoot medicine man reported the following:[21]

One night shortly after this, I dreamed that an old man and an old woman came into my tipi. The man had an iron whistle and the woman a wooden one. Each of them offered me their whistles, but I took the iron one. The old man said . . . "I live in the sky and as long as you live you will be protected by me. In a fight do not fear guns." . . . This old man was the morningstar.

That the old man is a manifestation of the morning star and not the sun is recognized according to the symbolic dress or paint of the dream-spirit. Rarely is such an identification made without some reference to accompanying symbolism.

Variability in the interpretation of various dream-spirits contributed to the divergent contents of the mythic discourse. Such visions reinforced the belief in the metamorphic quality of the mythic world, where various similar appearances might represent different topological referents. The old man may be any of numerous powers, depending on the specific content of the vision. Such variability resulted in the Hidatsa conviction that there were two basic sources for religious thought about life after death: the shared discourses of tradition and recent dreams and visions.[22] Such a twofold division of contents is quite appropriate for the entire Plains area.

Often the visionary, in an altered condition, is able to understand the language of the animals. The visionary might meet an animal, or an animal might come to the vision place and speak to him or her.[23] One Iowa dream faster had the following experience:[24]

This society (*tcé'unwaci*) was founded by a man who blackened his face and fasted to obtain power in the usual way. The white wolf took pity on him, and appearing in a dream spoke as follows: "I have interest in the Powers Above. I have pity on you people, for I am myself a sort of *wakanda* and I shall help you." The wolf then proceeded to give him the ritual of the society. When the leader had learned it he proceeded to call together his friends and impart the news to them.

Every vision experience in which an animal speaks to the visionary strengthens the religious bond, the reciprocity, between the people and the animals surrounding them.

Because of the difficulty of translating the vision into a verbal report, the narrative aspects of the experience are often shaped according to the structural aspects of oral narratives. The vision speech of an animal, such as the wolf in the preceding example, frequently becomes part of a patterned form of dream telling. Alanson Skinner notes the preceding as "typical wolf speech."[25] It would be more accurate to say that it is a typical form of dream narrative—the patterned language of dream telling. Dream speech attributed to an animal dream-spirit follows the patterned form of vision narratives and not the actual speech of the animal. The report is extremely brief and highly condensed, although the giving of the ritual could involve elaborate instructions and demonstrations. The condensed, literal report could be seen as a potential loss of the sacred power of the dream, particularly in the ethnographic context. Consequently, dream telling outside of its normally circumscribed, performative context was highly attenuated.

Many of the foundational dreams of a community are remembered long after the death of the original visionary. These dreams enter into the general structures of mythic discourse and contribute to the development of a shared body of sacred narratives. Such narration could be highly structured, particularly in the original language. The Lakota Sioux Tyon wrote of wolf dreamers in the following manner:[26]

A man who dreamed of wolves always went towards the enemies' tipis like a wolf, it is said. He was, therefore, very inconspicuous, hence nobody was able to see him. This is right, so far. A man was wandering, lost in the wilderness, when a wolf came there and they went together towards the camp, it is said. Therefore they believe the wolf to be very *wakan*. And so far, it is also right, it is said. The men who dreamed of wolves had certain customs, it is said. Some they told about, it is said. Those they told the people about, it is said.

This narrative is embedded in a customary way of speaking of visionary experiences, normally told in a structured context. The repetitions, used in Native American oral tradition to give emphasis; the evidential quotatives ("it is said"), which validate that the narrative is reported as heard from another; and the discourse bracketing ("it is right so far"), which confirms the accuracy of the report and links important themes (the *wakan* nature of wolves)—all reflect the typical oral style of a traditional Plains narrative.[27]

Unfortunately, few situated narratives have been recorded, because most of the dream narratives collected were not told in a performative context. Such context is referred to but is rarely, if ever, recorded in the moment, in the original language. Moreover, visionaries did not easily discuss their dreams because of the secret knowledge involved. "It is said," however, symbolizes the historical, intergenerational quality of the narrative and illustrates a form of expressive framing that acts to validate the sacred character of the tradition.

In the Sioux case, even greater difficulties are encountered because much of the vision speech was carried out in a special, esoteric language. The normal vision talk could be further encoded into the symbolic language of the shamans, according to the young Oglala shaman Sword, so that "the people may not learn those things that only the shamans should know."[28] This guarding of the vision contents is in keeping with the secret quality of the vision and is a way of further protecting the *wakan* or sacred quality of such speech, called *hanbloglaka*, or "relating visions," in Lakota.[29] In 1893, Stephen Riggs published one of the first rudimentary introductions to the Sioux practice:[30]

This sacred language . . . may be said to consist, first, in employing words as the names of things which seem to have been introduced from other Indian languages. . . . In the second place, it consists of employing descriptive expressions, instead of the ordinary names of things, as in calling . . . the wolf a quadruped. And thirdly, words which are common in the language are used far out of their ordinary signification; as *hepan, the second child if a boy,* is used to designate *the otter.*

Part of the structure of this sacred language originated in the visionary communication itself. James Walker was told that the dream-spirit "may speak intelligibly to him, or it may use words that he does not understand."[31]

For the Sioux, as for many other peoples, the religious specialist is the only one who possesses the appropriate knowledge to understand the dream communication. The obscure aspects of the vision could be interpreted by a visionary who had a thorough knowledge of religious symbolism and its linguistic correlates. The religious significance of such a sacred language is found in its symbolic referents, because the contents of mythic discourse are charged with diverse semantic associations. Certain of these associations came to have shared meanings that were only thoroughly synthesized by the shamans. Not only did this guard the sacred contents of the vision from those less familiar with sacred matters, but it also allowed the shamans to develop a symbolic language that expressed their personal collective experience. Thus the range of mythic discourse could extend from the esoteric language of the shamans and the shared knowledge of the foundational visions of individual dreamers to the broader communal patterns of narrative instruction, enactment, and story telling.

CEREMONIAL NARRATIVES

The communal basis of mythic discourse arises through a continuous dialogical process in a shared, oral setting. The discourse is not a "fixed text" but a dynamic process of interactive relations that are developed over generations of experience. The coherence of the narrated world, of the totality of the mythic potential, lies in both the telling and the recreation of the visionary event—in the reanimation and reaffirmation of its reality in all the intensity of the original encounter. The ongoing dynamics of narration, with its consensual recognition of the mythic structure of the lived world coupled with the dramatic enactment of the visionary experience, express a primary means by which the vitality of religious solidarity is created and maintained. Mythic discourse evokes the givenness of the religious world through its inclusive range of remembered and enacted encounters. This is not a static world of discourse but an emergent world of variable contents and interactions changing and evolving over time. In this sense, the traditional structures ("genres") of mythic discourse serve an integrative function: to form a coherent basis for communal identity in terms of a shared set of fundamental ideas and beliefs expressed in multiple forms, images, symbols, and enactments. Even so, these shared ideas and beliefs were subject to the powerful influence of the visionary encounter.

Dreams and visions are a means for both the confirmation and the elaboration of the spiritual potentials of the religious world. They expressively communicate the reality of their potency through the process of enactment—not through verbal report. The confirmation comes through the experience of dreaming; the elaboration comes about through the reenactment of the specific contents of the vision in acts of power. Thus it is possible for religious values to evolve spontaneously within a unified but unbounded mythic-religious context that is constantly undergoing subtle change and transformation. And yet that transformation is such that it maintains a certain pragmatic continuity with past experience and belief. Tradition in this sense is a process of gradual transformation of the historical and reflective consciousness of the individual and community over long periods of time. It is a dialogical process by which meaning, symbols, actions, and objects all reflect past interactions and present elaborations, regardless of how minute or subtle the changes may be. There is a continual process of "mythic elaboration" in which dream and visionary experiences contribute to the general structures of mythic discourse. Simultaneously, the symbols and forms of mythic discourse are incorporated into visionary experience or reenactment and form a mythic foreground for further interpretation. Therefore, dreaming among the Plains peoples acts both to validate cultural traditions and to facilitate their dynamic transformation.[32]

A central aspect of this process is the socially shared context of dream narration. A number of these contexts have been mentioned: during preparations for a vision fast; on return from the fast; among members of a visionary organization; in giving dreams to others; upon the purchase of power objects; after having a negative dream; among close relatives, such as husband and wife; during healing practices; in sponsoring a ceremony; and, of course, during the ethnographic interview. Most of these circumstances are highly circumscribed and private. The most public aspect of dream telling is in connection with the general ceremonial life of the community. This would also be the context in which both continuity and innovation in mythic discourse would be most visible. I do not mean to imply that it would be the most influential context, only the most visible. The more powerful shamans might have far more influence over the thinking of others on a one-to-one basis, as they were sought out for aid and guidance. The social domain of dream telling tends toward a more conservative maintenance of social expectation, because the telling is generally done in the context of highly structured ceremonial events. It should be remembered, however, that for the Plains people, religious behavior always had strong individual elements in terms of personal symbolism and visionary knowledge.

Many different types of ceremonial activities depended upon a dream or vision power to provide the necessary sanction for their performance. The specific contents of the relevant dreams were highly variable but had an underlying symbolism that identified them as appropriate. This symbolism frequently required the interpretation of the requisite ritual leader. Among the Assiniboine, the Watichaghe, or Make a Home, ceremony, which is related to the symbolic construction of the thunder bird nest during the sun dance rites, is undertaken by whoever first dreamed of the ceremony and gave public notice of the fact.[33] The performance of the Sioux Tatanka Lowanpi, the old time buffalo sing for the initiation of young girls into the rites of womanhood, was given by a shaman or sponsor who had received the appropriate vision and who narrated it during the ceremony.[34] The performance of a Sioux Heyoka ceremony might require the recitation of a dream or vision to other members of the society to legitimate its enactment.[35] A Gros Ventre man who had a dream of the Flat Pipe is required to participate in a special sweat-lodge ceremony, during which he paints the pipe and the faces of the children as directed in the dream.[36] Among the Absarokee, the tobacco society was developed around the visionary innovations introduced through dreams for the performance of the various ceremonies involved. In this case, Robert Lowie notes that various ceremonial chapters were formed as a consequence of variations in dreams sanctioning the planting of tobacco.[37]

Among the Mandan, the Okipa ceremony was sponsored as a result of a vision experience. The visionary would call the members of the Okipa ceremony to a feast in his lodge, after which he would relate the content of his vision. Alfred Bowers noted that "not all men dreaming of the buffalo bulls singing Okipa songs were permitted to give the ceremony. A young man having such a dream would tell his parents of his supernatural experience. They would know the qualities one must possess to go through the ordeals of the ceremony."[38] Here we are given a clue to the implicit symbolism that is part of the vision experience—the buffalo bulls singing the sacred songs of the society. The dream, which is discussed openly among members, must have certain contents that symbolize the ceremonial enactment. Then the dream contents must be weighed against the individual's ability for such an enactment. The vision does not predetermine the visionary's participation; other qualities and abilities must also be recognized. The vision is a powerful mediating influence, but the spiritual qualifications of the visionary must correspond to the dream's contents. The Naxpike ceremony of the Hidatsa had similar qualification dreams that a candidate must have to participate in the vision fasting and dance. These dreams were carefully discussed and analyzed by the elder members of the society.[39]

Among the Pawnee, the narration of visions is an integral part of the ceremonial ethnography. The corn-planting ceremony of the northern Skiri band was held annually by a woman who had received the appropriate dream or vision. She gave a special feast for the keepers of the skull bundle, who were in charge of the ceremony. She told her dream during the feast, and decisions about the performance of the ceremony were made.[40] If a Skiri man had a vision of the morning star, it could mean that it was necessary to perform a human sacrifice. The dream was told to the shaman who looked for the appropriate symbolism.[41]

During the performance of certain major ceremonials of the southern Pawnee bands, such as the white beaver ceremony, the buffalo dance and the bear dance, the visionary origins of each ceremony were recited.[42] Before the singing of many of the sacred songs throughout the ceremony, the visionary origins of each song were also recited.[43] Significantly, there could be different origin visions for the same songs. The songs of Young Bull, performed during the third day of the white beaver ceremony, had two origin narratives with similar but different contents. Both narratives were regarded as legitimate and were included in the ceremony.[44] Such variability is a normal feature of mythic discourse—it includes all versions because the oral structure of the culture is part of an ongoing process of shared events that are emphasized and interpreted differently by different individuals. Yet there is an inner symbolic coherence that is distinctly recognized and interpreted as such by the appropriate members of the society.

Another aspect of Pawnee ceremonial vision narratives is seen in the ability of a developed shaman to induce an altered state, journey to a place of the dream-spirits, and then return to narrate his experience. Fox Boy, during a time of famine, told the people that he was going on a four-day journey to seek aid:[45]

That night the tipi was cleared and made ready and Fox Boy put on a buffalo robe and tied it about his waist. He kept going round and round the fireplace all night. He took off his moccasins which the braves could see were all worn out. . . . He had been to the place where the four beings stood in the west. And these beings had told him when they blessed him that the buffalo would come in four days and then the people would eat. When he had spoken of taking a journey of four days he had referred to his dancing.

The symbolic act of dancing is a means for entering an altered state in which Fox Boy is able to communicate with the sacred beings. The journey motif acts as a unifying symbol of his vision experiences. He brings back a message to the people sent by the powers. This is a primary contribution to the structures of mythic discourse. The shaman is able to gain direct access to the powers through visions and to communicate that knowledge under public circumstances of symbolic and ceremonial enactment. Enactment and verbal report are united in a framework of religious experience and symbolic action, each element of which contributes to the ongoing processes of shared discourse.

A final aspect of Pawnee vision narratives is the metastructure of vision talk. In the performance of the Hako there is an enactment of calling the visions through the use of ceremonial speech that charts the flight of the visions down to earth, where they join the dancers and bestow their respective gifts. These visions could be summoned by the performance of a sacred dance with the feathered pipes. The bird spirits of the pipes would ascend to the visions and bring them down to the people. On making four circuits, the visions enter the lodge under the guidance of Kawas, the great female eagle:[46]

We go around the lodge and sing four times. As we walk, the visions walk; they fill all the space within the lodge; they are everywhere all about us.

We go around the second time. The visions which attend the *Hako* are now touching the Children, touching them here and there and by their touch, giving them dreams, which will bring them health, strength, happiness, and all good things. The visions touch all who are in the lodge.

We go around for the third time. As we sing, the visions are walking away; they have done what they came to do; they are now leaving the lodge. We pause and we think of the visions going away over the silent earth to ascend to their dwelling place.

Once more, for the fourth time, we go around the lodge singing. The visions ascend to their dwelling place; they have returned from where they came, to their home in the sky. When we reach the west, we lay the *Hako* down with the songs and movements which accompany the act. *Kawas* rests in her nest.

This ceremonial talk about visions—their reification—is an outstanding example of the way in which vision experience becomes incorporated into the general structure of mythic discourse. For the Pawnee, the visions are living beings who give dreams by touch and thus grant health and happiness. The intentional structure of such a discourse is meant to facilitate good dreams and visions in the children who were being adopted into the ceremony. Visionary power could be summoned if it were done in a ceremonially correct manner with the appropriate intent— in this case, to establish peaceful social relations. Good dreams and visions experienced after the ceremony were attributed to the sacred power of the Hako, or Feathered Pipe. In this sense, the good dreams of the people validated the sacred character of the pipe and the efficacy of the ceremony. Simultaneously, the contents of those dreams contributed to the general contents of the discourse. This is an example of how a ceremonially induced experience contributes to the elaboration of mythic ideas and yet maintains a symbolic coherence with the experiences of others. The ceremonial structure provides a shared context for later dream interpretations.

ENACTMENTS OF POWER

The enactment of the visionary contents often has no verbal expression other than the sacred song. A full understanding of mythic discourse requires a recognition of the highly significant nonverbal aspects of communication. The primary means for the communication of visionary experience among the Plains peoples is enactment, both dramatical and symbolical. While few spoke of their great visions directly or in any detail, most successful visionaries did use their power to produce visible results. This is particularly true of developed shamans. Reluctant to speak of their power, they are quick to demonstrate its use in appropriate circumstances. All forms of personal symbolism—paint, dress, and so on—contribute to the imagistic aspects of mythic belief, while acts of power demonstrate the efficacy of those symbols. The verbal aspects of this process, other than those I have related, were minimal and highly circumscribed. The visual aspects were dramatically evident and permeated many aspects of everyday life.[47]

The great vision experience of the Lakota holy man Black Elk resulted in a number of powerful demonstrations. The horse dance was one such example, in which the power of the vision was manifested in the rising of the storm and neighing of the horses. The synchronic structure of this event gave a dramatic and visible potency to the reciprocity between the vision, its enactment, and the thunder and horse powers. The enactment itself participated in the generally shared movement of all ritual recreations.

Before the enactment, Black Elk teaches the songs to the other shamans, and each morning they all take a sweat bath together. Sixteen horses are brought that match those seen in the vision, and Black Elk rides a bay as he did in the vision. Visionary objects are made and handled according to the instructions he had received. Movement is structured around the central rainbow tipi, representing the flaming tipi of the vision. Four young women dressed in red, with red faces and with sage wreaths on their heads, enter the tipi with Black Elk. Inside are six old men representing the grandfathers. An altar is made in the center of the tipi to represent the red and black roads the people must travel. Sacred songs are sung, and the riders move from the four directions toward the central tipi singing, each painted according to the images of the vision. All the riders face the opening on the west side of the camp, led by the four virgins. As the entire village circles the sacred tipi, a storm arises, sanctioning the enactment and validating the reality of the power invoked.[48]

The whole structure of this performance participates in a shared kinesthesis of movement in which space is ordered according to the vision and involves the entire population. The symbols displayed, their being handled by the virgins, the number four, the making of an altar, and the singing of sacred songs all communicate the vision in the visceral language of myth. The enactment is a physical translation of the vision into the language of imagery and gesture.

Other such enactments might involve the ritual preparation of a sacred lodge where dancing would be held, as in the vision experience of the Pawnee Fox Boy. The lodge would be cleaned and the participants assigned appropriate seating according to normal social conventions. Social space is communicative: the position of honor for the visionary communicates the importance of the vision's contents. Dance movement and physical action could express visually the nature of the received power, being highly imitative of the behavior of the dream-spirit. Movement in the Hako ceremony also illustrates this kinesthetic communication of meaning. As the dancers go around the circle, moving in a ritual manner, the visions join them to bless the people. The sacredness of the dance space is heightened by the intensity of the movement and the symbolic nature of gesture coupled with song. Movement is a communicative medium of great power and vitality that transcends the impact of the merely verbal report.

Another kind of enactment was the first healing done by Black Elk. In 1883, ten years after having his great vision, he healed a relative by enacting a specific portion of the vision:[49]

The power vision cannot be used until the duty we got with the part of the vision has been performed upon the earth. After that the power may be used. . . . When I sang this [sacred vision song] I could feel something queer in my body and I wanted to cry. . . . Then

I drank part of the water and started toward where the sick boy was and I could feel something moving in my chest and I was sure that it was that little blue man and it made a different sound from anything else. Then I stamped the earth four times standing in front of the boy. Then I put my mouth on the pit of the boy's stomach and drew the north wind through him. At the same time the little blue man was also in my mouth and I saw there was blood on it, showing that I had drawn something out of his body. Then I washed my mouth with some of the water of the cup. And I was now sure that I had power.

In performing this successful healing, Black Elk is giving another dramatic demonstration of his vision experience. He does not seek out explicit instruction from other holy men but goes ahead with the healing according to his own vision. Although he does mention that he has observed other medicine men at work, he also believes that he can "follow their way" because of his vision experience.[50] The symbolic presence of his healing power is manifested to him as the little blue man and the queer feeling, while to others it is manifested as a successful healing. The only verbal links are the sacred songs. The enactment is the primary context for communicating the vision experience. The personal symbols mediate between the sacred source of the vision and the consequential action of a successful healing.

Healing through enactment is the most common way of healing. The healer follows the vision and recreates it to heal the sick. There are hundreds of examples of such a procedure. In each, the healing takes a particular form that invokes the healer's personal powers, and it follows a unique pattern of action that usually includes the singing of sacred songs. The degree of variability in these procedures is extremely high, even within a single community: the use and type of power both overlap and are uniquely different.

The Blackfoot healer Spear Woman would prepare herbs and, while singing buffalo songs, would kneel by the patient's couch and imitate the actions of her dream buffalo, "pawing the ground, hooking with her head, and making sounds like a buffalo bull."[51] The Blackfoot shaman Rattler would spray yellow paint through the hollow wing-bone of an eagle onto the afflicted area of the sick person, all the while imitating a flying eagle and rocking his body in time to the chants sung by his helpers.[52] Another

Blackfoot shaman also had eagle power and was instructed by a female eagle to paint his own forehead to stop bleeding in his patient.[53] The variability here is typical of all Plains communities. Each has its own procedures and techniques given through visions and validated through healing. The songs, actions, dress, and symbolism all contribute to the mythic structure of the shared discourse.

Other types of enactment of vision powers might include weather control; special painting for ceremonials or for personal protection and luck during expeditions into enemy country; and the demonstration of new hunting techniques.[54] Visions also validated many variations in personal appearance, such as those noted among contemporary Shoshoni and Absarokee by Fred Voget:[55]

Since dream revelations validated an individual's right to possess a Sun Dance bundle and direct a performance, dreams offered a natural base for variations on ceremonial conventions. Mourner-pledgers, too, might introduce minor variations according to their dreams, as in the substitution of pine for cottonwood—a variation that may happen today.

Such variation and demonstration of vision and dream experience is part of a long tradition that was thoroughly integrated into the general structures of religious action. In each circumstance, the visionary demonstrated through nonverbal means the contents of the vision, and every successful demonstration was a validation of the efficacy of the vision's symbols. Yet all the variations participate in an ongoing discourse that has a structural integrity rooted in a shared topology and a seasonal patterning of communal life. Variation and development through dreams occurs incrementally and successively, each increment contributing to the overall pattern of relations and shared symbolism.

Certain enactments were of a more miraculous type. The ability to remain unharmed in battle was usually regarded as a dramatic and impressive demonstration of visionary power. The famous Shoshoni warrior Big Nez Perce demonstrated this power, which he obtained through visions: "Big Nez Perce was often knocked down by bullets but would get up with nothing worse than a blue spot on his body. Power such as that possessed by these men is obtained in dreams."[56] Such a demonstration necessitates certain dress, paint, and behavior to be effective, and it communicates to others the visionary means by which such protection could be obtained. The warrior's empowerment is a gift that must be handled appropriately to be effective.

Many shamans gave demonstrations of miraculous ability in order to prove that the power of visions exceeded normal human powers. Such enactment is the primary means of validating the gift of power. Talk about power is empty. The verbal aspect resides in the song; validity resides in the demonstration. When the Omaha Blue Smoke doubted the reality of visionary power, he was given a vivid demonstration by his father, who was a great shaman:[57]

Blue Smoke's father took him aside from the march of the buffalo hunters to a deserted spot, where, by the side of a knoll, there were many buffalo skeletons scattered. His father told him to assemble a skeleton complete with its skull facing east. . . . He did it accordingly. Then his father tied sweet grass bundles, placed a bundle between each set of adjoining vertebrae. His father then told Blue Smoke to sit down in front of the skull with his back to the skeleton, to face east, and not to stir a muscle. Blue Smoke heard his father sit down at the western end of the skeleton behind him. He heard his father sing his sacred songs. He suddenly heard a whirring sound go fast above him. His father said, "Come." He rose and looked behind. The skeleton was gone!

This remarkable example is only one of many in the ethnography. Such demonstrations, called conjuring in the ethnography, were carried out by shamans as a means of demonstrating their power, and they included activities such as walking on red-hot coals or handling red-hot rocks, calling various animals for hunters, making fresh fruits or grains appear in the midst of winter, suddenly producing gunpowder or lead, and foreseeing the movements of the enemy. Among the Pawnee, there was a thirty-day ceremony during which such abilities were demonstrated to the general public.[58] These enactments were the only displays of the dreams and visions of the shaman; such knowledge was considered highly secret and was never verbalized to others.

As I have discussed, the enactment of power is charged with

certain dangers and prohibitions. To transgress these prohibitions or to ignore the dangers could lead to disaster. These limits also enter into the general structure of mythic discourse, for the dreamer must not go beyond their power. Empowerment has boundaries that demand the respect of the visionary. The enactment is always directed toward specific ends and procedures, which are not to be transgressed. When the Sioux Black Horse had a great vision given by the Thunder Being, he received the following warning:[59]

As he stood there holding his pipe, the Thunder Voice sang and he joined them. The rain was violent, driven by wind. "Behold, my grandson, the birds of the air are rejoicing to see you following the footsteps of your forefathers. Look, this is the way we live." Whereupon a bolt of lightning struck the butte upon which he stood and shook it as if it were a leaf. "Look before you, take heed that you do not overdo what you have seen and heard." Ahead was a long straight trail as far as his eye could see. And it was lined with men's bodies with blood running from their mouths. "Those men overdid what they learned after undergoing what you are now endeavoring. They went beyond their power." Four bolts of lightning shook the butte and the Thunder Voice sang. Black Horse held his pipe and sang with them. As the rain fell, their song faded, yet not a drop had fallen within the square of offering.

This remarkable and profound vision shows the underlying possibility for abusing power. Visionary power can be mishandled and used for purposes other than those for which it was originally intended. This vision suggests that such abuse is not uncommon (the long line of bodies) and that there are always those who sing their songs for the wrong ends (blood from the mouth). The punishment is to be struck by lightning. There is a balance that must be maintained—a harmony and reciprocity with the dream-spirits. To maximize power, to overdo what has been given is dangerous and foolish. The visionary is often warned in the context of the vision that the enactment of power must be done correctly with the appropriate attitude of respect. The correct use of power requires humility and wisdom. Further, the responsibility could not easily be given away or dismissed.

When a young Ponca man tried to give his thunder power

away to a friend, at the urging of his father, who thought it was too dangerous, he was unsuccessful:[60]

My friend painted my face black with some dark earth and gave me a pipe and bid me hold it towards some clouds that lay at the horizon. I did as he told me. . . . The young man walked around me singing the song he had heard in his dream. A thunderstorm was seen coming up . . . but it did not come over us, it passed around. Then my friend said to me, "The Thunder does not want to speak to you. They want only me." . . . That summer he was struck by lightning because of what he had done. I never wanted to dream of thunder after that.

In other Dhegiha groups, mature power could be sold or transferred.[61] To transfer power that has been used appropriately and with care is sanctioned, but to fast for power and then reject it by trying to give it to another is considered dangerous in the extreme. The visionary cannot choose what form the power comes in or what the responsibilities will be, nor can someone easily give away powers that have been granted. The recipients of power, having made themselves pitiable, must act with humility when receiving and using the gift of power. They must recognize the limits of their abilities and not overstep the boundaries.[62]

CHAPTER TEN

The Visionary Arts

The seer painted the mystery objects on a robe or blanket, and prepared a feast, to which he invited all members of the order of Thunder shamans. When the guests had assembled the robe was hung up and shown to them. Then all who were present rejoiced. From that time onward the host was a member of the order, and he could wear the robe with safety.

—James O. Dorsey, *A Study of Siouan Cults*

OTHER THAN ENACTMENT, the most expressive means for communicating the dream experience, according to the ethnography, involves the use of visionary images and the making of an extremely wide range of objects. Although certain of these forms are part of a shared repertoire of symbolic items normally associated with visionary experience, any item of either nature or culture can be incorporated into a visionary assemblage that expresses the unique experience of the individual. Such an item is treated with care and attention as a means for evoking and manifesting power. The nature of such an assemblage varies in relationship to the contents of the vision and the instructions received. The visionary usually experiences visual imagery of a very explicit and vivid kind. This imagery is then transformed into objects or recreated in visual form symbolizing the presence of the power of the vision. Because the contents of the vision are highly variable, so also are the explicit images adopted by the visionary. The potential semiotic associations for such images are exceedingly rich and multifaceted. Every image communicates something of the experience, and every object, something of the power.

Dress, paint, and sacred objects such as feathers, stones, rattles, pipes, bundles, and robes are made to embody the presence of the visionary encounter. These objects or images are then handled with certain gestures and movements, along with specific prayers and songs. Such sacred praxis is learned primarily through imitation, not through detailed verbal instructions. To act as the dream power has acted or instructed and to handle one's objects in an identical manner are the essences of the dreaming situation. To use sacred objects—that is, to make exact copies of the things seen in the vision—is a way of making explicit the implicit power of the vision. This is another topological feature of the visionary episteme: the visible manifestation of the dream or vision object in the context of everyday life. The topos of the dream becomes the very place where the sacred bundle hangs or where the pipe is handled. The world of village life is filled with tangible objects and images that are the consequences of visionary experience. Ways of painting and singing, ritual acts, articles of clothing, and a multitude of animal-objects give visible testimony to the reality of the dreaming situation.

Because the contents of any sacred image embody a vital expressiveness, they have a communicative efficacy that functions nonverbally to convey the image's significance. The expressivity of the visionary image is holonomic: it dramatically communicates a totality of potential meanings, many of which are neither recorded, collected, nor verbally explicit in the mind of the culture member. Such knowledge is transmitted through the use of the symbols themselves, without verbal rationalization, on ritual occasions or through actions that bring the participant directly into contact with their implicit power. As the image or object functions to convey the immediacy of the sacred, it also expresses a synthesis of associated and implied meanings, unifying within itself a representation of the whole. The colors, the structure, the use, the meaning of the image—all participate in shared symbolic actions that reflect the visionary basis of Plains religions. The visionary event is encoded in objects and images that have powerful religious associations and are capable of transforming the very structures of perception through their correct use. The visionary object is a repository of both shared meanings and individual empowerment.[1]

Objects, as visible signs, express the presence or reality of the dreaming world in an immediate context of sensory awareness. They link the dreaming situation and the immediacy of the everyday, signifying the proximity of the spirit powers both to the dreamer and to any members of the community who are capable of interpreting or recognizing the signs. Such a world of signs creates a visible context in which the above and below powers can be seen as tangibly present. Thus the various powers that inhabit the strata of the world cosmology are not abstractions but visible realities embodied in the imagery of dress and act, in terms of the objects used and displayed. The dreaming world is a visually present world, a living reality constantly manifesting itself through highly charged, visible signs. These signs are codetermined and interactively defined through use, care, and imitative action. Every object or image participates in the shared repertoire of symbolic forms framed by mythic discourse, while also manifesting the specific experience of the visionary. The correct use of a visionary object, when united with appropriate intention and respect, produces a religiously defined result. Sacred objects are handled with great care because they are a primary means for expressing the reality of power.[2]

The power of the vision is frequently believed to be in the body of the visionary; it is not exclusively identified with its images or objects.[3] The objects used to evoke the power are an instrumental means that provide the external symbolic link with the implicit power and become a repository for that power, particularly during its use. The object itself is not the exclusive source of the power but only a means by which the power can be used or manifested.[4] Objects were perishable, subject to capture by enemies, capable of being lost or destroyed. This perishable quality, however, did not diminish the power of the vision, for among most groups, objects could be renewed or replaced when lost or damaged. Bundles were regularly opened and their contents renewed in ceremonial rites to maintain the potency of the powers contained therein. Among the Blackfoot, the loss of the object was not considered to be critical, because it could be remade by the visionary at any time.[5] In many ways, the object or image is a form of heightened presence. It contains the power of the mystery, in close association with the visionary experience, but it also enfolds the numinous quality of the visionary topology. Every object acted as a viable medium for connections with aspects or inhabitants of the less visible world.

Visionary images were not lightly used or displayed because of the powerful religious associations that imbued them with a sacred quality. Among the Ponca and the Omaha, as among other Plains peoples, the right to paint or wear a mystery image must originate in a dream or vision.[6] To wear an image that was not sanctioned by a vision subjected the visionary to repercussions from the dream-spirits: disaster and misfortune were expected, as well as the ever-present threat of lightning if the image was one of the thunder powers. Wearing such an image would also arouse the ire of other, legitimate members of the visionary societies.[7] For those who experienced the sanctioning vision, the imagery had certain characteristics by which its symbolic value could be interpreted. Such symbolism was generally highly esoteric and known only to the members of the various societies, although certain forms were part of a more conventional repertoire—such as the zigzag painting that represented lightning, or sun and moon symbols. Certain objects were recognized as representing specific powers or abilities. The Thunder Bow, or Thunder Lance, was a symbolic, visionary weapon held by a warrior society.[8] The flute was another such visionary implement believed to have a variety of powers associated with elk, such as the ability to seduce young women.[9]

Visions also helped to contribute new forms to the general repertoire. Women received new craft designs through visions, as recorded by William Whitman for the Ponca: "Visions frequently validated techniques in the arts. A woman went fasting. She was daubed with mud. She was going along a creek when she saw a little bush covered with yarn in pretty designs. That was how she learned those designs."[10] The design in this example would be a gift of spider to the woman and would have symbolic associations with that power.

Skill in crafts and in the production of beautiful and well-made articles is also a power received in visions. Many images are derived from vision experiences among the Ponca, as is seen in both small clay figures and in petroglyphs.[11] Among the Sioux, skill in crafts is a power given by dreaming of Double Woman, a mythic being who is credited with the discovery of quill working and its associated arts.[12] Among the Blackfoot, at least one shaman used a carved image of a man who appeared to him in a vision for the healing of bleeding.[13] In general, it is recognized that certain persons have visionary abilities when it comes to the making of sacred objects. Certain individuals could "talk to the object" and, by understanding what was communicated, could produce the most effective expression of the power being invoked.[14]

In all these examples, the image and the object are regarded as direct expressions of the vision and its associated power. To make the object or image is a way of communicating the specific nature of the power and a testimony that the visionary had a living relationship with that power. The imagery used is part of a pattern of communication that values these images as expressive of the profound reality of the sacred. The image is an opening into the sacred realm of the numinous—dangerous, powerful, and cathartic. It represents the visible portion of the enfolded order and serves as a constant reminder of those powers that remain yet concealed in the world strata and in every object that could potentially transform itself into a visionary appearance. The image is metamorphic and transformative. Through its use and manipulation, the shaman could enter into the visionary realm and return with remarkable knowledge. The image becomes a metonym expressing the shared structure of religious discourse. It is an immediate synthesis and condensation of an entire range of visionary experiences and mythic ideas that have a long and complex history. Images incorporate other images within themselves to create a complex of symbolic forms, all of which reflect interactively the nonverbal dimensions of religious experience.[15]

THE PAINTED LODGE

It is appropriate that an image should be the primary expression for the power and potency of the vision, because the vision itself is largely imagistic in nature. As the world metamorphoses and the vision manifests itself in discrete imagery, the visual impact of the encounter leaves a deep impression on the visionary and becomes an instrumental means for a return to the visionary state. The most immediate and personal aspects of that imagery are the vivid color and design that give a distinctive identity to the manifesting power. Alfred Kroeber recorded the following vision for an Arapaho man:[16]

A man painted green over his body, his hands red, and his face yellow with red streaks passing down from forehead to his jaw, was on foot in fight in the midst of the enemy. He wore a necklace from which hung medicine and an owl-feather, and which was swung around his back. . . . Then his dream or vision changed, and the people he had seen were small birds flying in flocks . . . and the man running between them was a yellow-jacket or wasp, flying back and forth.

A first thing to note about this vision is that the vivid description of color does not correspond to any "realistic" painting of a yellow jacket. The image of the yellow jacket or wasp as warrior is symbolized by color and design in a way that comes to represent the unique qualities of rapid movement and invulnerability rather than imitate physical appearance. The colors, when painted on the body, give the same qualities to the warrior. The owl association enhances that power—for example, through acuity of sight. The visionary must paint himself as the vision shows to express dramatically this power of action.

The use of color for symbolic expression is deeply rooted in a shared cultural repertoire enhanced by visionary experience. As self-expression, it is a visionary form of sacred art. The dream-spirits in most visions are dramatically painted and highly memorable, demonstrating that Native American visions were distinctly color laden and highly saturated with the patterned use of color.[17] Of the colors used, the most revered and sacred is red. Interestingly, this is not the color most frequently mentioned in visions—the most common are black and white, in approximately equal proportions.[18] Of all the colors, however, red is the one most representative of beauty and power. Its most frequent associations are the buffalo and the sun or stars. The buffalo often breathes red smoke from its nostrils when it bestows power, as is noted in this Kiowa-Apache vision: "On the same night a black buffalo came from the water and stood over him, snorting and pawing the ground, as if he would hook the man. His horns were like steel and he was throwing up dirt with them. From out of his nostrils came red paint when he snorted."[19]

This close association between the buffalo and its life-giving power, symbolized by the red color of its breath, imbues the color with highly positive meanings, for the buffalo expresses life and health. Stellar associations are also life affirming; the sun is an outstanding life-giving power for the Pawnee and many other Plains peoples.[20] Such associations are strengthened because red is the one color most often taken to express human beauty. Many visionary powers are painted red when they appear in human form. This color expresses the health, vitality, and power of Plains visionaries more than any other in the ethnography. It consequently has very positive sacred associations.[21] The uses of other colors are extremely variable and seem to undergo constant modification with regard to symbolic values.

Body paint might also be an expression of known ways of painting and thereby become a semiotic means for identifying the exact nature of the power. When the young Gros Ventre shaman Bull Lodge went crying around the deserted campground seeking visions, the following occurred:[22]

In his dream an old man approached, wearing a buffalo robe with the hair still on it. The robe was painted red where the old man's shoulders protruded. The waist line too had red paint going around the robe. The old man's hair was matted, and in his hand he held one of the sweat bath implements, made of buffalo tail. His face was painted with the same dark red paint, exactly as a Chief Medicine Pipe owner paints his face.

The painting and the manner of dress work together to convey the visual evidence that this is a vision of the power of the Feathered Pipe.

Among certain communities, the paint of an individual may denote a religious position, because certain types of painting were more socially symbolic than others. Such exact identifications, however, are uncommon in the visionary ethnography. Socially identified color imagery seems to play a far less significant role in determining visionary contents than does the generally shared recognition that color and design are the unique expressions of idiosyncratic relationships with specific dream-spirits.[23] Many visionaries received instructions for painting themselves or others to produce specific results—instructions that are entirely individual. For example, among the Blackfoot the result of such painting could determine weather patterns, keep away smallpox, give sun power to the women, or grant power in war.[24] The ultimate expression of body paint is, of course, tattooing, which was practiced by some Plains people, although not to the degree it was elsewhere. Among the Plains Cree, tattooing was closely associated with dream or vision experience.[25]

The most dramatic conventional expressions of imagery and design are painted lodges. These lodges are most prominently associated with well-known shamans. Painted lodges derive directly from visionary experience and are a result of the dreamer's having received the dream-spirits' command to make such a lodge. Once made, these lodges might be transmitted within the family or destroyed upon the death of the visionary. In general, the lodge or tipi has many symbolic associations and is considered to be an actual dwelling place for the powers that are painted in images on its outer surface. The symbolism involved is usually associated with one or more specific powers, as in this Piegan example:[26]

On the fourth night he fell asleep. In his dream a male and female bear appeared. They took pity on him. The female bear gave him her home, a handsome lodge with three red bears painted on each side. [She also gives a blackstone pipe in the shape of a bear.] Then the male bear spoke. "My son, I give you my lodge too." Two black bears standing on their hind legs were painted on this lodge, one on each side of the entrance. The father bear also gave him a pipe and a drum.

In this dream, the visionary, who had fasted in a bear's den because he wanted bear power, received what is believed to be one of the earliest examples of the painted lodge among the Blackfoot. The female bear gives the visionary "her home"; the lodge will be her dwelling place through the images painted on it, representing the power given to the visionary. He also receives a second lodge given by the male—a dual gender symbolism that is in keeping with the general structure of Blackfoot religious belief, in which sacred powers frequently appear in pairs. Many lodges of this type existed throughout the plains, each expressing the received powers through images painted life size.

Other lodges might have more complex symbolism representing many vision experiences, each adding its contents to the overall effect. The Assiniboine shaman Isto'egan had one such lodge that had multiple images and symbolic associations. He related his vision as follows:[27]

At a later period, I dreamt of several men who told me I was wanted in a certain tent. I walked to the lodge indicated. It was painted red all over. Right over the door was a picture of a man with outspread arms. As I entered, I bumped against something, it was a bell. An old man was sitting inside. He said, "My son, I am the one who has summoned you. I shall give you the painted lodge (wió'ha) and teach you how to use it." To the right of the entrance was the figure of a woman. I was told to copy it in my painted lodge. . . . About four feet from the ground there was painted a snake heading east; it was faced by another snake from the opposite side . . . . Their tails encircled the entire circumference of the [exterior] tent-cover. . . . The top of the lodge was explained to represent the sky-opening, and the bell the heart of a man speaking. The inmate of the lodge showed me his heart, and I saw it looked like a bell. Then he told me I was to get the wakan power to aid the sick.

The chthonic imagery of the power given in this dream—the dual snakes—is only part of a larger symbolism in which the lodge is represented as an image of a human being. Simultaneously, it is an image of the cosmos, uniting the underworld power with the sky power. As a macrocosmic image, it unites male and female symbolism with the life-giving power of its overall color, red. As human beings paint themselves and manifest the power given by doing so, the lodge in which they dwell is also a place of living power whose cosmological nature incorporates both the human and the transhuman sources that are represented in painted signs.

The bell is at once the heart of the power, the heart of the lodge, and the heart of the visionary. It is the unifying center of the entire symbolism and represents the most inward expression of the sacred power, the intent to grant the gift of healing. When Isto'egan wished to communicate with the sacred powers during a healing session, he would know they were present when the bell rang. The bell becomes a communicative means for establishing the presence of the sacred powers. After the bell rang, the shaman would receive instructions for healing the sick who were present. The combined symbolism creates a sacred place in which the sick come directly into the presence of the sacred images and actions, mediated through sacred sound.

Another example of the composite symbolism of the lodge is that of a well-known Cheyenne shaman:[28]

Old Spotted Wolf had a painted lodge, which he was advised to make by the buffalo, in a dream. A great snake-like animal was painted all around the lodge . . . about 45 buffalo cow heads, a night owl . . . a crescent moon over the door, a sun and on the back of the lodge . . . the constellation known as the "seven stars" was painted.

Once again the symbolism unites the above realm of the celestial power (the sun, moon, and stars) with that of the chthonic power of the below (the buffalo and the snake). The night owl may represent a messenger figure—an intermediary who transits between earth and sky. The unified cosmology of such a dwelling place empowered it with a sacred aura of mystery and presence that signified visually the immediacy of these powers. It also marked the dwelling place of the shaman as the home of one who had access to and communication with those sacred beings.

Such painting could also mark the dwelling place of a great warrior whose power was attributed to the dream-spirits painted on the lodge. Such was the case for the Kiowa warrior Screaming on High, whose power was given by the owl—an image of which was placed on a pole before his painted lodge and shrouded in red cloth.[29] The Kiowa turtle tipi is another example of how cosmological symbolism that originated in vision experience could unite the upper and lower realms. The tipi has a turtle and thunderbird fused into a single image with a pipe over each wing. The whole is unified by the drawing of a rainbow that brings together both color symbolism and the upper and lower worlds.[30] Other such visionary examples may be found among the Plains Cree and the Sioux.[31] The painted lodge is perhaps the most visually stunning example of religious cosmology and sacred art among the Plains people, and it represents a primary form for the communication of visionary experience.[32]

THE MEDICINE BUNDLE

The most central of all sacred objects is the medicine bundle in which all the objects used by the visionary to invoke the power of the vision are kept. Generally it consists of such objects as feathers or feather fans, sweet grass, sacred stones, tobacco, a pipe, small bags of powder for painting, various animal parts such as bone whistles, and, among the more agricultural Prairie people, one or more ears of painted or unpainted corn and certain beans or medicinal herbs. All these items are individually wrapped and then wrapped together in several layers of tanned animal skins (with fur side out); the bundle is tied up with buffalo- or horsehair rope or skin thongs. Occasionally an entire animal such as an otter is used to contain the various objects.

The typology of these bundles is threefold: the personal medicine bundle of the individual visionary; the kinship or society bundle, which belongs to a specific group; and the tribal bundle, which contains objects of the most sacred kind relating to the entire community.[33] When the bundle is stored in the lodge, it is usually kept in a place of honor, generally opposite the entrance and off the ground. On good days it might be hung on a tripod outside in the sunlight. At all times it is treated with care and respect and opened either when the visionary needs to perform the appropriate rites or during annual renewal ceremonies in which the contents are inspected and replaced if necessary.

The various types of bundles share a common theme: in most cases their contents are sanctioned by a vision. Certain objects meant to be displayed only during the time of their use bestow an aura of presence to the bundle, for the objects are regarded as the dwelling places of the powers. Yet in most cases the objects can be replaced or restored.[34] The communal objects that hold a prominent place in the tribal bundles—objects regarded as the primordial symbols of the visionary founders—are usually considered irreplaceable.[35] The loss of such a bundle is a calamity for the entire community. The more agricultural earth-lodge peoples, such as the Mandan, Hidatsa, and Pawnee, held the medicine bundle as most expressive of both communal organization and social identity.

The tribal type of bundle is part of a tradition of inherited ownership that is strongly allied to social status and organization. For example, leadership roles in Old Village among the southern bands of the Pawnee were organized according to the ownership of certain recognized tribal bundles. Later reorganization of tribal leadership was inspired by the power of the evening star in a vision to First Man, which established a new bundle and divided the roles of leadership between chiefs and doctors.[36] Among the Hidatsa and the Mandan, the possession of a hereditary society bundle was considered more significant than that of a personal vision bundle, even though both types originated in visions.[37] Thus bundles often became religiously founded symbols of social power, identity, and organization.

The primary concern of the visionary was to make a bundle that would contain those visionary objects necessary for the invocation of power. If the powers of a bundle proved to be efficacious and potent, they would secure increasing respect from others who had contact with the bundle. This in turn could lead to the formation of a society of similar dreamers. Over time such a process could result in a tribal bundle that had been passed on through the generations, from keeper to keeper. This was what happened in the case of the buffalo-stone bundle of the Blackfoot, which was given to Mink Woman in a winter vision long ago:[38]

Through the hundreds and hundreds of winters down to this day, the sacred [buffalo] stone has been not only a powerful healer of the sick, but has, to those for whom its owners have given its ceremony, prevented them becoming sick and preserved them from all dangers so they have lived to reach old age. . . . The Buffalo Stone was owned by women, and to them alone was the power given to call the buffaloes. . . . Mink Woman gave the stone to her daughter, and from her it went to woman after woman down to the time when it could no longer be used to call the buffaloes. It then became the property of a man, who used it for the curing of the sick, and ever since then it has passed from man to man, either by gift or by sale. Myself [Boy Chief], falling sick, some winters back, I bought it, for five horses, from Bull Turns Around, and its wonderful power soon made me well!

While this bundle did not have the same centrality within the religious worldview of the Blackfoot as did other tribal bundles, it illustrates the process by which the bundle acquires its sanctity. Only after its original purpose had diminished was the chain of tradition renounced by the women caretakers. Inevitably, such sanctity is tied to the efficacy of the original vision. In this case it was the visionary origin of the Blackfoot buffalo surround that proved highly successful, as did the bundle's later power to heal and give good health to its male owners.

The actual making of the bundle required the visionary to draw on the shared repertoire of symbolic forms that participated in the larger patterns of mythic discourse. For example, a Chawi Pawnee meteorite bundle was obtained by a young warrior who followed a bald eagle all day until, at about dusk, it landed in a tall tree. After a brief meal of parched corn, he lay down, for it had grown dark:[39]

He looked up at the stars in the sky and saw a meteor. The longer he looked at the meteor the more it seemed to resemble the bald eagle. The meteor appeared to make a circuit and fell where the eagle had alighted. The young man arose and began to cry. He was frightened because he was alone and had lost his party. [He prays to the meteor.]

He dreamed that standing near him was a man who wore a buffalo robe. . . . On his back he wore a bald eagle from under which seemed to come sparks of fire, just like the sparks he had seen when the meteor had fallen. . . . The man said, "My son, I am the meteor you saw shooting through the skies. I am the child of the heavens. I control the flock of eagles. My favorite bird is the bald eagle. . . . I like your spirit and will be with you always. I will come to you in dreams. I will make you a great warrior."

After the vision, in the morning, the young man follows the eagle, who circles a spot where the man finds a sacred meteorite, which he keeps. Then the eagle leads him back to the village. Later the man asks his mother for a piece of tanned buffalo hide (for the bundle wrapping), and he kills a bald eagle that he has consecrated by a shaman. He learns how to offer smoke and how to pray to Father Meteor, and he keeps the sacred stone and the eagle skin in the bundle with two ears of special corn and a pipe tied to the outside of the bundle. After this he has a series of dreams that give him further instructions in the use and contents of the bundle. He uses it in successful raids on the enemy; he dresses and paints in the manner of the visionary man who had appeared to him; and he takes the name Eagle Flying Under Heavens.[40]

The synthesis of sacred objects in this example involves both the unique experience of the visionary (meteorite and eagle) and shared symbolic forms (pipe, corn, and smoke) that are part of normal religious processes. Interestingly, the text notes that a bald eagle had never before been used by Pawnee shamans, and it therefore represents a new type of power that is subsequently identified with the successful war activities of the dreamer. In this way many Plains Indian visionaries acquired bundles that might be passed on with their power to others.

One object of prominence in many bundles was a sacred stone, an example of which is the meteorite just mentioned. The sacred stone, perhaps one of the oldest and most primordial religious objects among Native Americans, is prominent in the bundles of all the Plains peoples. The stone may embody a wide variety of powers according to its general form, as in the case of the Blackfoot buffalo stone. Generally, its symbolism is tied to an ancient knowledge that the earth alone possesses and that is known by the oldest members of earth, the stone people.

In the vision encounter of an Absarokee, a sacred stone might take on the appearance of a human being, or the dream-spirit might simply hold in his hand a sacred stone. The visionary was told in the vision where to find the stone and whether it was male or female.[41] There was a shared semiotics of stone lore among the Absarokee that allowed a visionary to identify its gender. Smooth or egg-shaped rocks were regarded as female, while more pointed shapes were regarded as male. Both types were generally fossil ammonites or baculites.[42] Many Plains people believed that when male and female stones were wrapped in a bundle they could reproduce. When the bundle was opened at a later date, it would contain smaller stones that were regarded as offspring of the male and female pair.

Such stones possessed many different kinds of power. One Blackfoot dreamer was given power to grow beautiful long hair by tying buffalo stones into his hair.[43] Members of the Omaha secret pebble society kept a translucent stone that symbolized the underwater powers as one of their most sacred objects. They wore little clothing but painted their bodies with designs that represented the power of the stone.[44] For the Lakota Sioux, stone (*Inyan*) was one of the great powers from which all creation ultimately originated. To dream of the sacred stones was considered highly significant because these stones granted many different powers: to cure illness, to predict the future, to find lost objects, and to obtain information by extrasensory means. The Sioux Chased by Bears described their symbolic contents as follows:[45]

The outline of the stone is round, having no end and no beginning; like the power of the stone it is endless. The stone is perfect of its kind and is the work of nature, no artificial means being used in shaping it. Outwardly it is not beautiful, but its structure is solid, like a solid house in which one may safely dwell. It is not composed of many substances, but is of one substance, which is genuine and not an imitation of anything.

These special stones, called *tunkan* in Lakota, could be of different types. The small, perfectly spherical stones found on the tops of high buttes and believed to be related to the thunderbird were packed with eagle down into small animal-skin pouches (some of which might be painted) and kept in the medicine bundle. According to Brave Buffalo, wherever lightning struck the earth, one of these thunder stones could be found buried in the ground.[46] Goose, a well-known shaman, used the power of his stones successfully to call a buffalo when the stones' power was doubted by a skeptical white trader. He also used his stones to find a lost rifle that had fallen into a river.[47]

The symbolism of the stones again unites the above and below powers in a single sacred object. The *tunkan* is from the earth, but it is simultaneously an expression of the celestial powers of the thunderbird. This cosmological theme of the unity of the above and the below is a primordial concept of the fundamental unity of the world order. The stones "know" the earth and what is happening on it at all times. A powerful shaman can send his stones after the requisite knowledge because they are capable of traveling throughout the world strata. Such knowledge was conveyed by dreams or visionary experience while the shaman was in a trance state.[48]

An extension of this stone symbolism was found in the sacred pipe. Made of stone, the pipe was a primary means for communicating with the sacred powers and represented the powers of both heaven and earth. The stone bowl, the wood of the stem, and the tobacco used in the pipe were from the earth, but often special bird down or feathers were attached to represent the celestial powers, as they were on Black Elk's pipe. The fire and smoke from the pipe carried the prayer addressed to the powers. This smoke had been mixed with human breath and thereby went out to unite the visionary with the sacred powers.[49]

Many pipes were given by dream-spirits in visions. These would be kept in a medicine bundle or a special pipe bag to be used according to the instructions received. According to the Cheyenne, one of the first pipes ever made was received in a vision given long ago to a shaman who fasted on a hilltop and was taken into the hill, where he was instructed in the making of the pipe.[50] Among the Blackfoot, the Children's Pipe originated in a dream that came to Middle Calf; it gave him and his descendants health and good fortune.[51] Other visionary origins account for tribal pipes such as the Gros Ventre Feathered Pipe or the Lakota Buffalo Calf Pipe.[52] Of all objects kept with the medicine bag, the pipe was the supreme example of the means by which the visionary could both communicate with the sacred powers and demonstrate knowledge of correct religious behavior. As a unifying symbol, the pipe was a means for establishing correct relations with the powers. Handling the pipe respectfully was a demonstration of religious knowledge and signified to others the seriousness of such communication.

Another unifying object in many bundles of the river-valley peoples, such as the Pawnee, is Mother Corn. Symbolized by a particular kind of white corn, Mother Corn is also a holonomic symbol of the cosmos.[53] Called *Atira*, "Mother," she manifests the fruitfulness of the earth and gives blessings through visions, dreams, and ceremonies. During the Hako, Mother Corn plays a central role. The symbolism of the special ear used to represent her was explained by the elders (*Ku'rahus*) as follows:[54]

The ear of corn represents the supernatural power that dwells in *Uraru*, the earth which brings forth the food that sustains life; so we speak of the ear of corn as *Atira*, mother bringing forth life. The power that allows it to bring forth comes from above; for this reason we paint the ear of corn with blue. Blue is the color of the sky, the dwelling place of *Tira'wahut*. . . . As we sing the *Ku'rahus* marks with his finger four equidistant lines of blue paint on the ear of corn. . . . Mother Corn having reached [through the ceremony] the blue dome where dwells the great circle of powers . . . descends to earth by the four paths.

Thereafter, Mother Corn leads the ceremony because she knows all that happens to human beings everywhere, having come forth out of the earth. This unifying symbolism is embodied in a religious object that was revealed through visions to the Pawnee elders.[55]

Among many Plains people, the medicine bundle with all its sacred objects could be transferred through inheritance or purchase. Once the new owner had acquired all the necessary rites, songs, and objects of the bundle, he or she would be as able to invoke the sacred powers as the original visionary had been. Traditionally, a Mandan male was expected to buy his father's bundle on reaching maturity, and he might be condemned for failing to do so.[56] Among the Hidatsa, and the related Absarokee, a man would purchase a hereditary bundle only if he dreamed of the appropriate powers; otherwise he followed his own dreams, from which he constructed a personal medicine bundle.[57] A Pawnee chief would pass his bundle to his son on his death.[58] An Arapaho elder summarized the practice:[59]

Generally, when such powers were transferred, they were either sold, or given to sons or nephews. A young man might pray to an old man for his power. Then, instead of going out on the hills and suffering hardships to acquire it, he received his power by instruction. He paid the old man for each sitting with him. He learned the old man's medicine-roots and their uses, his way of painting, his songs, and so on. By the time the old man was dead, the young man had his power.

In all these cases, the power of the vision could be passed on. The primary symbols of this transfer were those contained in the bundle, the symbolism of paint, the songs, and the correct behavior for invoking the power. The bundle itself came to be a primary expression of religious tradition and visionary history. Without anyone's maintaining knowledge of its use and contents, the bundle ceased to have the appropriate religious significance. The vitality of the medicine bundle, its sacred quality, was wholly dependent upon a shared context of religious discourse that both heightened and specified its place in the religious life of the community. In many ways it expressed the very heart of Plains religious life.

THE WARRIOR SHIELD

Perhaps the most important aspect of a warrior's shield was its religious symbolism. The shield, one to two feet in diameter and made of rawhide on a round wooden frame, was painted with images evoking the dream-spirits of the vision. In this way it gave protection and power to the warrior. The shield was a religious symbol of warfare reflecting the primary relationship between warrior visionaries and their powers. Once the relationship with the dream-spirit was established, the primary form of the bond made with the power was one of protection and inspiration for daring and courageous acts. The ethnographic record discusses the symbolism of the shield more explicitly than that of many other religious objects.[60] The primary symbolism always involved its religious and visionary associations. The shield was not only a protective device but also a highly expressive religious symbol that combined color, abstract design, and naturalistic form to communicate a religious worldview. Shields also expressed a high degree of holonomic symbolism, for they frequently synthesized Plains cosmology in miniature through imagery, color, and form.

Among the Cheyenne, George Grinnell recorded three types of shields that were also typical for many other Plains groups: common, unpainted shields used by those without dream powers and considered of only minimal protection; dream shields that were created and cared for by the original visionary; and shields that were under the care of a particular group that had inherited it from the original visionary.[61] These last-mentioned shields could be quite old. Like society medicine bundles, they were believed to possess powerful influences that could work for the protection and success of an entire group in warfare. Bear Butte, or Medicine Lodge, near the Black Hills in North Dakota was believed by the Cheyenne to be the home of the sacred powers that gave the first painted shield. During a vision fast, a young man was led into Bear Butte where he had the following encounter:[62]

The man found himself in a lodge, and about it he saw hanging many shields. An old man—the chief man of the lodge—gave the young man seven differently painted shields. . . . The man who brought these shields told his people that they must make their shields like them; so henceforth all the tribal groups had shields which were always the same.

In this manner, group shields are used to symbolize social identity in a way similar to that of tribal medicine bundles. The vision is a natural means for establishing such identity and also for giving religious sanction to social organization. In all cases, the shield embodies a set of images that express the specific content of the vision encounter. Consequently, Bear Butte became a widely recognized sacred place in which to seek visions, and it is still regarded as a holy place.

The gaining of a sacred shield is considered to be a sign of good fortune and to indicate the path of the shaman-warrior. Most shields are used to protect the owner in times of danger and to gain power over those whom the warrior fought. The power attributed to the shield is instrumental; that is, the shield conveys, through images and accompanying songs and ritual use, a transmission of the power of the dream-spirits. The images on the shield communicate to others the nature of the shield as a sacred object and the fact that its power derives from a source greater than human beings. The power is communicated in a complex use of colors, design, and both abstract and realistic figures. Essentially the shield, like the painted lodge and the medicine bundle, is a mystery object. Its exact meaning is known only to the visionary or the inheritors of the object, and this knowledge is rarely verbalized. Among the Kansa, the image on the shield was sacred, powerful, and mysterious; one shield was painted with the image of a flying serpent believed to dwell in the Black Hills and whose power was known only to the visionary.[63]

The mysterious nature of the shield is recorded in the vision experience of the Gros Ventre Bull Lodge. After praying to the Feathered Pipe in the deserted campgrounds, he lay down on the ground and stared into the sky:[64]

As he gazed up at the sky, an object appeared, very small, but he could see that it was moving. It looked like a circling bird. . . . It came closer and closer, and the closer it came, the bigger it got, until it came within arm's length. It was a shield, with a string or fine cord attached to it leading up into the sky. . . . The surface presented to him was painted half red and half dark blue. A painted rainbow went all around the edge. In the center a black bird was painted, and from each side of the bird's head, green streaks of lightning, ending at the rainbow's inside rim. Eagle feathers hung in a double row from the outside rim. In the center of the shield hung a single soft, fluffy feather.

The shield, representing thunder power, descends from the above realm and is an emblem of the eagle power of thunder.[65] The rainbow is a unifying symbol that unites heaven and earth, while the fine cord is an element that is represented on many shields and other objects as a lifeline or spiritual link drawn between the object and its source. It symbolizes the inseparability of the object from its source and points to the sacred origin of the vision. Its religious symbolism usually refers to breath as the spiritual principle that gives life to the object. Because Bull Lodge is still very young, he must prove himself to the powers through other vision fasts before he can receive instructions for the correct use of the shield. As I have mentioned, this is a typical trait in shamanistic dreams—a series that culminates in complete and thorough knowledge of the power and its invocation.

The full complexity of shield art is beyond the scope of this work, because it requires a knowledge of the mythic patterns of discourse and the shared symbolism of each community involved, coupled with the unique visions of each dream fast. Furthermore, the shield designs contributed to the shared symbolism of

imagery and mythic discourse that extended over the generations. The following is an example of a Cheyenne vision shield
and its complex interpretation by its owner, Whistling Elk. Having gone to a rocky point that projected into a lake, he fasted
with a buffalo skull and had the following experience:[66]

On the morning of the fourth day, a buffalo raised its head above
the water and sang a song, directing Whistling Elk to make a shield
and describing how it should be made. The painting on the shield
should consist of a pair of long, slender, upward-directed horns, a
little above the center of the shield; below them is a large disk
surrounded by dots; between the horns is a red disc also surrounded
by dots, and there are four disks evenly distributed near the border
of the shield. These disks on the outer rim represent the four directions; the disk below the horns is the moon; the red disk between
the horns, the sun; the dots are stars. The horns represent the animal that took pity on Whistling Elk and taught him how to make
this shield. The moon is the spirit that during the night protected
the brave who carried the shield, and the sun protected him during
the day. The upper round spot to the left of the horns represents the
wind which comes from the setting sun. The upper spot at the right
of the horns represents the wind from the north, the lower spot on
the right, the wind from the east, and the lower spot on the left, the
wind from the south. The spirit which controls the south wind is
supposed to have the greatest power when prayed to for help. When
carried in battle, a piece of lodge skin was fastened to the bottom of
the shield, hanging down, and across this lodge skin were four
rows of eagle feathers.

While the prominent aspects of the symbolism are celestial,
their origins are chthonic—from the buffalo. Heaven and earth
are united, and the shield includes a representation of the cosmos with the four directions, the four winds, and the sun, moon,
and stars. The horns symbolize the buffalo that emerges out of
the water of earth, and the feathers, the eagle that flies through
the heavens. Not only are the above and below represented, but
also day and night. The symbolism is holonomic and expresses a
unified cosmology and a multiplicity of sacred powers, each of
which contributes to the effectiveness of the shield. The symbols
are arranged in a concentric manner that emphasizes an inner
protective power in the moon-stars-sun conjunction at the center
embodied in the form of the buffalo power. At the outer frame
are the four winds, which send their moving energy toward the

center. The prominence of the south wind is a common element for many Plains people, because this wind was a source of warmth and healing. Thus the symbolism, using shared geometric forms and associated meanings, has a specific interpretation and embodies a multitude of shared symbols in a unique, individualized form.

The only one empowered to make the shield is the visionary who has the experience. Among the Comanche, there are three recorded ways to obtain a shield: one could ask someone who had a vision shield to share his power; one could ask a shaman to fast for him and then make the shield; or one could fast and make the shield himself with or without the guidance of a shaman.[67] If more than one shield is made for another person, the design is exactly the same for all, though many groups limited the number of copies of a particular shield. Among the Sioux, as among other Plains people, the making of the shield required a special procedure. Prayers, offerings, and songs must be given, and a certain order of construction had to be followed. This was true also for the Blackfoot, who had some very elaborate rites involving medicine shields of great antiquity.[68] The shields had to be handled in a special manner before going into battle. For example, the shield might have to be incensed or held up to the sun and prayers offered.[69] The shield-making procedure and its visionary origins were later transferred by the Sioux to the making of the Ghost Dance shirt with its elaborate designs and protective symbols. Clark Wissler mentions that ghost shirt visions often occurred to women, who would then make many copies of the shirts with the help of female relatives.[70] The purpose of the design and the visionary art was to protect wearers from injury and empower them with the various qualities represented by the figures drawn.[71]

VISUAL ECONOMY

The communication of vision experience is part of a shared context in which the image is a primary form for the expression of meaning. From the phenomenological point of view, there is a powerful visual economy at work in which a minimal symbol such as a circle or star can express a maximum of meaning. Here

I use the term symbol to mean an identifiable form that participates in a context of possible meanings, both presently and historically, and that also points beyond itself to express those meanings in a highly condensed and simplified manner. By identifiable form, I mean that symbols communicate recognizable aspects of visual culture. The symbolic contents of the religious form express through imagery both specific ideas and shared meanings, which work together to create a focused representation of the cosmos. The relationships among form, color, and design give a structural picture of the organization of the sacred world. There is a geometry of symbolic relations that reflects not only the world order but also the ritualization of space itself, as in the pervasive use of the circle or the four directions. The image reflects the presence of various dream-spirits and the meaningful interrelation among them in the context of a visually structured field of variable elements. This symbolization also expresses a timeless present rather than a historical moment. It images the ever-present reality of the mythic world.

In all the objects discussed, the images reflect the holonomic quality of a religiously unified epistemé. This type of condensation in imagery is a direct expression of the visionary condition, an imagistic compression of meanings and form. The imagery functions for the edification of both the visionary and the community. The holonomic nature of the image reflects a strong visual, right-hemispheric emphasis sustained through a historical process by which the imagery interactively enhances, enriches, and complements the experiences of other visionaries in a context of shared beliefs. Mythic discourse is the means by which those forms accrue verbal meaning and depth over time, particularly when they are enhanced by demonstrable and remarkable manifestations. Yet the image and its symbolic contents always remain open to new interpretation because the imagery is variable and not dogmatically defined.

One significant aspect of the holonomic image is that while it represents the structure of belief and experience, it is also capable of continuous explication, unfoldment, and refinement. It develops in a cyclical, repetitive manner based on shared, interactive themes and symbolic expressions. Such an image expresses both the actual (explicit) whole and the possible (implicit) whole yet to be known or experience. In this sense, holonomic symbols cannot be limited to strict cultural definitions because the culture concept itself generally reflects an analytical norm, a rational description, that often misses the emergent processes of human experience as both multifaceted and heterogeneous. Thus a collective, normative description cannot express enfoldment in its totality, but can only give an explicit example that is charged with conflictive, manifest fragments or subtotalities of other possible meanings. The rational tendencies of any cultural analysis tend to work toward a logical description involving refractory elements of culture while frequently ignoring the actual complexity and diversity of many underlying tensions and disparate subtotalities. The view of culture as process, as reflective of a dynamic condition of constant change, modification, adaptation, and encounter structured by an unbound and visionary worldview, allows for the recognition of an underlying or implicit wholeness, along with an understanding that the field of actual events is fragmentary and conditioned by multiple and varying circumstances, many of which are often contradictory.

The function of the image, explicitly the religious image, is to bear witness to this implicit unity in the face of diversity. The highly compressed, often stylized and abstract image with its vibrant color and design draws together this diversity and expresses, in the context of both revelation and enactment, the unique synthesis of the cosmological whole in a visual language of shared symbols. This is the holonomic aspect of the symbol, its ability to center the visionary within a unified cosmos. The symbolism itself participates in an interactive dialogue of religious ideas joined to other visionary experiences that sustains the continuity of shared communication. Mythic discourse provides the foreground through which individual experience becomes incorporated into various subtotalities of meaning. The largest part of this discourse is imagery—highly compressed, holonomic, and mythically expressive of the sacred. Another important aspect is holonomic sound—the sacred song or chant that expresses the vision experience in a condensed verbal formula. A third holonomic feature is movement or stylized dance in the context of ritual enactment. A fourth lies in the collective stories, tales, and shared beliefs conveyed among individuals. A fifth is the esoteric knowledge of the medicine society or the shaman's lodge. Finally, social organization and kinship relations contribute their essential social structures to the mythic discourse. Thus the dream or vision must undergo a whole series of interactive encounters, all of which contribute, in sometimes contradictory ways, to the ongoing processes of interpretation.

Another aspect of visual economy is the way in which the visionary image is fused with a practical object. The image as such is rarely presented apart from an object that has pragmatic value and usefulness. Even a simple, natural object, such as a feather, has a degree of instrumentality through which the power is expressed. It transmits, it effects change, it invokes a presence. As such, all visionary art is sacred and more than decorative or purely aesthetic. The quality of art that makes it sacred is this instrumentality and expressiveness through which the more transcendent and less visible aspects of religion are given a pragmatic and existential form. It is not art for the sake of art; it is an expression of the sacred that has an impact and an instrumental effect on the awareness and actions of the individual or group. The shield expresses its instrumentality to the enemy as a protective device, both pragmatically and symbolically. The painted lodge protects the dweller practically and spiritually. The medicine bundle is a means for containing the objects of power, and it provides a blessing for the keeper. Quill work as a sacred art enhances the usefulness and power of a moccasin; painting a horse makes it both beautiful and one with the Thunder powers.[72]

The power of this imagery would have been particularly strong for children, whose early learning experience is primarily imagistic and eidetic.[73] In a context of ritual enactment where parents and relatives all paint themselves with vivid colors and images, using objects of mystery and power to invoke the mythic world through singing and dancing in a ritual manner, the child would be highly susceptible to the power of the imagery as well as to its evocative emotional contents. All the rich imagery on tipis, horses, and clothing would constantly be communicating its contents nonverbally to a receptive child. Those special times of collective ceremony and enactment would strongly reinforce the importance and primacy of the imagery. In certain circumstances, a receptive child would be painted and asked to play a role in an enactment, as Black Elk was during a bear curing ceremony. He was given no verbal instructions, yet after being painted, he became possessed by the bear power through imitating the actions of the instructing shamans, all of whom were dressed as bears.[74] Such powerful imagery would be constantly impacting the child and sensitizing him or her to future visionary experience—all in a nonverbal context of vivid enactment and object symbolism.

This fusion of the object and the image in a context of religious experience and enactment expresses the intentional nature of the vision. The intent of the vision quest is to seek empowerment through contact with more-than-human beings. The dream-spirit conveys the fulfillment of this intention through multiple instrumental means. The visionary is given a song, various objects, designs, and a unique color combination, as well as instructions in the use of these things. Through making the necessary objects, using them in a prescribed manner, painting in the correct way, and singing the sacred song, the visionary actualizes the gift of power. The dreamer must look carefully at the dream-spirit in order to observe clearly all the nonverbal aspects of its appearance and actions, all of which have potential symbolic meanings and applications. The image serves to unify and organize the experience, and it acts as a template for reproducing the mysterious power. Subsequently, there is a shift in intentionality. The fast is a search for power; the enactment is the expression of power. The consequence of the successful vision is in the reformation of intentionality, guided by contact with the sacred, to express through primarily nonverbal and instrumental means an *act* of power. Such action is strongly assisted by the making and use of sacred images. The sacredness of these images resides in their ability to invoke the appropriate state of intentionality in all who have contact with them. Thus, the image reflects the core of both the visionary experience and its many social and religious manifestations.

Afterword

TRANSFORMATION THROUGH visionary experience—the ability to cross into the mysterious world of dreams that empower the dreamer in healing, warfare, or a vast array of ritual-life patterns—is a primary means for constituting the world of Native American religious specialists, or shamans. The dreamer's world is also the shaman's world. It is a world that lacks precise boundaries, that speaks in imagery and affect, that constitutes itself around the heart of a sacred mystery. The link between the mythic world of religious imagery and conception and the bounded world of "ordinary perception" is the bridge of dreams—the visionary encounters that inform and validate a religious worldview. The languages of dreaming, being highly imagistic and affective, are only with great difficulty translated into rational systems of interpretation and thought. The shaman's art is not the translation of dreams into verbal interpretations; rather, it is the use of dreams, the praxis though which events are transformed or guided in accordance with dream or visionary experience.

The shaman's world is the world in which all human beings live, a world seen and enhanced through dreams and visionary experiences in which the boundaries between waking and sleeping have retained their transparency. It is a world in which flights of soul are considered normative and journeys are not confined to the physical limitations of the body. The perceptual basis for entering the shaman's world lies in direct experience, through increased development of perceptual clarity and deep sensitivity to alternate states of awareness. The shift from waking to dreaming is continuously broken down into subtler states and gradations until the metaphor "life-as-dream" takes on an increasingly vivid signification. In this sense, the shaman's art is dramatically linked with the art of dreaming and to the sacred world of shamanistic powers.

Encoded in highly symbolic imagery and language, resonant with multifaceted expressions of meaning, and capable of radically transforming the individual, shamanistic dreams and visions are primarily expressions of a mysterious potential or power that imbues the visionary world. Therefore, my concern in this book has been to recognize the dynamic patterns of relations that constitute the complexity of the traditional Plains Indian dreaming world. It is not a complexity merely of inherited forms, but one of an emergent, revelatory pattern whose intent continues to make known the sacred character of the world. Whatever the medium of expression—be it song, dance, or a shaman's fan—the intent involves the constant and direct solicitation of power so that the dynamic pattern of mythic relations, perfectly congruent with the natural world, stands forth as a validation of the dreaming experience. These patterns are a matter not only of the clarity of the shaman's vision but also of the immediacy of impact that allows the power of the vision to work effectively in the life of the individual or the community.

Most importantly, the dreamer's art is not accessible to purely objective analysis. Arising in a stream of historically congruent symbols and formal expressions, the visionary experience cannot be wholly separated from the complexity and richness of those forms and the variety of multifaceted interpretations that imbue the social world with power. Many of these forms are nonverbal and object oriented, and they arise in a purely visionary context, much of which is retained privately by the individual as sacred and inviolable. Though many of these forms tend toward communally transmitted and recognized collective expressions, it would be inappropriate to regard such expressions as dogmatically determined by members of the dreaming community. Shamanism, prophecy, and dreaming among Native Americans have a highly idiosyncratic character, one in which the collective expressions of consciousness are subject to radically distinct interpretations.

Yet interpretation is by no means the primary goal of visionary experience. The vision, its manifestation in acts of power, its capacity to reveal the complexity and mystery of the pattern of relations, and its overwhelming imagistic and affective potency are far more significant than the capacity of the individual rationally to interpret the experience. Consequently, it has been my intent not to rationalize shamanistic dream experience but to enrich our awareness of its far-reaching potential and power.

What I have not discussed are the diverse ways in which shamans attain or maximize the power of their dreams. This is because of the richness and diversity of ways in which every group sanctioned and recognized its visionary members. Generally speaking, however, the ethnography supports the idea that shamans—that is, religious specialists of all sorts, men and women of power, and those with remarkable or unusual ability—had quantitatively more and richer dreams. These dreamers were qualitatively different only in their ability to have, naturally and spontaneously, very rich and complex visions. Yet someone who made great effort and was persistent could also achieve a high degree of social recognition if he or she could demonstrate an unusual degree of power. Visions were not the only important criteria for becoming a healer or religious leader. Social standing, kinship affiliation, gender, age, society membership, and inheritance patterns all played significant roles in an individual's development. What constituted the specific contents of the "shaman's dream" remains to be explored, but the underlying principle is not the type of dream but the richness, quantity, and continuity of the dreaming state maintained by the advanced dreamers. Life-as-dream means the continual merging of the waking and dreaming states to form a mastery of control and expertise that allowed the developed dreamer consciously to enter the visionary state and effect a positive result. The shaman's art is the mastery of human potential, however it is achieved.

The Visionary Ethnography

THE FOLLOWING LIST identifies the Plains Indian communities for which dream and vision materials are readily availible in the existing ethnography. While most material used in this book has been drawn from the greater plains, other materials were instrumental in helping me gain a comprehensive overview of dreaming throughout North America. This is by no means a comprehensive list; almost every group for which there is an ethnographic history mentions the importance of dreams. Archival materials and unpublished manuscripts abound for the further study of Native American religion, along with journals, letters, and popular press publications.

Among the Plains nomadic peoples—followers of the buffalo herds—are the northern groups: Absarokee (Crow), Assiniboine, Blackfoot, Cheyenne, Gros Ventre, and Teton-Dakota Sioux; and the southern groups: Apache (Jicarilla), Arapaho, Comanche, Kiowa, Kiowa-Apache, Quapaw, and Wichita. The river-valley peoples, who follow an agricultural, dual cycle of planting and hunting, are the Dhegiha-speaking peoples of the middle Missouri River Valley (Kansa, Omaha, Osage, Ponca); the Arikara, Hidatsa, and Mandan on the upper Missouri River; the Pawnee of the northern and southern Platt River; and the Chiwere-speaking Iowa and Oto-Missouri. The northern woodland and prairie peoples are the Plains Cree, the Plains Ojibwa, and the Winnebago; the western mountain and plains peoples are the Nez Perce, Shoshone, and Ute. While Plains Indian studies tend to emphasize high plains nomadic religious culture, the river-valley peoples have a very distinctive religious orientation that should be distinguished from that of the more nomadic Plains groups.

Dream Ethnography by Geographic Area

NORTHWEST

Bella Coola
Gitksak
Haida
Kwakiutl
Nootka
Salish
Tlingit
Tsimshian

PLATEAU

Flathead
Nez Perce
Tenino
Thompson

CALIFORNIA

Chumash
Hupa
Klamath
Mono
Pomo
Shasta
Yokuts

GREAT BASIN

Mohave
Paiute
Paviotso
Shoshone
Ute
Washo

GREATER PLAINS

Northern

Absarokee (Crow)
Assiniboine
Blackfoot
Blood
Piegan
Cheyenne
Gros Ventre
Sioux
Dakota
Lakota

River Valley

Arikara
Dhegiha
Kansa
Omaha
Osage
Ponca
Hidatsa
Iowa
Mandan
Oto-Missouri
Pawnee

Southern

Arapaho
Comanche
Kiowa (Apache)
Quapaw
Wichita

SOUTHWEST

Apache
Hopi
Navajo
Tewa
Yuma
Zuni

SUBARCTIC

Beaver
Carrier
Cree
Kutchin
Plains Cree
Plains Ojibwa
Ojibwa/Salteaux
Winnebago

NORTHEAST

Algonkian
Chippewa
Delaware
Huron
Iroquois
Cayuga
Mohawk
Oneida
Onondaga
Seneca
Menominee
Micmac
Penobscot
Potowatami

SOUTHEAST

Cherokee
Chickasaw
Choctaw
Creek
Seminole

APPENDIX TWO

Indigenous Terms

THE FOLLOWING TERMS have appeared in the main body of the text or in footnotes. The translations do not represent actual linguistic translations, but English approximations based on their usage in English texts that often give little or no explanation. The phonemic representations reflect those found in the texts used for this study.

Assiniboine:
    Watichaghe: Make-a-Home ceremony, 200
    Wió´ha: painted lodge, 219

Blackfoot:
    Kshá´kom-mitapi: Earth People, 30
    Spómitapi: People Above, 30
    Piskan: buffalo surround, 193

Cheyenne:
    Aktovo: Blue Sky Space, 30
    Aktunov: Deep Earth, 30
    Heammahestonev: Earth Surface, 30
    Hestenov: world cosmos, 30
    Hohnuhk´e: thunder dreamer, 54
    Maiyun: mysterious beings, 282n.23
    Setovo: Near Sky Space, 30
    Taxtavo: atmosphere, 30
    Votoso: upper-layer Earth, 30
    Wu-wun: fasting, 101

Gros Ventre:
    Behä´tixtch: Leader of All, 115

Plains Ojibwa:

Kini'u: golden eagle, 74

Ogima: superior person (spirit), 74, 256n.33

Pawakan [Pawágan]: dream spirit, 268n.31, 280n.62

Sioux:

Akicita: messenger, 122, 124

Cansasa: smoking mixture, 112, 113

Hanble: vision, 122

Hanblecheyapi: crying for a vision, 112

Hanbloglaka: vision talk, 122, 197

Haye: it is said, 179

Hepan: otter, second male child, 180

Heyoka: thunder dreamer, 54, 156, 200

Inyan: stone, 225

Ohakaya: caused to be blocked, 177

Tatanka Lowanpi: buffalo sing, 200

Tobtob kin: four times four, 256n.24

Tunkan: thunder stone, 225

Tunkashila: grandfather, 128

Unktehi: Water Monster, 30, 39, 72

Wacinksapa: attentive understanding, 115

Wakan: mysterious power, 69, 71, 123, 129, 135, 136, 172, 177, 178, 179, 196, 197, 219

Wakan-Tanka: Great Mystery, 122

Wakinyan: thunder being, 130

Wakinyan-Tanka: great thunder being, 179

Wiwanyag wacipi: sun dance, 50

Notes

THE FOLLOWING CONVENTIONS have been adopted for longer quotations in both the main body of the text and the notes: any break in a narrative that is longer than two or three sentences, or that contains a digression of any length not relevant to the actual vision experience, is indicated by a space between quoted block paragraphs. Paragraph indentations either follow the original text or indicate a distinct change in action or subject. Indentation does not imply a break in the text. Shorter omissions are indicated in the conventional way (. . .), and square brackets [ ] contain explanatory information or a synopsis indicating a compression of the text. Native language is indicated by italic type.

Prologue

1. Ruth Benedict, *The Concept of the Guardian Spirit in North America*, p. 43.

2. See Lee Irwin, "Myth, Language and Ontology Among the Huron," "Visionary Dialogues: The Huron-Jesuit Relations," and "Cherokee Healing: Myth, Dreams and Medicine," for the significance of Native American dreams and visions outside of the greater plains area. See the appendix One for a brief overview of the threefold division of the plains and a list of resources from other geographical areas.

3. The earliest ethnographic sources written by the Spanish, French, and English all record the importance of dreaming among indigenous groups. For a French example written in 1636, see Reuben G. Thwaites, *The Jesuit Relations and Allied Documents: Travels and Explorations of the Jesuit Missionaries in New France*, 10:169–173. Early 1760s Plains Indian examples are found in John Parker, *The Journals of Jonathan Carver and Related Documents, 1766–1770*, pp. 103–105; Henry R. Schoolcraft, "Indian Theory of the Mind During Sleep," records some early theoretical notes on the subject.

4. See G. A. James, "Phenomenology and the Study of Religion: The Archaeology of an Approach," p. 323.

5. See Stanford Krolick, "Through a Glass Darkly: What is the Phenomenology of Religion?" p. 197.

6. Ingvild S. Gilhus, "The Phenomenology of Religion and Theories of Interpretation," pp. 29–30.

Chapter 1. Culture, Dreams, and Theory

1. Jackson S. Lincoln, *The Dream in Primitive Cultures*; Dorothy Eggan, "The Significance of Dreams for Anthropological Research"; Clyde Kluckhohn and William Morgan, "Some Notes on Navaho Dreams"; George Devereux, *Dream and Reality: The Psychotherapy of a Plains Indian*; Roy G. D'Andrade, "Anthropological Studies in Dreams"; Weston LaBarre, "The Dream, Charisma, and the Culture-Hero."

2. Andrew Samuels, *Jung and the Post-Jungians*, p. 231.

3. Clyde Kluckhohn and William Morgan, "Some Notes on Navaho Dreams," pp. 120 and 124, give a remarkable example of a Freudian approach:

> The facts uncovered in my own field work and that of my collaborators have forced me to the conclusion that Freud and other psychoanalysts have depicted with astonishing correctness many central themes in motivational life which are universal.... [For example] Jennie, a Navaho Mother [said] "I used to have a dream lots of times and thought I was walking in a garden and there were lots of beautiful flowers and there were roses as high as that gas tank. And there were lots of squash and melons and fruits. And I went everywhere looking for the very best flowers and ripest melons." ... The flowers and melons may be equated with phallus and testes (note the height of the roses). The picking of the flowers may represent castration or hostility activity on the part of the dreamer.... It may even be that the dreamer is here in a masculine role, with the walk into the valley equalling insertion.

4. R. E. Haskel, "Cognitive Psychology and Dream Research: Historical, Conceptual, and Epistemological Considerations," p. 135.

5. Ruth Benedict, *The Concept of the Guardian Spirit in North America*, p. 7.

6. Lincoln, *The Dream in Primitive Cultures*, p. 22; also Eggan, "The Significance of Dreams for Anthropological Research."

7. D'Andrade, "Anthropological Studies in Dreams," p. 306.

8. Devereux, *Dream and Reality: The Psychotherapy of a Plains Indian*, pp. 143–44, writes:

> The quest for visions, which started with masochistic self-pity and appeals for compassion, and culminated in aggression and competitiveness, can be understood in terms of ... the dynamics of masochism and dependency.... The segment of the unconscious reflected in these dreams is primarily the unconscious segment of the ego—i.e., the defense mechanisms—because, in Wolf culture, dreams are, themselves, major psychic defenses.... Dreaming itself may be thought of as a defense mechanism, which, due to cultural conditioning, sometimes occupies a pivotal position in the individual's total system of psychic defenses.

9. A. Irving Hallowell, "The Self and Its Behavioral Environment."

10. Anthony Wallace, "Dreams and the Wishes of the Soul: A Type of Psychoanalytic Theory Among the Seventeenth-Century Iroquois," p. 238.

11. D'Andrade, "Anthropological Studies in Dreams," p. 319. John Honigmann, "North America," p. 199, summarizes the tendency: "The prevailing tendency in culture and personality research is to observe with the aid of appropriate theory and with clinical exactness living people in their normal environment in order to infer the underlying psychological states by which they can be characterized."

12. William Dement and Nathan Kleitman, "The Relation of Eye Movements during Sleep to Dream Activity"; Barbara Tedlock, *Dreaming: Anthropological and Psychological Interpretations*, pp. 12–16.

13. Haskel, "Cognitive Psychology and Dream Research: Historical, Conceptual, and Epistemological Considerations," p. 140.

14. D'Andrade, "Anthropological Studies in Dreams," pp. 307–308.

15. The Jungian approach to dream interpretation offers a still unexplored potential in the study of Native American dreaming. The general approach has been founded on a recognition of the genuinely symbolic content of dreaming, as distinct from Freudian semiotics. This was first expressed clearly by Jolande Jacobi, *Complex, Archetype, Symbol in the Psychology of C. G. Jung*, p. 80; see also Samuels, *Jung and the Post-Jungians*, p. 231.

16. See David Foulkes, *Dreaming: A Cognitive-Psychological Approach*, p. 158. Haskel, "Cognitive Psychology and Dream Research: Historical, Conceptual, and Epistemological Considerations," p. 151, has challenged the idea that dreaming is an expression of "random" psychophysical processes by pointing out that, on the cortical level, these underlying processes are selectively organized by the same mechanisms that operate in waking consciousness. The development of the continuity hypothesis between sleeping and waking is strengthened if similar cognitive operations function to organize meaningfully both REM sleep states and waking consciousness.

17. A. P. Dubrov and V. N. Pushkin, *Parapsychology and Contemporary Science*; Roland Fischer, "Toward a Neuroscience of Self-Experience and States of Self-Awareness and Interpreting Interpretations"; Stanley Krippner and L. George, "PSI Phenomena as Related to Altered States of Consciousness"; Charles T. Tart, "The World Simulation Process in Waking and Dreaming: A Systems Analysis of Structure." Erika Bourguignon, *Psychological Anthropology: An Introduction to Human Nature and Cultural Differences*, has dedicated a long chapter to reviewing the whole concept of ASC in this anthropology textbook.

18. Richard Noll, "Mental Imagery Cultivation as a Cultural Phenomenon: The Role of Visions in Shamanism," p. 448.

19. Akhter Ahsen, "The New Structuralism: Images in Dramatic Interlock," p. 33; for an overview see Akhter Ahsen, "Rewriting the History and Future of the Imagery Movement," and David F. Marks, "Imagery Paradigms and Methodology."

20. Ahsen, "Rewriting the History and Future of the Imagery Movement," p. 275.

21. Ahsen, "Prolucid Dreaming: A Content Analysis Approach to Dreams," p.63, makes the following observation with regard to the continuity between the waking and dreaming states:

> Obviously, we find the dynamic logic in the expansive world of the dream separated from the linear logic of waking life. However, when we wake up, remembering a dream represents a state of exile into that kind of linear logic which defines the sad conventional world around us. What we are saying is that perhaps waking cognition really needs to learn more from the dream cognition rather than the other way around. The problem lies in the fact that waking cognition just does not let the dream into waking life, let the dynamic logic happen.

22. Michael H. Stone, "Dreams, Free Association, and the Non-dominant Hemisphere: An Integration of Psychoanalytical, Neurophysiological, and Historical Data"; Robert G. Ley, "Cerebral Asymmetries, Emotional Experience, and Imagery: Implications for Psychotherapy"; Paul Bakan, "Imagery, Raw and Cooked: A Hemispheric Recipe"; T. B. Rogers, "Emotion, Imagery, and Verbal Codes: A Closer Look at an Increasingly Complex Interaction"; Anthony Stevens, *Archetypes: A Natural History of the Self*; Jon Tolaas, "Transformatory Framework: Pictorial to Verbal"; Gordon Globus, "Three Holonomic Approaches to the Brain."

23. Bakan, "Imagery, Raw and Cooked: A Hemispheric Recipe," p. 36, has argued for a "dual dominance model" but has not considered the general problem of cultural developmental patterns that emphatically stress left-brain learning.

24. Stevens, *Archetypes: A Natural History of the Self*, p. 253; see also Tolaas, "Transformatory Framework: Pictorial to Verbal," p. 38.

25. Ley, "Cerebral Asymmetries, Emotional Experience, and Imagery: Implications for Psychotherapy," pp. 42–46.

26. Ley, "Cerebral Asymmetries, Emotional Experience, and Imagery: Implications for Psychotherapy"; Stevens, *Archetypes: A Natural History of the Self*; Tolaas, "Transformatory Framework: Pictorial to Verbal"; and others have specifically considered the problem of the cognitive development of hemispheric specialization. Stevens is particularly interesting in this respect. In discussing susceptibility to environmental influences, he notes the high degree to which contemporary Euro-Americans have been conditioned to left-hemisphere activities.

27. Ley, "Cerebral Asymmetries, Emotional Experience, and Imagery: Implications for Psychotherapy"; Waud Kracke, "Myths in Dreams, Thoughts in Images: An Amazonian Contribution to the Psychoanalytic Theory of Primary Process."

28. Stone, "Dreams, Free Association, and the Non-dominant Hemisphere: An Integration of Psychoanalytical, Neurophysiological, and Historical Data," p. 279; Ley, "Cerebral Asymmetries, Emotional Experience, and Imagery: Implications for Psychotherapy," p. 46; Rogers, "Emotion, Imagery, and Verbal Codes: A Closer Look at an Increasingly Complex Interaction," p. 300.

29. Ley, "Cerebral Asymmetries, Emotional Experience, and Imagery: Implications for Psychotherapy," p. 55, writes:

Because of the relatively greater development and influence of the right hemisphere during this developmental period, early childhood experiences are primarily processed, coded, and stored in the right hemisphere. This *coding* is most likely to be of a nonverbal, imagistic, or sensory-affective kind. As a result, these experiences are difficult to *decode* or "remember" by a verbal, linguistic or cognitive means, which is the typical recollective strategy employed by adults. . . . Simply put, one cannot use a left hemisphere key to open a right hemisphere lock.

30. Tolaas, "Transformatory Framework: Pictorial to Verbal." The average individual will have over 150,000 (REM) dreams in his or her lifetime, yet how many will draw on this rich pleroma of affective, imagistic experience to enhance the cognitive quality of their awareness, having been educated in a dominantly left-hemispheric culture?

31. Stone, "Dreams, Free Association, and the Non-dominant Hemisphere: An Integration of Psychoanalytical, Neurophysiological, and Historical Data," p. 279; Stevens, *Archetypes: A Natural History of the Self*, p. 255.

32. Many psychologists have challenged this viewpoint and articulated the importance and significance of working with dream materials. The following is from Montague D. Ullman and Stanley Krippner, *Dream Telepathy: Experiments in Nocturnal ESP*, p. 223:

> The dream is, in effect, a frank and honest pictorial statement of the issue as he [the dreamer] experiences it, of the connection of the issue with his past, of the resources as well as character defenses that are mobilized in response to it, and of his ability, in the face of all this, to cope with it. There is an essential honesty, truthfulness, and transparency to dream imagery that escapes us in waking life, mainly because we can't summon the same degrees of truthfulness about ourselves. While awake we are participants in a social drama and are called upon to enact many and often conflicting roles. While asleep our being is all that exists in the universe and we dare to look more deeply at our true selves.

33. For a further discussion of epistemé, a term first popularized by Michel Foucault, see J. G. Merquior, *Foucault*. Merquior writes, p. 38:

> An *epistemé*, therefore, may be called a paradigm, providing it is not conceived of as an exemplar, a model of cognitive work. It is a basement ("sous-sol") of thought, a mental infrastructure underlying all strands of knowledge at a given age, a conceptual 'grid' ("grille," in Foucault's Levi-Struassian wording) that amounts to an 'historical a priori'—almost a historicized form of Kant's categories.

34. During the last decade, the "continuity hypothesis" has been gaining ground. This hypothesis postulates an unbroken continuity between waking and sleeping states both on the microlevel of brain physiology and on the macrolevel of perceptible mental events. See also H. Hunt, "Some Relations between the Cognitive Psychology of Dreams and Dream Phenomenology," p. 216, and Ahsen, "Prolucid Dreaming: A Content Analysis Approach to Dreams," p. 5. Haskel, "Cognitive Psychology and Dream Research: Historical, Conceptual, and Epistemological Considerations," p. 151, writes:

> It seems reasonable to invoke and extend the continuity-hypothesis between waking and dreaming to its logical conclusion: that the same general cognitive operations function during certain stages of sleep as they function in the waking state—the basic difference being that thoughts and stimuli ordered during the waking state are, by social consensus, considered to be real, while those ordered during the sleep state are considered to be imaginal. It is doubtful, however, if neurocognitive processes, or brain tissue, make this rather fine distinction. The brain probably attempts to render all stimuli meaningful.

35. It may seem that I wish to avoid a "psychological" interpretation altogether but I actually have the deepest interest in the psychological approach. On the other hand, I do not wish to consider dreams as strictly psychological phenonema. They are far more complex events manifesting rather poorly understood subtotalities of higher-order synthesis than most

present psychological theory allows for; this higher order is explicitly recognized by Plains Indian dreamers, and dreaming is consequently reified in terms of a more cosmological and religious espistemé.

36. David Bohm, *Wholeness and the Implicate Order*; John P. Briggs and David F. Peat, *Looking Glass Universe: The Emerging Science of Wholeness*; B.J. Hiley and David F. Peat, *Quantum Implications*; Richard Morris, *The Edges of Science: Crossing the Boundary from Physics to Metaphysics*.

37. This part-whole analogy represents the process of learning as a continuing unfolding of potential meaning—meanings and significations that become relevant to the struggles and discoveries of a particular generation of researchers. This does not mean that the process is necessarily "evolutionary" in the lineal sense, but that various experiences and discoveries of a particular age or culture may need to be reintegrated (such as the values and practices found in Native American spirituality) as essential to the greater wholeness. Also, the insights and emphasis of a particular generation may prove to be faulty, inaccurate, and grossly misleading and represent a contraction and an obscuring of that wholeness.

38. As a particular designated subtotality, such as social organization, is explored and understood (through social sciences, etc.), it becomes more explicit in our understanding of the cultural whole; it is part of the process of unfoldment. Emerging disciplinary perspectives are already implicate in the original cultural totality and gradually become more and more explicit as analytic reflection continues to explicate specific features, patterns, symbols, and so on. Consequently, there is no such thing as a "final interpretation"; there is only the process of continually unfolding layers of increased awareness and insight, each investigation contributing its "quantum" to making the implicate explicit. For more about the "bootstrap" idea, first articulated in the field of quantum physics by Gregory Chew, see F. Capra in Ken Wilber, *The Holographic Paradigm and Other Paradoxes: Exploring the Leading Edge of Science*, p. 114; and Stanislav Grof, *Beyond the Brain: Birth, Death, and Transcendence in Psychotherapy*, p. 57.

Chapter 2. Greater Plains Cosmography

1. The term topology derives from the Greek *topos*, meaning place, spot, or position, or, secondarily, occasion or opportunity. Thus the original meaning involves both a spatial and a temporal character, where time is noted as a particular occasion. A *topos* is a "place where something occurs."

2. While some individuals felt, like the Hidatsa Edward Goodbird (*Goodbird the Indian: His Story Told to G. L. Wilson*, p. 22), that "all dreams were from the spirit," many others, like the Comanche eagle-healer Sanapia (David Jones, *Sanapia: Comanche Medicine Woman*, p. 38) and the Mandan warrior Crow Heart (Alfred Bowers, *Mandan Social and Ceremonial Organization*, p. 169), distinguished "real dreams" from all others, and these were the dreams narrated and discussed.

3. This type of distinction has been noted earlier by Native Americans, particularly in terms of the breakdown of the normally rigid separation between "material" and "spiritual" realities. See the Lakota artist Authur Amiotte, "Our Other Selves: The Lakota Dream Experience," p. 27.

4. E. Adamson Hoebel, *The Cheyennes: Indians of the Great Plains*, pp. 87–89. Karl Schlesier, *The Wolves of Heaven: Cheyenne Shamanism, Ceremonies, and Prehistoric Origins*, discusses similar ideas among the Cheyenne.

5. Edward Curtis, *The North American Indian*, 6:65.

6. Alanson Skinner, "Menomini Social Life and Ceremonial Bundles," p. 87, writes about the Algonkian Menomini of upper Wisconsin as follows: "The Memomini divide [the world] into two main sections: the upper and lower worlds. These in turn are divided into four parts or tiers each, and are separated by the earth [i.e., the "middle" realm]. Each world has its presiding deity." The Delaware have an even more complex twelve-fold division of the universe; see Anthony Wallace, "New Religions Among the Delaware Indians, 1600–1900."

7. James O. Dorsey, *A Study of Siouan Cults*, p. 442.

8. James R. Walker, pp. 93–96, has noted a somewhat similar system among the Teton-Dakota; see also DeMallie and Lavenda, "Wakan: Plains Siouan Concepts of Power."

9. Alice Fletcher and Francis La Flesche, *The Omaha Tribe*, p. 589.

10. For the various types of dream-spirits, which Benedict, *The Concept of the Guardian Spirit in North America*, discusses as "guardian spirits," her book gives a good overview of the general subject. The concept of a "guardian-spirit," however, is a rather limited translation of the role of visionary experience in Plains Indian religious thought.

11. David G. Mandelbaum, "The Plains Cree," p. 252.

12. Mandelbaum, "The Plains Cree," p. 252; see also Paul Radin, "The Winnebago tribe," p. 305.

13. Mandelbaum, "The Plains Cree," p. 251.

14. Leonard Bloomfield, *Plains Cree Texts*, p. 151.

15. While a number of indigenous categorizations of dream types exist, very few conceptual or linguistic distinctions are made by Plains groups between "dreams" and "visions." Furthermore, very few phenomenological distinctions are given as descriptive of the "state" of the visionary. Note the ease with which observers enter into the experience of seeing a buffalo transform itself into a human being. It just happens, suddenly. Categorical distinctions simply do not apply, nor are they relevant to the epistemology involved here.

16. Alfred L. Kroeber, *The Arapaho*, p. 419.

17. The appearance of multiple animals is more characteristic of some tribes than others. It seems to be particularly true of the Pawnee (Gene Weltfish, *The Lost Universe: The Way of Life of the Pawnee*, pp. 404–406), the Ute (Marvin K. Opler, "Dream Analysis in Ute Indian Therapy," p. 103), and the Dhegiha-speaking people (Alanson Skinner, "Societies of the Iowa, Kansa, and Ponca Indians," p. 707).

18. Examples of this reflexive imagery and symbolism are scattered throughout the ethnography. For a classic example see Raymond DeMallie, *The Sixth Grandfather: Black Elk's Teachings Given to John G. Neihardt*, p. 119.

19. Frances Densmore, *Teton Sioux Music*, pp. 176–79.

20. Clark Wissler, "Ceremonial Bundles of the Blackfoot Indians," pp. 265–66; Stanley Vestal, *Warpath: The True Story of the Fighting Sioux Told in a Biography of Chief White Bull*, p. 94.

21. Wissler, "Ceremonial Bundles of the Blackfoot Indians," p. 77.

22. Ernest Wallace and E. Adamson Hoebel, *The Comanches: Lords of the Southern Plains*, p. 204.

23. Wallace and Hoebel, *The Comanches: Lords of the Southern Plains*, p. 197. Deward E. Walker, "Nez Perce Sorcery," p. 207, gives a good summary of

the types of dream-spirits that might be encountered among the Plateau Indians:

> Sources from which a person could gain power in the aboriginal system ranged from inorganic to organic and superorganic phenomena. Tutelary spirits have been recorded for the following sources: sun, moon, and stars; clouds, lightning, spring floods, ice, mountains, trees, and rivers; a large number of land mammals, birds, reptiles, fish, and insects; day ghosts, [and] night ghosts.

24. John Stands in Timber and Margot Liberty, *Cheyenne Memories*, p. 90. This butte has a long history of being a particularly powerful place for visions. The Sioux medicine man Fools Crow tells of his experience at the butte during a vision fast he was leading there; see Thomas E. Mails, *Fools Crow*, pp. 179–83.

25. Weltfish, *The Lost Universe: The Way of Life of the Pawnee*, pp. 404–406.

26. Many other examples of visionary contact with underwater beings can be found among the Plains peoples. For a Kiowa example, see Wilbur S. Nye, *Bad Medicine and Good: Tales of the Kiowas*, p. 257; for the experience of the Absarokee medicine woman Pretty Shield, see Frank B. Linderman, *Pretty Shield: Medicine Woman of the Crow*, pp. 127–28. These experiences are similar to those found among the Great Basin Washo (see Edgar E. Siskin, *Washo Shamans and Peyotists*, pp. 24–25) and among the central California Yukuts (Richard B. Applegate, *'Atishwin: The Dream Helper in Southern California*, p. 43). Leslie Spier, "Klamath Ethnography," p. 93, reports that among the Klamath of southern Oregon, "diving beneath lonely pools" was a typical way of seeking visionary power.

27. William Whitman, *The Oto*, p. 86.

28. James W. Schultz, *Friends of My Life as an Indian*, p. 65.

29. Alfred Bowers, *Mandan Social and Ceremonial Organization*, p. 178.

30. Robert H. Lowie, "The Assiniboine," p. 48.

31. William Wildschut, *Crow Indian Medicine Bundles*, p. 137.

32. For another good example of the ambiguity of the rattlesnake figure, see the famous Tipi Sapa dream as told by Vine Deloria, Sr., about the visionary experience of his famous Sioux grandfather, Francis Deloria. When Brown Bear, a cousin of Francis Deloria's, went to see how he was doing during his vision fast, he discovered him entirely covered with rattlesnakes and assumed he had been killed. Later, Deloria returned to camp unharmed but with new visionary power; see Raymond DeMallie and Douglas Parks, *Sioux Indian Religion: Tradition and Innovation*, p. 94.

33. Mary Eastman, *Dahcotah, or Life and Legends of the Sioux around Fort Snelling*, p. 241.

34. Fletcher and La Flesche, *The Omaha Tribe*, p. 565; see also R. F. Fortune, *Omaha Secret Societies*, p. 27.

35. Densmore, *Teton Sioux Music*, pp. 160ff.

36. DeMallie, *The Sixth Grandfather: Black Elk's Teachings Given to John G. Neihardt*, p. 120.

37. See Anthony Wallace, "The Dream in Mohave Life," pp. 105ff.

38. J. Gilbert McAllister, "The Four Quartz Rocks Medicine Bundle of the Kiowa-Apache," pp. 216–20.

39. David Rockwell, *Giving Voice to Bear: North American Indian Myths, Rituals, and Images of the Bear*, passim.

40. Densmore, *Teton Sioux Music*, p. 195.

41. Deward E. Walker, "Nez Perce Sorcery," p. 70.

42. John C. Ewers, *The Blackfeet: Raiders of the Northwestern Plains*, p. 166.

43. Other examples may be given of the chthonic nature of bear power. The Mandan healer Cherry Necklace "cried all night until nearly morning when a bear came out of the water and led him into his den under the water" (Bowers, *Mandan Social and Ceremonial Organization*, p. 178). Among the Absarokee, the medicine man Fringe received his powers from beneath Medicine Springs in the Bighorn Mountains, where he met an otter and a white bear (Linderman, *Plenty Coups: Chief of the Crows*, p. 302). The white bear as a distinctive chthonic power appears among the Ojibwa (Johann G. Kohl, *Kitchi-Gami: Life Among the Lake Superior Ojibway*, p. 207) and in the cosmology of the Menominee (Alanson Skinner, "Menomini Social Life and Ceremonial Bundles," p. 87).

44. Linderman, *Plenty Coups: Chief of the Crows*, pp. 61–65.

45. Densmore, *Teton Sioux Music*, pp. 173–74. The buffalo dream-spirits were not strictly confined to underworld existence, though in most cases they were strongly associated with the earth and the powers of the earth. They might emerge out of a buffalo wallow or appear mysteriously before the unsuspecting traveler. Some accounts have them emerging out of the water, as one did to the Cheyenne Whistling Elk (George B. Grinnell, *The Cheyenne Indians: Their History and Ways of Life*, 1:196).

46. DeMallie, *The Sixth Grandfather: Black Elk's Teachings Given to John G. Neihardt*, pp. 114ff.

47. The idea of "passivity" is not an exclusive feature of the visionary encounter. Frequently, the dreamer or visionary must make various choices or act in an aggressive or dynamic fashion to achieve the visionary goal. In this case, Black Elk must, later in the vision, lead a fight against the blue man who emerges from the Missouri, whom he defeats (DeMallie, *The Sixth Grandfather: Black Elk's Teachings Given to John G. Neihardt*, pp. 121–22).

48. My thanks to Ray DeMallie for a number of enlightening conversations on this topic. His initial observation that kinship relations were perhaps the most apt description for the relationship between the dreamer and his power has certainly been supported by the dream ethnography. The kinship bond functions to establish qualities of intimacy and relatedness that integrate the dream-spirit into a meaningful social context.

49. For other Plains Indian examples see Elsie C. Parsons, *Kiowa Tales*, p. 117; Alice Fletcher, *The Hako: A Pawnee Ceremony*, p. 122; Clark Wissler, "Some Dakota Myths," p. 204, and "Some Protective Designs of the Dakota," p. 23; Royal Hassrick, *The Sioux: Life and Customs of a Warrior Society*, pp. 232ff. For the Woodlands, see Paul Radin, "The Winnebago Tribe," pp. 275 and 279; for the Northwest Coast Indians, see John R. Swanton, "Social Condition, Beliefs and Linguistic Relationship of the Tlingit Indians," p. 452.

50. Linderman, *Plenty Coups: Chief of the Crows*, p. 39.

51. Wissler, "Ceremonial Bundles of the Blackfoot Indians," p. 76.

52. Gideon H. Pond, "Dakota Superstitions," p. 46; James W. Lynd, "The Religion of the Dakotas," pp. 166–67.

53. Densmore, *Teton Sioux Music*, p. 251. For a similar vision among the Osage, see Francis La Flesche, *A Dictionary of the Osage Language*, p. 194; among the Oto, see Whitman, *The Oto*, p. 93.

54. Mandelbaum, "The Plains Cree," p. 313.

55. Schultz, *Friends of My Life as an Indian*, pp. 170–76.

56. Schultz, *Friends of My Life as an Indian*, p. 182.

57. Wissler, "Ceremonial Bundles of the Blackfoot Indians," p. 73; Alfred L. Kroeber, *The Arapaho*, p. 427.

58. Alice Fletcher, "The Elk Mystery or Festival: Ogallalla Sioux," p. 281; Nancy O. Lurie, "Winnebago Berdache," p. 708.

59. Alfred Bowers, *Hidatsa Social and Ceremonial Organization*, p. 326.

60. Fletcher and La Flesche, The Omaha Tribe, p. 132.

61. Wildschut, *Crow Indian Medicine Bundles*, pp. 44–45.

62. Linderman, *Pretty Shield: Medicine Woman of the Crow*, pp. 215–17.

63. John R. Murie and Douglas R. Parks, *Ceremonies of the Pawnee*, p. 115; see also pp. 186, 190, 193.

64. Murie and Parks, *Ceremonies of the Pawnee*, p. 199.

65. Robert H. Lowie, "The Religion of the Crow Indians," pp. 330–31.

66. Wilson D. Wallis, "The Canadian Dakota," p. 81.

67. Clark Wissler, "Societies and Ceremonial Associations in the Oglala Division of the Teton-Dakota," p. 83; Wallis, "The Canadian Dakota," p. 82.

68. Grinnell, *The Cheyenne Indians: Their History and Ways of Life*, 2:85.

69. This happened to the young Black-Elk; see DeMallie, *The Sixth Grandfather: Black Elk's Teachings Given to John G. Neihardt*, pp. 213–14.

70. Densmore, *Teton Sioux Music*, p. 159.

71. Dorsey, *A Study of Siouan Cults*, p. 392.

72. Densmore, *Teton Sioux Music*, pp. 160–64.

73. Clark Wissler, "Some Protective Designs of the Dakota"; James R. Walker, *Lakota Belief and Ritual*, pp. 101 and 138–39.

74. Vestal, Warpath: *The True Story of the Fighting Sioux Told in a Biography of Chief White Bull*, pp. 12–15.

Chapter 3. Space, Time, and Transformation

1. Raymond DeMallie, *The Sixth Grandfather: Black Elk's Teachings Given to John G. Neihardt*, p. 114.

2. Thomas E. Mails, *Fools Crow*, pp. 154–55.

3. For more about color symbolism see James O. Dorsey, *A Study of Siouan Cults*, passim. The order of frequency in the ethnographic materials used for this work is as follows: white (223), black (183), red (129), blue (42), yellow (39), green (17).

4. Marla Powers, *Oglala Women: Myth, Ritual, and Reality*, p. 191.

5. The typical Cartesian description of the "normative" topology of space-time (see A. P. Dubrov and V. N. Pushkin, *Parapsychology and Contemporary Science*, p. 158) needs to be prefaced by the observation that this is a pre-quantum, basically Newtonian description that has deep philosophical roots in the late medieval alienation of man from nature. Dorothy Eggan, "Hopi Dreams in Cultural Perspective," pp. 250–53, notes the Hopi response to the Cartesian world of space-time in relation to the Hopis' structure of time as a multidirectional moral influence.

6. Douglass Price-Williams, "The Waking Dream in Ethnographic Perspective," p. 259.

7. Frank B. Linderman, *Plenty Coups: Chief of the Crows*, pp. 300–301.

8. Robert H. Lowie, "The Assiniboine," p. 48.

9. Linderman, *Plenty Coups: Chief of the Crows*, p. 63.

10. DeMallie, *The Sixth Grandfather: Black Elk's Teachings Given to John G. Neihardt*, p. 215.

11. James W. Schultz and J. L. Donaldson, *The Sun God's Children*, pp. 177–78.

12. John R. Murie and Douglas Parks, *Ceremonies of the Pawnee*, p. 107.

13. Deward E. Walker, "Nez Perce Sorcery," p. 69; Clark Wissler, "Societies and Ceremonial Associations in the Oglala Division of the Teton-Dakota," p. 81; R. F. Fortune, *Omaha Secret Societies*.

14. Alfred W. Bowers, *Mandan Social and Ceremonial Organization*, p. 315.

15. George B. Grinnell, *The Cheyenne Indians: Their History and Ways of Life*, 2:128–29.

16. David G. Mandelbaum, "The Plains Cree," p. 261.

17. A. Irving Hallowell, in "The Role of Dreams in Ojibwa Culture," has written most perceptively on this subject and demonstrates a penetrating understanding of the Woodlands point of view. Concerning the Ojibwa, he writes in a way reminiscent of many other Native American dreaming traditions; see "Ojibwa Ontology, Behavior, and World View," p. 165:

> Dream experiences function integrally with other recalled memory images in so far as these, too, enter the field of self-awareness. When we think autobiographically we only include events that have occurred when awake; the Ojibwa include remembering events that have occurred in dreams. And, far from being of subordinate importance, such experiences are for them often *of more vital importance* than the events of daily waking life. [My emphasis.]

18. I refer here largely to the general character of the dreaming ethnography and to the approach of many cultural analysts outside the area of religious studies. Rudolf Otto, *The Idea of the Holy*, pp. 143ff., has certainly spoken to the issue of the "inmost core" of religious experience as fundamental to all religious discourse, but he has differentiated the holy as something quite distinct from its manifestations and as fundamentally incomprehensible and "Other." Mircea Eliade, *Patterns in Comparative Religion*, p. 367, has discussed the concept of the manifestation of the sacred as a "hierophany" insofar as a manifestation sanctifies the space and time in which it occurs. His definitions, however, are static and categorical and fail to describe the richness of visionary experience (as a mediating, agent-centered activity) beyond the dialectic tension he posits between myth and history, a tension reflective of European philosophical traditions.

19. Frances Densmore, *Teton Sioux Music*, p. 214.

20. James R. Walker, *Lakota Myth*, passim.

21. Densmore, *Teton Sioux Music*, pp. 160–64.

22. Edward Curtis, *The North American Indian*, 5:19; see also Bowers, *Mandan Social and Ceremonial Organization*, p. 335.

23. Dorsey, *A Study of Siouan Cults*, p. 433; Edward Goodbird, *Goodbird the Indian: His Story Told to G. L. Wilson*, pp. 21–22; Paul Radin, "The

Winnebago tribe," p. 286; John Fire and Richard Erdoes, *Lame Deer: Seeker of Visions*, pp. 155–56.

24. George Sword's *tobtob kin* arrangement of the mythic beings of the Lakota worldview (James R. Walker, *Lakota Belief and Ritual*, pp. 98–99) is not confirmed by other ethnographic sources and represents the unique synthesis (definitely hierarchical) that expressed his own view, or possibly the secret oral tradition of a select few Lakota shamans. Furthermore, there were secret societies and shamanistic traditions that were not recorded and in which greater systemization may have occurred.

25. Alice Fletcher and Francis La Flesche, pp. 597–99.

26. The influence of Christianity has made a tremendous impact on the conceptualization of the "sacred" among many Plains peoples, but the actual ethnography of dreams shows very little of this impact. While many have come to equate the "mysterious presence" with the Judeo-Christian God, the entire theology of Western civilization is remarkably absent in actual dream experience. Nevertheless, there is a degree of Christian symbolism and syncreticism in the texts that has not been used in this work. The problem of prophetic movements and Christian influences deserves a separate work. See, for example, Mandelbaum, "The Plains Cree," p. 256; Alred Bowers, *Hidatsa Social and Ceremonial Organization*, p. 311; Goodbird, *Goodbird the Indian: His Story Told to G. L. Wilson*, p. 28; and William Fenton, *Parker on the Iroquois*, pp. 24ff.

27. Fletcher and La Flesche, *The Omaha Tribe*, p. 598.

28. A. Irving Hallowell, "Ojibwa Ontology, Behavior, and World View," p. 163.

29. See Lee Irwin, "Cherokee Healing: Myth, Dreams and Medicine," for a more thorough discussion.

30. Curtis, *The North American Indian*, 3:188.

31. Fletcher and La Flesche, *The Omaha Tribe*, p. 583; Dorsey, *A Study of Siouan Cults*, p. 394; Wilson D. Wallis, "The Canadian Dakota," pp. 94–101.

32. A. Irving Hallowell, "Some Empirical Aspects of Northern Salteaux Religion," p. 399.

33. Hallowell's translation of *ogima* as "chief, superior person" reflects his differentiation between the dreamer and the dream-spirit as a social-political distinction (chief) and as a hierarchic difference (superior person). From the visionary point of view, however, the *ogima* is a uniquely empowered "sacred" being. Success in "secular" leadership (a Western category) was inevitably attributed to assistance or guidance by dream-spirits or specially empowered beings. The surplus of power inherent in the visionary realm was always concieved of as issuing through the dream-spirits, who were regarded reverently for their ability to transmit that mysterious power. The degree of difference is relative but fundamentally part of a religious way of thinking that recognized the "more-than-human" quality of the spirits.

34. There are innumerable examples of this kind of identity with the dream-spirit. Clark Wissler, "Ceremonial Bundles of the Blackfoot Indians," p. 80, records it among the Blackfoot. Alfred L. Kroeber, *The Arapaho*, p. 421, finds it among the Arapaho. John M. Cooper, *The Gros Ventres of Montana: Religion and Ritual*, p. 284, writes: "In many cases power objects were swallowed by the power-recipient when first given to him and were so retained within his body until he forfeited his power through breach of

code or instruction or until just before his death. These objects would come out of his body, usually his mouth." The Sioux holy man Fools Crow commented that he had seven small stones in his body that gave him prophetic and other kinds of knowledge; see Thomas E. Mails, *Fools Crow*, p. 183.

35. Kroeber, *The Arapaho*, p. 433.

36. Alanson Skinner, "Societies of the Iowa, Kansa, and Ponca Indians," p. 707.

37. The possible Christian influence in this experience in no way detracts from the phenomenological description. On the other hand, the use of the term "father" (or "grandfather") is very consistent with the normative kinship metaphors used to symbolize traditional ideas about the "highest" power.

38. Robert H. Lowie, "The Northern Shoshone," p. 225.

Chapter 4. Isolation and Suffering

1. Very little attention has been paid to the spontaneous nature of the vision experience, even though the Plains Indian ethnography contains numerous accounts of such dreams and visions. This is a consequence of the early anthropological interest in actual structures of Native American social and cultural life. Also, ethnographers have tended to ignore women's spontaneous vision experiences as less important than men's structured quests. The unstructured, spontaneous vision, however, is intimately tied to a natural ability and inclination for visionary experience frequently demonstrated by strongly imagistic cultures and reflective of a recognized acquisition of power. This tendency, when coupled with the normal frequency of dreaming in a cultural context that does not sharply distinguish between waking and dreaming, provides a tentative theoretical basis for the arising of spontaneous visions; see David F. Marks, "Imagery Paradigms and Methodology," p. 21; and Ellen Basso, "The Implications of a Progressive Theory of Dreaming," p. 87.

2. Ernest Wallace and E. Adamson Hoebel, *The Comanches: Lords of the Southern Plains*, p. 159, record that certain types of knowledge gained in visionary experience among the Comanche were a "life-and-death secret." Alice Fletcher and Francis La Flesche, The Omaha Tribe, p. 459, distinguish between two types of Omaha visionary societies: social and secret. John M. Cooper, *The Gros Ventres of Montana: Religion and Ritual*, p. 409, notes the general tendency to keep all dreams secret among the Gros Ventre. Edward Curtis, *The North American Indian*, 3:133, gives the following example of Assiniboine "witchcraft":

> This power was obtained through dreams, which must be kept secret, and whose commands it was essential to obey implicitly. The *Waéchonsa* in his conjuration made an image of birchbark (or rawhide), punched four holes through the vital parts, and buried it in a freshly raised mound on a hilltop. These things were of course done secretly.

3. Cooper, *The Gros Ventres of Montana: Religion and Ritual*, pp. 273–74.

4. Cooper, *The Gros Ventres of Montana: Religion and Ritual*, p. 283.

5. Alfred Bowers, *Mandan Social and Ceremonial Organization*, p. 174.

6. Robert H. Lowie, "The Religion of the Crow Indians," p. 332.

7. Morris E. Opler, *Apache Odyssey: A Journey between Two Worlds*, p. 201.
8. Alfred L. Kroeber, *The Arapaho*, p. 434.
9. Robert H. Lowie, "The Assiniboine," p. 47.
10. James W. Schultz, *Friends of My Life as an Indian*, pp. 170–76.
11. George B. Grinnell, *The Cheyenne Indians: Their History and Ways of Life*, 2:92–93.
12. Wallace and Hoebel, *The Comanches: Lords of the Southern Plains*, p. 168.
13. Wilbur S. Nye, *Bad Medicine and Good: Tales of the Kiowas*, p. 47.
14. Alanson Skinner, "Societies of the Iowa, Kansa, and Ponca Indians," p. 784.
15. John R. Murie and Douglas R. Parks, *Ceremonies of the Pawnee*, pp. 156–57 and 319.
16. James R. Walker, *Lakota Belief and Ritual*, p. 79.
17. For the Hidatsa, see Alfred W. Bowers, *Hidatsa Social and Ceremonial Organization*, pp. 61 and 73; for the Mandan, see Bowers, *Mandan Social and Ceremonial Organization*, p. 164. For the Dhegiha, see Alanson Skinner, "Societies of the Iowa, Kansa, and Ponca Indians," p. 769; and William Whitman, *The Oto*, p. 81. For the Comanche, see Wallace and Hoebel, *The Comanches: Lords of the Southern Plains*, p. 157. A similar structure for young males and females existed among the Woodlands peoples. Jennifer S. Brown and Robert Brightman, *The Orders of the Dreamed: George Nelson on Cree and Northern Ojibwa Religion and Myth, 1823*, p. 140, note the following for the Woodlands Cree:

> The typical age of the faster showed some some regional variations, ranging from the age of ten, through fourteen to sixteen. Girls sometimes underwent an isolated fast as well. More typically, however, they acquired spirit guardians during their first menstrual isolation or during dreams or trances not purposely induced.

18. Fletcher and La Flesche, *The Omaha Tribe*, p. 128.
19. Wallace and Hoebel, *The Comanches: Lords of the Southern Plains*, p. 156.
20. Robert H. Lowie, *The Crow Indians*, p. 248; Bowers, *Hidatsa Social and Ceremonial Organization*, p. 310; Hoebel, *The Cheyennes: Indians of the Great Plains*, p. 94.
21. Clark Wissler, "Ceremonial Bundles of the Blackfoot Indians," p. 104.
22. Frances Densmore, *Chippewa Customs*, p. 79.
23. For a discussion of liminality, see Victor Turner, *The Ritual Process: Structure and Anti-Structure*, passim.
24. Robert H. Lowie, "The Tobacco Society of the Crow Indians," p. 182.
25. Francis La Flesche, "Death and Funeral Customs Among the Omahas," p. 5.
26. Cooper, *The Gros Ventres of Montana: Religion and Ritual*, p. 293.
27. Bowers, *Mandan Social and Ceremonial Organization*, p. 175.
28. Maurice Boyd, *Kiowa Voices: Myths, Legends and Folktales*, vol. 2, pp. 127–29.
29. Schultz, *Friends of My Life as an Indian*, pp. 170–76.
30. Schultz, *Friends of My Life as an Indian*, p. 182.

31. Hoebel, *The Cheyennes: Indians of the Great Plains*, p. 91; Skinner, "Societies of the Iowa, Kansa, and Ponca Indians," p. 784.

32. Cooper, *The Gros Ventres of Montana: Religion and Ritual*, p. 323.

33. Willard Z. Park, *Shamanism in Western North America: A Study of Cultural Relations*, p. 110.

34. Morris E. Opler, *Apache Odyssey: A Journey between Two Worlds*, p. 202.

35. Robert H. Lowie, "Notes on Shoshonean Ethnography," pp. 291–96.

36. Elsie C. Parsons, *Kiowa Tales*, p. xix.

37. DeMallie, *The Sixth Grandfather: Black Elk's Teachings Given to John G. Neihardt*, pp. 109–11.

38. Clark Wissler, "Some Dakota Myths," pp. 204–207.

39. Alanson Skinner, "Societies of the Iowa, Kansa, and Ponca Indians," p. 710.

40. Whitman, *The Oto*, p. 87. For other examples of childhood visions, see Densmore, *Teton Sioux Music*, p. 173; Lowie, "The Assiniboine," p. 48; Mandelbaum, "The Plains Cree," pp. 313–14; and Parsons, *Kiowa Tales*, p. 115.

41. Lowie, "The Religion of the Crow Indians," pp. 330–31.

42. Similar examples can be found among the Blackfoot, such as one in which an old man and his son were trapped by a severe winter storm and buried in a hastily constructed shelter for over four days. A vision experience of the father's resulted in his receiving the Winter Tipi from the chief of the winter people, which protected him from becoming cold (Clark Wissler, "Ceremonial Bundles of the Blackfoot Indians," pp. 234–35).

43. Wilbur S. Nye, *Bad Medicine and Good: Tales of the Kiowas*, p. 47.

44. Frank B. Linderman, *Pretty Shield: Medicine Woman of the Crow*, p. 120. An interesting example of a woman's founding a predominantly male society, one of crucial importance to communal leadership, is that of Short Woman, whose vision experience was responsible for the founding of the Cheyenne tribal council (see E. Adamson Hoebel, *The Cheyennes: Indians of the Great Plains*, p. 91).

45. George B. Grinnell, "The Cheyenne Medicine Lodge," p. 250.

46. Grinnell, *The Cheyenne Indians: Their History and Ways of Life*, 2:92–93.

47. The concept of a "free-soul" as distinct from the body is widespread throughout native North America and has been extensively written about in Ake Hultkrantz, *Conceptions of the Soul among North American Indians*. For further discussion of the subject, see Lee Irwin, "Myth, Language and Ontology Among the Huron."

48. Curtis, *The North American Indian*, 4:56–57.

49. DeMallie, *The Sixth Grandfather: Black Elk's Teachings Given to John G. Neihardt*, p. 111.

50. This entire area needs to be more fully explored and developed. The whole circumstance of emotional expression and its intensity needs to be considered from the point of view of religious beliefs, particularly in relation to cathartic rites. The psychological and spiritual patterns of denial in contemporary culture have been explored by such writers as Elizabeth Kübler-Ross, Stanislav Grof, Joan Halifax, and Michael Grosso.

51. La Flesche, *A Dictionary of the Osage Language*, pp. 41–42.

52. Cooper, *The Gros Ventres of Montana: Religion and Ritual*, p. 293.

53. Lowie, "The Religion of the Crow Indians," p. 332.

54. Linderman, *Pretty Shield: Medicine Woman of the Crow*, p. 166.

55. Wildschut, *Crow Indian Medicine Bundles*, p. 139.

56. The use of dreams as a medium of interpretation for earlier visions will be explored more fully in a later work. For other examples of spontaneous male mourning visions, see for the Blackfoot, Wissler, "Ceremonial Bundles of the Blackfoot Indians," pp. 84–85, and for the Oto, Whitman, *The Oto*, p. 93.

57. Stanley Vestal, *Warpath: The True Story of the Fighting Sioux Told in a Biography of Chief White Bull*, p. 250.

Chapter 5. Rites and Preparations

1. James R. Walker, *Lakota Belief and Ritual*, p. 79.

2. Alfred Bowers, *Hidatsa Social and Ceremonial Organization*, p. 59.

3. Willard Z. Park, "Paviotso Shamanism," p. 99.

4. Edgar E. Siskin, *Washo Shamans and Peyotists*, p. 73.

5. Robert H. Lowie, "The Northern Shoshone," p. 224; "Notes on Shoshonean Ehnography," p. 291.

6. Elsie C. Parsons, *Kiowa Tales*, p. xix.

7. Robert H. Lowie, "The Religion of the Crow Indians," p. 232.

8. John M. Cooper, *The Gros Ventres of Montana: Religion and Ritual*, p. 293.

9. Alfred Bowers, *Mandan Social and Ceremonial Organization*, p. 165; *Hidatsa Social and Ceremonical Organization*, p. 285.

10. George B. Grinnell, *The Cheyenne Indians: Their History and Ways of Life*, 1:80–81. Many accounts are given of those who fasted and received no vision: see Cooper, *The Gros Ventres of Montana: Religion and Ritual*, p. 296; Bowers, *Mandan Social and Ceremonial Organization*, p. 165; Walker, *Lakota Belief and Ritual*, p. 86.

11. John R. Murie and Douglas R. Parks, *Ceremonies of the Pawnee*, p. 364; J. Gilbert McAllister, "Dávéko: Kiowa-Apache Medicine Man," p. 36; David G. Mandelbaum, "The Plains Cree," p. 252.

12. Alice Fletcher and Francis La Flesche, *The Omaha Tribe*, pp. 129–31; R. F. Fortune, *Omaha Secret Societies*, p. 40.

13. William Whitman, *The Oto*, p. 82.

14. Alanson Skinner, "Societies of the Iowa, Kansa, and Ponca Indians," p. 769.

15. John R. Murie and Douglas R. Parks, *Ceremonies of the Pawnee*, p. 364.

16. Bowers, *Hidatsa Social and Ceremonial Organization*, p. 106.

17. Bowers, *Hidatsa Social and Ceremonial Organization*, p. 287.

18. David E. Jones, *Sanapia: Comanche Medicine Woman*, p. 31.

19. Walker, *Lakota Belief and Ritual*, p. 130.

20. Lowie, "The Religion of the Crow Indians," p. 326; Cooper, *The Gros Ventres of Montana: Religion and Ritual*, p. 277.

21. Walker, *Lakota Belief and Ritual*, p. 85.

22. For more about the religious importance of the pipe, see Jordan Paper, *Offering Smoke: The Sacred Pipe and Native American Religion*.

23. Ake Hultkrantz, *Conceptions of the Soul among North American Indians*, p. 52.

24. Fletcher and La Flesche, *The Omaha Tribe*, p. 130. The subject of prayer and its related forms and meanings is one that needs to be further

explored, particularly in terms of its religious contents and associated symbolism in both material culture and ritual action. For an important contribution to the concept of the metalinguistic structure of prayer and sacred language in Native American religion, see Sam Gill, *Sacred Words: A Study of Navajo Religion and Prayer*; William Powers, *Sacred Language: The Nature of Supernatural Discourse in Lakota*; and Joseph Epps Brown, "Evoking the Sacred through Language, Metalanguage and the 'Arts'."

25. Cooper, *The Gros Ventres of Montana: Religion and Ritual*, p. 280.

26. Wilbur S. Nye, *Bad Medicine and Good: Tales of the Kiowas*, p. 257; Murie and Parks, *Ceremonies of the Pawnee*, p. 160.

27. Ernest Wallace and E. Adamson Hoebel, *The Comanches: Lords of the Southern Plains*, p. 157; Bella Weitzner, "Notes on the Hidatsa Indians Based on Data Recorded by the Late Gilbert L. Wilson," p. 315.

28. Lowie, "Notes on Shoshonean Ethnography," p. 296.

29. Mandelbaum, "The Plains Cree," p. 252.

30. Cooper, *The Gros Ventres of Montana: Religion and Ritual*, pp. 27–75.

31. A notable exception to the springtime fasting rites was the Hidatsa and Mandan pattern of fasting for a vision during the winter buffalo-calling rites; Bowers, *Hidatsa Social and Ceremonial Organization*, pp. 59–60.

32. For the Sioux, see Walker, *Lakota Belief and Ritual*, p. 151; for the Blackfoot, Clark Wissler, "Ceremonial Bundles of the Blackfoot Indians," p. 104; and for the Comanche, Wallace and Hoebel, *The Comanches: Lords of the Southern Plains*, p. 157. A point of interest is that a great deal of the ethnography on dreams and visions does not explicitly mention the exact role of the shaman in the preparation of the visionary. The shaman's role appears far more significant in the interpretation of visions than in the preparation of the candidate. This may be the consequence of a lacuna in the general ethnography. Ritual preparation of the faster specifically by a shaman or medicine man is not highly documented in the pre–World War II materials other than for those communities mentioned above.

33. Wallace and Hoebel, *The Comanches: Lords of the Southern Plains*, p. 157.

34. Walker, *Lakota Belief and Ritual*, p. 85.

35. Cooper, *The Gros Ventres of Montana: Religion and Ritual*, p. 280.

36. Robert H. Lowie, "The Tobacco Society of the Crow Indians," p. 190.

37. David Rodnick, "An Assiniboine Horse-Raiding Expedition," p. 612; Wissler, "Ceremonial Bundles of the Blackfoot Indians," p. 105; Mandelbaum, "The Plains Cree," p. 252; John Fire and Richard Erdoes, *Lame Deer: Seeker of Visions*, p. 14.

38. Joseph Epps Brown, *The Sacred Pipe: Black Elk's Account of the Seven Rites of the Oglala Sioux*, p. 59.

39. George Horse Capture, *The Seven Visions of Bull Lodge*, pp. 30ff.

40. Bowers, *Mandan Social and Ceremonial Organization*, p. 167.

41. Lowie, "The Religion of the Crow Indians," p. 332.

42. The so-called "torture" feature of Native American vision practice has been discussed in Ruth Benedict's classic article, "The Vision in Plains Culture." As she notes, it seems to have been a practice highly associated with the northern Plains people. See also Lowie, "The Religion of the Crow Indians," p. 332; Horse Capture, *The Seven Visions of Bull Lodge*, p. 35; and Bowers, *Hidatsa Social and Ceremonial Organization*, p. 135. I have met and

talked with a number of persons who have the scars of Sun Dance piercing, which are regarded as honor marks, similar to war wounds, and as indicating seriousness of commitment in religious participation.

43. Wissler, "Ceremonial Bundles of the Blackfoot Indians," p. 104.

44. Brown, *The Sacred Pipe: Black Elk's Account of the Seven Rites of the Oglala Sioux*, p. 58.

45. Elsie C. Parsons, *Kiowa Tales*, p. 114.

46. Bowers, *Hidatsa Social and Ceremonial Organization*, p. 73.

47. Fletcher and La Flesche, *The Omaha Tribe*, p. 131.

48. See Frank B. Linderman, *Plenty Coups: Chief of the Crows*, p. 36; Alred L. Kroeber, *The Arapaho*, p. 419; John Cooper, *The Gros Ventres of Montana: Religion and Ritual*, p. 4; and Edward Curtis, *The North American Indian*, 6:123.

49. Walker, *Lakota Belief and Ritual*, p. 85.

50. For example, see Wallace and Hoebel, *The Comanches: Lords of the Southern Plains*, p. 157.

51. Fletcher and La Flesche, *The Omaha Tribe*, p. 129.

52. The technique of free association is a good example of this condition. Other work done in meditative disciplines and altered states of consciousness has demonstrated the necessity of clearing the mind of its normal, rational preoccupations while simultaneously focusing attention. See Stanley Krippner and L. George, "PSI Phenomena as Related to Altered States of Consciousness," p. 349; Charles T. Tart, "The World Simulation Process in Waking and Dreaming: A Systems Analysis of Structure," p. 149.

53. Walker, *Lakota Belief and Ritual*, p. 133.

54. Densmore, *Teton Sioux Music*, p. 157.

55. Cooper, *The Gros Ventres of Montana: Religion and Ritual*, p. 280.

56. Wissler, "Ceremonial Bundles of the Blackfoot Indians," p. 104.

57. Walker, *Lakota Belief and Ritual*, p. 85; Bowers, *Hidatsa Social and Ceremonial Organization*, p. 59.

58. Cooper, *The Gros Ventres of Montana: Religion and Ritual*, p. 280.

59. Raymond DeMallie and Douglas Parks, *Sioux Indian Religion: Tradition and Innovation*, p. 38.

60. Brown, *The Sacred Pipe: Black Elk's Account of the Seven Rites of the Oglala Sioux*, p. 58.

61. Walker, *Lakota Belief and Ritual*, p. 152.

62. For a more contemporary example, see William Powers, *Oglala Religion*, pp. 138–39.

63. John Stands in Timber and Margot Liberty, *Cheyenne Memories*, p. 90.

64. Cooper, *The Gros Ventres of Montana: Religion and Ritual*, p. 281.

Chapter 6. The Mystery of Presence

1. Historical origins of the vision quest lie outside the range of this analysis and are highly complex and difficult, if not impossible, to assemble. Various ritual activities, such as the Sun Dance, had definite associations with visionary experience; general ceremonial patterns would have influenced the structure of the vision quest, as would have various visionary societies. Furthermore, shamanistic individuals would also have known how to induce vision experiences and would have had an oral tradition as

well as recognized communal paradigms to work with in the structuring of any fasting rites. Finally, the spontaneous vision is pervasive in the ethnography. In essence, the history of the vision is intrinsic to the history of dreaming in human development.

2. By autopoiesis, or "self-making"—a term originally coined by Erich Jantsch (see John P. Briggs and David F. Peat, *Looking Glass Universe: The Emerging Science of Wholeness*, p. 180)—is meant any structural organization that maintains an equilibrium through the constant, dynamic input of energy and the continual consumption of that energy. In social terms this would refer to continued human effort and activity that is constantly "in process," maintaining existing social structures, but in a restrictive manner according to shared social norms and beliefs. It is the propagation and "self-making" of any and all social environments that have become established through repetitive actions. That these structures require continuous input and effort to be maintained is a function of resisting a tendency toward inertia and collapse. Emergent structures, on the other hand, have a low degree of autopoiesis and generally reflect less well-defined structural organization, thereby demanding higher degrees of energy and action, which may have a catalytic effect on normative structures. See Briggs and Peat, *Looking Glass Universe: The Emerging Science of Wholeness*, pp. 153–209.

3. Only with the coming of the Euro-Americans and their oppressive cultural domination did the visionary contents become more radically apocalyptic, culminating in the widespread Ghost Dance phenomenon—an emergent structure that failed to catalyze the necessary social transformations. This is a theme I hope to pursue in a future work.

4. The qualitative flow of visionary experience has been recognized as a constant feature of dreams in contemporary research. It was first noted by Allan Rechtschaffen, "The Single-Mindedness and Isolation of Dreams," in which he discusses the way in which dreams tend to reflect a low degree of awareness beyond the immediate dream context and to have a thematically similar content without the intrusion of alternative images and thoughts. Research in lucid dreaming has shown, however, that self-conscious awareness can clearly exist while the dream is in process, and this fact is recorded in the Native American ethnography. See also Roger T. Broughton, "Human Consciousness and Sleep/Waking Rhythms," p. 467; H. Hunt, "Some Relations between the Cognitive Psychology of Dreams and Dream Phenomenology," p. 217; and on lucidity, see Steven LeBerge, *Lucid Dreaming*. Akhter Ahsen, "Prolucid Dreaming: A Content Analysis Approach to Dreams," p. 3, discusses the threshold concept as a normal aspect of the indeterminate quality of certain kinds of experience (vivid imagining, daydreams, hypnogogia, etc.) that accompanies the conscious intent to induce such experience.

5. James R. Walker, *Lakota Belief and Ritual*, p. 79.

6. Frances Densmore, *Teton Sioux Music*, p. 184.

7. John M. Cooper, *The Gros Ventres of Montana: Religion and Ritual*, p. 278.

8. A few examples of the waking-sleeping distinction are mentioned as follows: the Gros Ventre and the Arapaho agree that the vision could occur both in sleep and while awake, with the most frequent condition being sleep (Alfred L. Kroeber, "Ethnology of the Gros Ventre," p. 222; Cooper,

The Gros Ventres of Montana: Religion and Ritual, p. 281). The Hidatsa called the waking vision "seeing with their own eyes" (Alfred Bowers, *Hidatsa Social and Ceremonial Organization*, p. 286). Among the Oto (William Whitman, *The Oto*, p. 85), the vision was the experience by which one received power, in contrast to the non–power-bestowing dream. Yet waking and sleeping, as conditions for either, are not distinguished. Ernest Wallace and E. Adamson Hoebel, *The Comanches: Lords of the Southern Plains*, p. 155, following Leslie Spier's "Klamath Ethnography," p. 253, make the distinction between dreams and visions synonymous with sleeping and waking, a categorization that is completely at odds with the ethnographic record. Most vision narratives never mention the sleeping or waking condition of the visionary—only a description of what was seen.

9. Clark Wissler, "Ceremonial Bundles of the Blackfoot Indians," p. 104.

10. Cooper, *The Gros Ventres of Montana: Religion and Ritual*, pp. 278–79.

11. Walker, *Lakota Belief and Ritual*, p. 151. For a Pawnee example, see John R. Murie and Douglas R. Parks, *Ceremonies of the Pawnee*, p. 364. Anyone who has had a frightening dream and awakes during it and attends to his or her emotional condition may easily realize how disturbing such an experience could be in a waking state far from friends and family.

12. Alfred L. Kroeber, *The Arapaho*, p. 433; Cooper, *The Gros Ventres of Montana: Religion and Ritual*, p. 7; Frances Densmore, *Teton Sioux Music*, p. 185.

13. Wissler, "Ceremonial Bundles of the Blackfoot Indians," p. 79.

14. Lowie, "The Assiniboine," p. 48.

15. George Horse Capture, *The Seven Visions of Bull Lodge*, p. 52.

16. Walker, *Lakota Belief and Ritual*, p. 84.

17. Raymond DeMallie, *The Sixth Grandfather: Black Elk's Teachings Given to John G. Neihardt*, p. 114.

18. David G. Mandelbaum, "The Plains Cree," p. 313.

19. Peter Nabokov, *Two Leggings: The Making of a Crow Warrior*, pp. 146–48.

20. J. Gilbert McAllister, "Dävéko: Kiowa-Apache Medicine Man," pp. 36–37.

21. Cooper, *The Gros Ventres of Montana: Religion and Ritual*, p. 159; Densmore, *Teton Sioux Music*, p. 181.

22. David E. Jones, *Sanapia: Comanche Medicine Woman*, p. 31; Willard Z. Park, *Shamanism in Western North America: A Study of Cultural Relations*, p. 38; Morris E. Opler and William E. Bittle, "The Death Practices and Eschatology of the Kiowa-Apache," p. 391.

23. Alice Fletcher and Francis La Flesche, *The Omaha Tribe*, p. 489.

24. R. F. Fortune, *Omaha Secret Societies*, p. 42.

25. Fortune, *Omaha Secret Societies*, p. 78.

26. John Fire and Richard Erdoes, *Lame Deer: Seeker of Visions*, p. 65.

27. This does not mean that dreams and visions were never questioned or doubted. Sometimes they were, particularly if the vision was not clearly seen or if something unrecognizable appeared to the visionary. But there is a very distinctive, predominant collection of visionary experiences in the existing ethnography that clearly shows an unquestioning belief in the reality of the experience.

28. Fire and Erdoes, *Lame Deer: Seeker of Visions*, p. 135.

29. Fire and Erdoes, *Lame Deer: Seeker of Visions*, pp. 14–15.

30. Fire and Erdoes, *Lame Deer: Seeker of Visions*, p. 16.

31. An example of the sensate nature of power was explained to me by the Absarokee medicine man Tom Yellowtail. He told me that when he received his power from the Shoshone shaman John T., he felt the power go into his body while John T. stood behind him and blew through his fist onto Yellowtail's back. He clearly expressed that he could feel the power in his body after the transfer.

32. David E. Jones, *Sanapia: Comanche Medicine Woman*, p. 40.

33. Peter Nabokov, *Two Leggings: The Making of a Crow Warrior*, p. 51.

34. Frank Linderman, *Plenty Coups: Chief of the Crows*, p. 37.

35. George B. Grinnell, *The Cheyenne Indians: Their History and Ways of Life*, 2:92.

36. Clark Wissler, "Some Dakota Myths," p. 204; Densmore, *Chippewa Customs*, p. 84.

37. Alfred L. Kroeber, *The Arapaho*, p. 428.

38. Wissler, "Ceremonial Bundles of the Blackfoot Indians," p. 78. For more about the "free-soul," see Ake Hultkrantz, *Conceptions of the Soul among North American Indians*, passim. Johann G. Kohl, *Kitchi-Gami: Life among the Lake Superior Ojibway*, pp. 205ff. and 238, gives an extensive example of a flying dream and discusses the "free-soul" concept as held by the Ojibwa.

39. Alfred L. Kroeber, *The Arapaho*, p. 421.

40. Alanson Skinner, "Menomini Social Life and Ceremonial Bundles," p. 51.

41. Wilson D. Wallis, "The Canadian Dakota," p. 87.

42. Belief in reincarnation is widespread among peoples outside the Great Plains, according to the ethnographic record. Among the Huron, Chippewa, Winnebago, Kutchin, Kwakiutl, and many other people it is a central tenet of belief. See Elizabeth Tooker, *An Ethnography of the Huron Indians, 1615–1649*, p. 100; Richard Slobodin, "Kutchin Concepts of Reincarnation," p. 69; Paul Radin, "The Winnebago Tribe," pp. 271–75.

43. Fletcher, *The Hako: A Pawnee Ceremony*, pp. 155–56.

44. Cooper, *The Gros Ventres of Montana: Religion and Ritual*, p. 415.

45. For another example of mass vision, consider the following Assiniboine example witnessed by a hunting party under the leadership of White Dog. David Rodnick, "An Assiniboine Horse-Raiding Expedition," p. 613, writes:

> White Dog made preparations to receive a vision.... As soon as two songs were finished, the [buffalo] skull suddenly disappeared and in its place, furiously pawing the snow, stood a huge buffalo bull, which made ready as if to attack the men. Just as quickly the buffalo disappeared and the men saw that the skull was back in its place.

Chapter 7. The Transfer of Power

1. James O. Dorsey, *A Study of Siouan Cults*, p. 367.

2. Alice Fletcher and Francis La Flesche, *The Omaha Tribe*, p. 131.

3. John R. Murie and Douglas R. Parks, *Ceremonies of the Pawnee*, p. 156.

4. For other examples of female visions sanctifying warrior activities,

see Johann G. Kohl, *Kitchi-Gami: Life among the Lake Superior Ojibway*, p. 126; and Oscar Lewis, "Manly-Hearted Women among the North Piegan."

5. Edward Curtis, *The North American Indian*, 6:123.

6. Frank B. Linderman, *Plenty Coups: Chief of the Crows*, pp. 301–302.

7. John R. Murie and Douglas R. Parks, *Ceremonies of the Pawnee*, p. 396.

8. James R. Walker, *Lakota Belief and Ritual*, p. 86.

9. Clark Wissler, "The Whirlwind and the Elk in the Mythology of the Dakotas," p. 265.

10. Charles Brant, *Jim Whitewolf: The Life of a Kiowa-Apache Indian*, p. 111.

11. Frank B. Linderman, *Pretty Shield: Medicine Woman of the Crow*, p. 120.

12. It is interesting to consider the possibility of the reflexive quality of the vision experience. While most vision narratives do not specify whether the visionary was conscious of being in a vision, the dialogue between the visionary and the vision power might be taken as a form of reflexivity insofar as the dream-spirit brings to the forefront the motivations of the dreamer through questioning. This might be a form of socially structured reflexivity by which the dreamer comes to know himself or herself more deeply through the vision encounter. This would be congruent with the general structure of kinship relations, which are meant to facilitate spiritual growth and development. The vision always seems to reveal something intrinsic about the individual to the individual so that he or she may have an enhanced sense of empowerment through the use of new symbolic structures.

13. Jackson S. Lincoln, *The Dream in Primitive Cultures*, p. 97, contends, following Freud, that all dream instruction is based on wish fulfillment and that a substitute father figure cannot be supported. He writes, regarding the purpose that motivated the vision quest:

> The wish of the individual [is] to receive the blessings and favours from the "totem" father or ancestor. Since in some areas these dreams occur at puberty, when the individual must renounce his infantile attitudes toward the parents and face his own cultural milieu as an adult, he instinctively turns to the ancestor or father for guidance, or is compelled to do so by the tribal custom to go out and seek a vision.

While it is true that there is an authoritative or imperative mood in most visionary communications, such a mood is support by a religious worldview grounded in a complex network of authoritative kinship relations. The visionary power can in no way be seen as a "substitute" for that kinship network. Rather, it is an extension of that network into the visionary world. Furthermore, it is clearly evident that dream and vision figures are of both sexes and all ages. Also, many appearances are animal in nature and cannot be conceived of in any way as a "totem," if this refers to communally sanctioned symbolism and ancestral clan organization. An elder male figure may represent any number of kinship relations, and "father" is only one form of such manifestations.

14. Murie and Parks, *Ceremonies of the Pawnee*, p. 298.

15. Wissler, "Ceremonial Bundles of the Blackfoot Indians," p. 104. The Blackfoot belief in the primacy of the dream song over the dream object is a culturally specific belief. As previously discussed, the Gros Ventre, Arapaho,

Absarokee, and other communities believed that the real power was internalized—literally in the body of the visionary. Specific objects related to that power were crucially linked to the individual. The point of Wissler's observation refers to the external object, which was frequently remade or replaced when it became worn, broken, or lost.

16. Murie and Parks, *Ceremonies of the Pawnee*, pp. 351–52.

17. Murie and Parks, *Ceremonies of the Pawnee*, p. 352.

18. The area of Native American song and its religious contents and significance needs a great deal more research and has been dealt with here in a strictly introductory manner. The nature of Plains and Prairie Indian songs and their religious structure and content were originally studied by Frances Densmore in "The Belief of the Indian in a Connection between Song and the Supernatural," *The American Indians and Their Music*, and *Teton Sioux Music*. For a more extensive bibliography on Native American music, see William Clements and Frances Malpezzi, *Native American Folklore, 1879–1979: An Annotated Bibliography*, pp. 28–32 and index. The relationship between song, dance, and religious contents is certainly a fruitful area for future research. Another article deserving close attention is that by George Devereaux, "Dream Learning and Individual Ritual Differences in Mohave Shamanism," regarding the various semantic levels that are compacted into dream "catch-words" out of which the song is constructed. Unfortunately, much of Devereaux's article is prejudiced by his obvious Freudianism. Also, dual-language texts are becoming increasingly available and represent the most desirable sources for future work—e.g., John R. Murie and Douglas R. Parks, *Ceremonies of the Pawnee*, and Douglas Parks, *Traditional Narratives of the Arikara Indians*.

19. The dream song as the epitome of the visionary encounter may represent a unique kind of speech act: a linguistic representation of right-hemispheric activity. Robert G. Ley, "Cerebral Asymmetries, Emotional Experience, and Imagery: Implications for Psychotherapy," p. 58, has described such activity by saying:

> When imagery-laden or emotionally evocative words are used, especially in a creative, non-linear, non-syntactic fashion, the right hemisphere is primed. . . . In short the difference between right hemispheric language and left hemispheric language is like the difference between the language of poetry and economics.

He goes on to mention five distinct characteristics of the right-hemispheric use of language: it is generally figurative, condensed, aphoristic, and allusive, and constituent parts can substitute for or represent complex wholes (*pars pro toto*). See also Michael H. Stone, "Dreams, Free Association, and the Non-dominant Hemisphere: An Integration of Psychoanalytical, Neurophysiological, and Historical Data," p. 257; and Akhter Ahsen, "The New Structuralism: Images in Dramatic Interlock," p. 74.

20. The translation of various indigenous terms into the blanket term "power" appeared in the earliest ethnography and quickly became an anthropological convention. Yet a thorough understanding of the concept would require a major work that would approach the problem from the point of differentiating various types of power, their indigenous linguistic roots, and their socioreligious manifestations with regard to the various ideas implicit to distinct social groups. The concept of power has been

imported into the ethnography of dreams and visions as the most comprehensive term for otherwise difficult or obscure meanings, and it seems to be acceptable to many Anglo-American ethnographers. The concept has been used in a manner similar to that of "family resemblances," as articulated by Ludwig Wittgenstein; the term "power" overlaps with many indigenous ideas but is identical to none. Yet the phenomenology of power remains a challenging area of research that has by no means been fully explored. A full analysis would need to address the question of the types and functions of power, complemented with an understanding of the various semantic and symbolic levels of meaning that were understood by religious specialists in the context of mythic belief, experience, and ritual. Only the briefest introduction to this complex subject is given here. For a preliminary overview of the anthroplogy of power with regard to native North America, see Raymond D. Fogelson and Richard N. Adams, *The Anthropology of Power: Ethnographic Studies From Asia, Oceania, and the New World*. For the Plains Indian area, see Raymond DeMallie and R. H. Lavenda, "Wakan: Plains Siouan Concepts of Power."

21. Patricia Albers and Seymour Parker, "The Plains Vision Experience," p. 208. The social implications of the vision quest are discussed as motivating goal-directed behaviors and acting as a medium for explaining social behavior. Albers and Parker qualify these observations by noting also that such implications of the vision require a fully developed religious worldview to be effective.

22. Alfred L. Kroeber, *The Arapaho*, p. 419.

23. DeMallie and Lavenda, "Wakan: Plains Siouan Concepts of Power."

24. Gene Weltfish, *The Lost Universe: The Way of Life of the Pawnee*, p. 406.

25. Deward E. Walker, "Nez Perce Sorcery," p. 70.

26. Alanson Skinner, "Notes on the Eastern Cree and the Northern Saulteaux," p. 67; Stanley Vestal, *Warpath: The True Story of the Fighting Sioux Told in a Biography of Chief White Bull*, p. 94, n. 3.

27. J. Gilbert McAllister, "Dävéko: Kiowa-Apache Medicine Man," p. 36.

28. Elsie C. Parsons, *Kiowa Tales*, p. 114.

29. Morris E. Opler, *Apache Odyssey: A Journey between Two Worlds*, p. 204. Similar visionary tests of courage and endurance imposed by dream-spirits are recorded for the Pawnee (Murie and Parks, *Ceremonies of the Pawnee*, p. 571) and the Gros Ventre (George Horse Capture, *The Seven Visions of Bull Lodge*, p. 36).

30. William Powers, *Oglala Religion*, p. 138. Such a temptation is probably tied to the Sioux mythology of the black-tailed deer and its mythic correlate, Double-Woman, who sometimes appeared as black-tailed deer who wished to seduce men. This temptation would then be sexual in nature. See Wissler, "Societies and Ceremonial Associations in the Oglala Division of the Teton-Dakota," p. 93.

31. The ambiguity of the vision experience, particularly for the neophyte, is noted by Jennifer S. Brown and Robert Brightman, *The Orders of the Dreamed: George Nelson on Cree and Northern Ojibwa Religion and Myth, 1823*, p. 145, among the Ojibwa. The *pawakan* is the dream-spirit that appears to the visionary:

Although the human-*pawakan* relationship was ideally one of love, respect, and assistance, uncertainty attached to this most central of spiritual relationships as it did to other areas of interaction between human beings and spirits. Some individuals experienced their guardians as unpredictable, demanding, and dangerous. As Nelson also emphasized, the spirits reacted angrily to skepticism about their powers or existence.

32. Kroeber, *The Arapaho*, p. 434.

33. John M. Cooper, *The Gros Ventres of Montana: Religion and Ritual*, p. 265.

34. Cooper, *The Gros Ventres of Montana: Religion and Ritual*, pp. 266–67 and 40.

35. McAllister, "The Four Quartz Rocks Medicine Bundle of the Kiowa-Apache," p. 217.

36. Paul Radin, "The Winnebago Tribe," p. 300.

37. Edward Curtis, *The North American Indian*, 6:124.

38. Edgar E. Siskin, *Washo Shamans and Peyotists*, p. 34.

39. Opler, *Apache Odyssey: A Journey between Two Worlds*, p. 203.

40. Wallace and Hoebel, *The Comanches: Lords of the Southern Plains*, pp. 165 and 168. This attitude is typical throughout the dreaming ethnography of North America. It should be kept in mind, however, that it represents only a minor portion of that ethnography. A similar attitude prevailed among the California Indians. Richard B. Applegate, *'Atishwin: The Dream Helper in Southern California*, p. 49, notes the following:

One might feel it is too cumbersome to fast and follow the other disciplines necessary to cultivate a relationship with the dream helper. One might also hesitate to accept the responsibility, from fear of making some mistake and incurring the helper's ill will; some helpers are quite demanding. . . . Finally, a person might not want the specific power offered by a particular helper.

41. Wilson D. Wallis, "The Canadian Dakota," pp. 82 and 110. A similar example is recorded for the Ponca in Alice Fletcher, "The Indian and Nature," pp. 440–41.

42. Robert Lowie, "Dance Associations of the Eastern Dakota," p. 122.

43. William Whitman, *The Oto*, p. 101.

44. Power, however, might also be rejected because the expected results failed to materialize. Bowers, *Mandan Social and Ceremonial Organization*, p. 170, recorded the following Mandan practice: "When a leader goes out to war as a result of the promise of a certain animal and loses one of his men, he will reject that animal's instruction if sent to him again in a dream."

45. Lowie, "The Assiniboine," p. 47.

46. Kenneth M. Stewart, "Spirit Possession in Native America."

47. Kroeber, *The Arapaho*, p. 436; McAllister, "The Four Quartz Rocks Medicine Bundle of the Kiowa-Apache," p. 220.

48. McAllister, "Dävéko: Kiowa-Apache Medicine Man," p. 38.

49. William Powers, *Yuwipi: Vision and Experience in Oglala Religion*, p. 49.

50. Because sacred objects always had a specific context for their use and handling, the display of these objects in museums has caused a great deal of concern among many Native Americans. Such display completely

decontextualizes the object and actually makes it dangerous to handle for those unfamiliar with its intended use and purpose. This is particularly true for objects that are most closely associated with major religious ceremonies and that were owned by recognized shamans. The handling of these objects in a traditional context would require the closest supervision and care. For other examples of such prescriptions, see Wissler, "Ceremonial Bundles of the Blackfoot Indians," p. 79; James W. Schultz, *Friends of My Life as an Indian*, p. 184; Cooper, *The Gros Ventres of Montana: Religion and Ritual*, pp. 40–41.

51. DeMallie, *The Sixth Grandfather: Black Elk's Teachings Given to John G. Neihardt*, p. 214.

52. Curtis, *The North American Indian*, 6:204–205.

53. A. Irving Hallowell, "The Role of Dreams in Ojibwa Culture," p. 280.

Chapter 8. Sharing the Dream

1. Contemporary Euro-American ideas about the "deep structures" of language that function to shape communal awareness and perception are relative and partial ideas regarding the nature of consciousness. I firmly disagree with the basic presupposition that language plays such a strong role in the development of perception. The attempt to place langauge so centrally in the formative stages of human development has always struck me as a reflection of the inordinant role language plays for the proponents of the idea. Most scholars are fascinated by and absorbed in the "language game," and it is no surprise that a left-hemispheric culture so bound to its output of words and books should also celebrate language as the ultimate source of human consciousness. Nevertheless, the basis of human awareness is far more grounded (over tens of thousands of years) in visual perception and imagery communication. The action, kinesthetic gesture, color, form, sound of nature, music, dance, and object construction that reflect personal experiences are more primary and fundamental than language, a derived and secondary phenomenon.

2. H. Hunt, "Some Relations between the Cognitive Psychology of Dreams and Dream Phenomenology," pp. 224–25, has made an important statement with regard to the phenomenological contents of the dream experience, stressing the "complex interdependence of the processes of perception, mnemonic imagery, and symbolic imagination." He goes on to emphasize that there is no single "deep structure" for symbolic cognition, "but rather multiple and potentially independent faculties, each developing a self-referential, recombinatory capacity in its own fashion." The vision expresses complex structures of religious thought and experience that simply cannot be rendered into a fully meaningful, strictly verbal form. For other references to the dual code model, see Robert G. Ley, "Cerebral Asymmetries, Emotional Experience, and Imagery: Implications for Psychotherapy."

3. Because positivism has tended to discredit language that refers to non-immediate, non-observable experience and has granted an inordinate "reality" to the immediate, sensory world, analysts face the paradox of having no reliable language or verbal means with which to discuss the

non-empirical. Such a situation only adds to the difficulty of "making sense" of reported dream materials. Emotional and imagistic experience has its own language, which suffers serious contraction in a purely verbal explanation. The poetic character of many dream songs in part reflects the attempt to create a verbal link with the imagistic events of the vision.

4. On the synergy of converting images into language, see Jon Tolaas, "Transformatory Framework: Pictorial to Verbal," p. 60.

5. The problem of translating the dream into verbal formulation is discussed by Akhter Ahsen, "Prolucid Dreaming: A Context Analysis Approach to Dreams," p. 2, where he notes the problematic aspects of verbalizing the dream:

> Verbal reports are themselves inadequate because they add something to the reported image which may not exist at the experiential levels and thus do not exactly report the experienced image. Semantic research also has convincingly showed that verbal statements themselves are not experientially faithful in their communication, there being verbal descriptions which do not even tell us how to translate the verbal command into a concrete effect which matches the intended reality.

6. Exceptions to this piecemeal gathering of dream texts are Franz Boas, "Contributions to the Ethnology of the Kwakiutl," a small volume of dreams (with no ethnographic notes!); also Clark Wissler, "Ceremonial Bundles of the Blackfoot Indians"; Jackson S. Lincoln, *The Dream in Primitive Cultures;* Wilson D. Wallis, "The Canadian Dakota"; and William Wildschut, *Crow Indian Medicine Bundles.* Dream materials in these collections are scattered but are consistently presented as a significant aspect of Native American religion.

7. Kracke, "Myths in Dreams, Thoughts in Images: An Amazonian Contribution to the Psychoanalytic Theory of Primary Process," p. 36.

8. As noted by Mikhail Bakhtin ("The Problem of the Text," p. 7), the "chain of texts . . . [form] special dialogical relationships" that contribute to the richness of meaning implicit in both the various texts under consideration and the associations between texts and the entire interactive field of the cultural and historical environment. I do not concieve of this interaction as dialectic. I understand the dialectic as a product of abstract analysis based on a propositional set of binary categories that are generally the creation of the analyst. Dialectic analysis is often represented by agonistic tensions posited by the analyst as "implicit" in the cultural data. Such analysis lacks the richness and complexity of the heterogeneous dialogical context and expresses the inherent logical structures of language in a static setting. To write about the rational versus the irrational in any cultural setting is dialectic. To discuss the rational in a context of other, equally significant processes of knowing or understanding, such as dreams or visions, trances, or ritual enactments, is dialogical. That texts may speak with each other through the medium of the reader means that the reader contextualizes the contents of the texts through increasingly richer associations and implied meanings reflective of the cultural milieu both of the text and of the reader. In this sense, a great deal of deconstructive analysis is dialectic.

9. John Fire and Richard Erdoes, *Lame Deer: Seeker of Visions,* p. 137.

10. This is what Carl Jung discusses as the "transcendent function" of

the dream, which is the process of the inherent tensions of the individual working toward greater integration and maturity (Carl Jung, "The Transcendent Function," p. 90). It is also what Roland Cahen, *The Psychology of the Dream*, p. 133, following Jung, called the "energy gradient" by which dream contents are resynthesized following any analytic effort.

11. For more on the subject of the tensions in sacred discourse, see Richard Bauman, *Let Your Words Be Few: Symbolism of Speaking and Silence among Seventeenth-Century Quakers*, pp. 20–31.

12. Raymond DeMallie, *The Sixth Grandfather: Black Elk's Teachings Given to John G. Neihardt*, p. 126.

13. Frances Densmore, "The Belief of the Indian in a Connection between Song and the Supernatural," p. 220.

14. Alanson Skinner, "Ceremonies of the Plains Cree," pp. 70–71.

15. A. Irving Hallowell, "Ojibwa Ontology, Behavior, and World View," p. 165, records similar sanctions among the Ojibwa: "Dream experiences are not ordinarily recounted save under special circumstances. There is a taboo against this, just as there is a taboo against myth narration except in the proper seasonal context."

16. David G. Mandelbaum, "The Plains Cree," p. 252.

17. John M. Cooper, *The Gros Ventres of Montana: Religion and Ritual*, p. 409.

18. Alice Fletcher and Francis La Flesche, *The Omaha Tribe*, p. 131.

19. James O. Dorsey, *A Study of Siouan Cults*, p. 395.

20. Ernest Wallace and E. Adamson Hoebel, *The Comanches: Lords of the Southern Plains*, pp. 159 and 155.

21. Fletcher and La Flesche, *The Omaha Tribe*, p. 459.

22. Edward Curtis, *The North American Indian*, 3:133.

23. Deward E. Walker, "Nez Perce Sorcery," p. 70.

24. In contrast to the Plains and Prairie peoples, the southwestern Mohave shaman dreamers were obliged to dream the primal myth of origins as a sign of shamanistic calling. Dream recitation must fit the existing oral narrative dream patterns (see Anthony Wallace, "The Dream in Mohave Life," p. 253). Even in such a highly patterned group, however, dream narratives of the mythic events of creation differed with each shaman, even among those who dreamed of the same medicine powers (George Devereux, "Dream Learning and Individual Ritual Differences in Mohave Shamanism," p. 20). More significantly, new techniques for healing and ceremonial behavior were dreamed as a hitherto unrevealed portion of the creation narrative (Devereux, "Dream Learning and Individual Ritual Differences in Mohave Shamanism," p. 23). Thus it was likely that a shaman, while dreaming of the recognized myth, simultaneously personalized that myth in terms of his dreams and added completely novel elements to the known record.

25. Such esoteric knowledge was recognized by various visionaries. In discussing sacred powers, the Sioux Little-Wound told James R. Walker, *Lakota Belief and Ritual*, p. 67: "In my boy vision, the Buffalo came to me and when I sought the shaman's vision, the Wind spoke to me. . . . I can tell you of the Buffalo but I cannot tell you of the Wind for that is my secret as a shaman." There is obviously a distinction here between the early experiences of youth and the secret or esoteric knowledge of the shaman. In Thomas E. Mails, *Fools Crow*, p. 86, Fools Crow talks of the secret things he

learned in the vision by which he became a medicine man. In fact, Black Elk told Fools Crow he must not speak about his shaman's vision to anyone (see Thomas Mails, *Fools Crow*, p. 88).

26. George B. Grinnell, *The Cheyenne Indians: Their History and Ways of Life*, 2:128–29.

27. Patricia Albers and Bea Medicine, *The Hidden Half: Studies of Plains Indian Women*, p. 257. See also Walker, *Lakota Belief and Ritual*, p. 242, for a discussion of the powerful influences of a young woman's first menstrual flow.

28. For the Comanche, see Wallace and Hoebel, *The Comanches: Lords of the Southern Plains*, p. 168; for the Blackfoot, see Walter McClintock, "Saítsiko, the Blackfoot Doctor," p. 83; for the Gros Ventre as represented by First Woman and First Man, see Cooper, *The Gros Ventres of Montana: Religion and Ritual*, pp. 451–54. The high frequency of male and female dream-spirits appearing as dual helpers suggests the Absarokee attitude; see Robert H. Lowie, "The Religion of the Crow Indians," p. 329.

29. Frances Densmore, *Teton Sioux Music*, p. 184.

30. David G. Mandelbaum, "The Plains Cree," p. 252.

31. Peter Nabokov, *Two Leggings: The Making of a Crow Warrior*, p. 24.

32. Walker, *Lakota Belief and Ritual*, p. 153.

33. Joseph Epps Brown, *The Sacred Pipe: Black Elk's Account of the Seven Rites of the Oglala Sioux*, p. 61.

34. For an overview of the key aspects of verbal art, see Richard Bauman, *Verbal Art as Performance*. In the general collection of the Plains Indian dream and vision narratives, there is little evidence of the patterning of formal features that normally marks verbal art as such. This may be because most narratives were given in English, frequently through the mediating influence of an interpreter, and not in the original language. Also, they were given in the unusual situation of a more general ethnographic study and were rarely, if ever, recorded in the appropriate ceremonial circumstance. Tyon's report is translated directly from the Sioux as recorded by Tyon himself for Walker, *Lakota Belief and Ritual*, p. 147. The study of Plains Indian verbal art, to be effective, needs to be done in the original language.

35. Brown, *The Sacred Pipe: Black Elk's Account of the Seven Rites of the Oglala Sioux*, p. 61.

36. For a more contemporary example, see Fred W. Voget, *The Shoshoni-Crow Sundance*, p. 182, who notes the following for the Shoshone-Crow: "Those who lied about dreams in order to sponsor a Sun-Dance could expect to be brought down with a disease. . . . Those who disregarded the mandates of their power dreams reaped nothing but bad luck and an early death."

37. The Absarokee shaman Big Shadow saw in his dreams the experience that Bull Chief had while dragging the skull in search of a vision. Bull Chief was reluctant to speak until Big Shadow told him what Bull Chief had seen in his vision (Curtis, *The North American Indian*, 4:198). Another Absarokee example is given by Robert H. Lowie, "Notes on Shoshonean Ethnography," p. 292.

38. Frank B. Linderman, *Plenty Coups: Chief of the Crows*, pp. 300–301.

39. Linderman, *Plenty Coups: Chief of the Crows*, p. 303.

40. Such a narrative goes a long way toward pointing out that symbolic

interpretation was a normal feature of Plains and Prairie religion. Such interpretation had varying degrees of sophistication and depth, depending on the experience and background of the interpreters. My own reading of Native American religious tradition is that symbolic interpretations have always been an essential aspect of the shaman's role. As religious practitioners, their use of symbolism is an extremely widespread and highly conscious part of all Native American religious activities. As dream interpreters, Native American shamans demonstrate a knowledge of the cultural symbolism of their own environment that is usually unattainable by non–culture members.

41. Walker, *Lakota Belief and Ritual*, pp. 134–35.

42. Walker, *Lakota Belief and Ritual*, p. 135.

43. This process of discussing the dream in a group context has strong parallels with work done in contemporary research on dream interpretations in group settings. Montague Ullman, "Access to Dreams," pp. 531–33, notes the following with regard to helping a dreamer understand his or her dream in a group context:

> Working on a dream in a group the intent is to mobilize the collective imagination of the group in order to come up with an array of feelings and metaphorical potentialities that the members of the group might connect to the dream if it were their dream. . . . They speak of the dream as their own, and they speak to each other, not to the dreamer. The dialogue is the most difficult part of the process and the one that requires the most skill. . . . The goal of the dialogue is to effect a sense of closure between the dreamer and the dream. . . . The point of closure is reached when everyone, especially the dreamer, has a felt sense that the dreamer recognizes the issues raised by the dream.

There is a definite sense in the ethnography that discussions in interpretive settings are in fact seeking some sense of closure for the dream, while all participants realize that further dreams or visions might alter the interpretation. Also, it seems true that collective imagination is at work, though in the Native American context this would be highly structured by religious beliefs and the mythic background of those beliefs. Finally, the visionary does, in fact, continue to reflect on his experience and seek alternative interpretations.

44. R. F. Fortune, *Omaha Secret Societies*, pp. 78–79. For Southwestern parallels, see Dorothy Eggan, "The Significance of Dreams for Anthropological Research," p. 179; and Barbara Tedlock, *Dreaming: Anthropological and Psychological Interpretations*, p. 117.

45. John R. Murie and Douglas R. Parks, *Ceremonies of the Pawnee*, p. 319.

46. Wallis, "The Canadian Dakota," p. 84.

47. Francis La Flesche, "The Omaha Buffalo Medicine-Men: An Account of Their Method of Practice," p. 217; Mandelbaum, "The Plains Cree," p. 254.

48. Densmore, *Teton Sioux Music*, p. 248.

49. Cooper, *The Gros Ventres of Montana: Religion and Ritual*, p. 454; J. Gilbert McAllister, "The Four Quartz Rocks Medicine Bundle of the Kiowa-Apache," p. 220. The Plains Cree attitude toward such narration is summarized by Mandelbaum, "The Plains Cree," p. 254, as follows:

The prime blessing which could be granted in a vision was the ability to cure. . . . The shaman repeated the circumstances of the dream, told when and where it was received, and notified the powers that he was about to demonstrate the procedure revealed to him. Thus the doctor publicly asserted his right to undertake the cure by reminding the spirit powers that he was upholding his part of their pact and it was incumbent upon them to fulfill their promises.

50. Nabokov, *Two Leggings: The Making of a Crow Warrior*, p. 131.

51. Alfred Bowers, *Hidatsa Social and Ceremonial Organization*, p. 265.

52. For the Ponca, see William Whitman, *The Oto*, p. 186; for the Blackfoot, John Ewers, *The Blackfeet: Raiders of the Northwestern Plains*, p. 163; for the Absarokee, Robert H. Lowie, *The Crow Indians*, p. 248; for the Mandan, Alfred Bowers, *Mandan Social and Ceremonial Organization*, p. 182; for the Hidatsa, Bowers, *Hidatsa Social and Ceremonial Organization*, pp. 238 and 286.

53. Fortune, *Omaha Secret Societies*, p. 40.

Chapter 9. Mythic Discourse

1. It is possible on this basis to differentiate between mythic discourse and philosophic discourse: philosophic discourse may be described as the rational framing of projects and concerns—the verbal means through which beliefs and ideas are given logical and systemic expression. Generally, this requires the use of abstract language to explain or justify a particular line of concern or argument. Both are rhetorical. The existentialists have challenged the idea that such abstract discourse can ever be an accurate presentation of the complexity of human existence at the experiential level, or that reason and logic are adequate to the task.

2. A distinction can be made, heuristically, between religion and myth in terms of discourse typology. I conceptualize mythic discourse as a type of religious communication. Theology is another type, as are philosophical or historical discourses on religion. The unique characteristics of mythic discourse are its story form, its correlation with dramatic enactment, and its powerful embeddedness in actual people and places. Narratives of the "sacred beings" (angels, prophets, culture heroes, dream-spirits, gods, and goddesses) all cohere around acts of power and exceptional knowledge. The drama of the mythic narrative is, in this case, existential and not literary, insofar as it is rooted in actual encounters, visions, and powerful emotional and spiritual transformations. The recitation is evocative, has an imperative mood, and directs attention toward the actual manifestation of the powers involved. However, this is a heuristic distinction—the conceptual overlap between "religion and myth" is usually extensive in indigenous traditions and in many ways cannot be reduced to such distinctive categories.

3. Rudolph Bultman, "New Testament and Mythology," p. 4.

4. Bultman, "New Testament and Mythology," p. 4, discussing the religious worldview of the New Testament with its three-layered structure of heaven above, hell below, and earth between, writes:

Man's knowledge and mastery of the world have advanced to such an extent through science and technology that it is no longer possible for anyone seriously to hold the New Testament view of the world. . . . We no longer believe in a three storied universe. . . . The only honest way of reciting the creeds is to strip the mythological framework from the truths they enshrine.

Karl Jaspers, *Myth and Christianity*, p. 15, has expressed the belief that "mythical thinking is not a thing of the past but characterizes man in any epoch." This is because the contents of the mythic are captured in dramatic images and symbolic acts and not in purely rational discourse. Subsequently Jaspers, *Myth and Christianity*, p. 47, wrote: "Rational and mythical modes of awareness are only the foreground of a never-ending process of existential clarification and comprehension." The contemporary challenge is to comprehend mythic processes in terms of this ongoing transformation of the meaning and value of myth in the contemporary world and not just in the past.

5. Patricia Albers and Seymour Parker, "The Plains Vision Experience," p. 225. This is summarized as follows:

In many ways the difference between visions and certain kinds of myth is not one of kind but degree. While visions seem to justify adequately the personal attributes of individuals or the characteristics they should hold as members of a social group, myths have a much broader point of reference: namely, they justify the characteristics and functions of clans, non-kin sodalities, and/or the society as a whole.

But they do not necessarily do so in a socially consistent or homogeneous way, because the social collective is influenced by its various members and the power and significance of individual dreams or visions. The collective power of the vision was actually shared among a small number of members, but there were many such groups within a single community. The larger impact on the collective would come through performances and other symbolic expressions.

6. An example of this may be seen in the vision of Plenty Coups. After reciting the dream to Frank B. Linderman (*Plenty Coups: Chief of the Crows*, p. 75) several of those present began to discuss its significance: "Coyote Runs and Plain Bull began a conversation between themselves when Plenty Coups left off talking. Both said that the dream was well known to all the tribe, even the day after his return from his dreaming. 'We travelled by that dream,' said Coyote Runs." Significantly, this dream had strong apocalyptic contents that warned of coming disasters (such as the end of the buffalo) and provided a symbolic language for considering how to meet such powerful events.

7. To what degree may the contents of a dream be attributed to the culturally influenced mentality of the dreamer? I regard this as one of those paradoxical "scientific" problems that plague the modern conscience, a problem rooted in a deep-seated insecurity about the exact nature and role of creativity in culture coupled with a profound skepticism about all metaphysical realities. Various models proposed for the transformation and growth of culture have depended on a Nietzchean will-to-power genealogy, perceiving conflictive and agonistic human relations as a primary source for change. While the conflictive model may account for some changes in social and historical existence (e.g., Victor Turner, "Social Dramas and Stories about Them"; J. C. Heesterman, *The Inner Conflict of Tradi-*

tion), it does not account for the rise and expression of aesthetic, ethical, philosophical, religious, or scientific creativity. My own approach has been to emphasize the religious basis of cultural organization and to show how religious thought and experience (the world over) can facilitate cultural transformations.

8. For the creative role of dreaming in the Western traditon, I can think of no better example than the following citation from Montague D. Ullman and Stanley Krippner, Dream Telepathy: Experiments in Nocturnal ESP, p. 220:

> While he was in the army, Descartes spent a winter of inactive duty in a hotel room. He was discontent with army life and ideas spun through his brain in an angry, disconnected, and contradictory way. One night he had a dream in which all his previously clashing thoughts fell suddenly into harmony. That dream began the philosophical and mathematical formulations that were to change the course of Western thinking.

9. Mythic discourse may be generally summarized for the Plains Indians as non-empirical, with its own criteria for validation; inclusive and structured by its own symbolic coherence; value laden but not rigidly hierarchical; represented by dynamic patterns of changing relations; transformative because it allows for a wide variety of mythic identifications; heterogeneous and highly variant; capable of innumerable interpretive responses; multigenetic, containing potentially agonistic as well as creative possibilities; highly complex; referring to the unbound world of human potential through interactions with the sacred powers; and, therefore, revelatory.

10. Raymond DeMallie, *The Sixth Grandfather: Black Elk's Teachings Given to John G. Neihardt*, p. 311.

11. James W. Schultz, *Friends of My Life as an Indian*, pp. 26–28.

12. Other communities had, of course, differing views on this subject. For the Asarokee, flint arrows had their origins in the death of the first woman, Red Woman, whose bones were made of flint and burst in the fire when she was burned, most likely for practicing sorcery (see Frank B. Linderman, *Pretty Shield: Medicine Woman of the Crow*, p. 54). Among the Plains Cree, the arrowheads were made by the powerful little people, *memkwe'ciwak*, who lived in the sand hills and riverbanks (Mandelbaum, "The Plains Cree," p. 263). It is interesting to consider that wherever there is a known technology for making arrowheads, there are visionary origins, whereas the discovery of preexistent arrowheads is attributed to other mythic sources.

13. James W. Schultz and J. L. Donaldson, *The Sun God's Children*, p. 24.

14. Schultz, *Friends of My Life as an Indian*, p. 184.

15. James R. Walker, *Lakota Belief and Ritual*, p. 260.

16. Presently, the earliest records may be found in Reuben G. Thwaites, *The Jesuit Relations and Allied Documents: Travels and Explorations of the Jesuit Missionaries in New France*, volumes 1–73, covering a period beginning early in the seventeenth century and reporting on the Iroquois and similar tribes. The letters contain extensive references to dreams and visions as the origins of many practices and beliefs central to the Iroquois way of life. See also Lee Irwin, "Visionary Dialogues: The Huron-Jesuit Relations," and J. N. B. Hewitt, "The Iroquoian Concept of the Soul." For the Great Plains,

see James W. Lynd, "The Religion of the Dakotas," pp. 166–67; and James O. Dorsey, *A Study of Siouan Cults*, pp. 436 and 483.

17. Alice Fletcher and Francis La Flesche, *The Omaha Tribe*, p. 565.

18. John R. Murie and Douglas R. Parks, *Ceremonies of the Pawnee*, pp. 323 and 364.

19. Paul Radin, "The Winnebago Tribe," p. 299.

20. Clark Wissler, "Ceremonial Bundles of the Blackfoot Indians," p. 76.

21. Wissler, "Ceremonial Bundles of the Blackfoot Indians," p. 73.

22. Alfred Bowers, *Hidatsa Social and Ceremonial Organization*, p. 173.

23. William Powers, *Oglala Religion*, p. 138; John Fire and Richard Erdoes, *Lame Deer: Seeker of Visions*, p. 14.

24. Alanson Skinner, "Societies of the Iowa, Kansa, and Ponca Indians," p. 701.

25. Skinner, "Societies of the Iowa, Kansa, and Ponca Indians," p. 710, n. 2.

26. Walker, *Lakota Belief and Ritual*, p. 160.

27. See Douglas Parks, *Traditional Narratives of the Arikara Indians*, 3:64–82, for an excellent overview of Plains oral style, using original Arikara text materials.

28. Walker, *Lakota Belief and Ritual*, p. 94.

29. Ray DeMallie and Douglas Parks, *Sioux Indian Religion: Tradition and Innovation*, p. 39.

30. Stephen R. Riggs, *Dakota Grammar, Texts, and Ethnography*, p. 166. Further work has been done by William Powers, *Sacred Language: The Nature of Supernatural Discourse in Lakota*, p. 25, in which he discusses differences among several variations in sacred language as used by a Sioux shaman.

31. James R. Walker, "The Sundance and Other Ceremonies of the Oglala Division of the Teton Dakota," p. 68. The visionary ethnography does not highlight any other Plains group as using a similar language, but this could well be a function of the ethnographic context, in which such speech would be inappropriate. Cherokee shamans seem to have developed something very similar; see James Mooney and Frans M. Olbrechts, *The Swimmer Manuscript: Cherokee Sacred Formulas and Medicinal Prescriptions*, p. 14, and Lee Irwin, "Cherokee Healing: Myth, Dreams and Medicine," p. 250. Most likely this special use of language is far more common than is presently recognized.

32. An important contribution to this point of view is made by Stanley Krippner, "Dreams and the Development of a Personal Mythology," p. 454, in his work with personal mythology in dreams: "While personal myths are derived, in part, from the myths of the culture, the process moves in both directions. Each individual's personal mythology contributes to the ongoing development of the surrounding culture's mythology as well." This theory is developed also by David Feinstein, "Myth-Making Activity through the Window of the Dream." Recently, the two authors have combined their efforts in an important work on the mythological character of dreams in contemporary culture; see David Feinstein and Stanley Krippner, *Personal Mythology: The Psychology of Your Evolving Self*.

33. Edward Curtis, *The North American Indian*, 3:128.

34. Walker, *Lakota Belief and Ritual*, p. 244.

35. Wilson D. Wallis, "The Canadian Dakota," p. 86.

36. John M. Cooper, *The Gros Ventres of Montana: Religion and Ritual*, pp. 116–19.

37. Robert H. Lowie, "The Tobacco Society of the Crow Indians," p. 112, writes:

> The visionary and his ceremonial descendants constituted the original Tobacco society. New visions by members of this fold led to the segregation of chapters, all sharing the right to plant Tobacco but distinguished by ceremonial details and songs. The same result was also achieved by independent visions of the Tobacco granted to outsiders, who were thereby empowered to start new lines of descent.

38. Bowers, *Mandan Social and Ceremonial Organization*, p. 123.

39. Bowers, *Hidatsa Social and Ceremonial Organization*, p. 311.

40. Murie and Parks, *Ceremonies of the Pawnee*, p. 77.

41. Murie and Parks, *Ceremonies of the Pawnee*, p. 115.

42. Murie and Parks, *Ceremonies of the Pawnee*, pp. 221, 319, and 395.

43. It is remarkable that while the Pawnee did not institutionalize the vision quest as a normative religious practice, almost all ceremonials, songs, and sacred bundles have their origins in visionary experience. In most cases this is a consequence of a spontaneous vision encounter. The underlying belief seems to be that if individuals are chosen to receive a vision from the powers, it will come whether they seek it or not. The people must depend entirely on the sacred powers to guide them and to reveal the appropriate ceremonies.

44. Murie and Parks, *Ceremonies of the Pawnee*, pp. 298–99.

45. Gene Weltfish, "The Vision Story of Fox Boy," p. 73.

46. Alice Fletcher, *The Hako: A Pawnee Ceremony*, pp. 119–22.

47. Albers and Parker, "The Plains Vision Experience," p. 206–207. The authors discuss briefly the distinction between systems of action and systems of belief in relation to the vision:

> As a system of action, the vision experience provides linkage between the social structure and ideology. . . . The vision could be used to compete for and to defend claims to positions of prestige and privilege . . . as a mechanism for identity formation, serving to legitimate his actions and status in the community.

I take ideology here to refer to religious ideas. Such ideas allowed the actions of the individual to be primarily structured according to the vision, which in some cases did not have immediate ties to existing social structures. In and of itself, the vision was initially only a potential source of empowerment. The crucial test was the actual ability of the individual to manifest the vision in acts of power—it was these acts that could secure social recognition. In this sense, actions legitimated the vision and thereby social status.

48. DeMallie, *The Sixth Grandfather: Black Elk's Teachings Given to John G. Neihardt*, pp. 215–26.

49. DeMallie, *The Sixth Grandfather: Black Elk's Teachings Given to John G. Neihardt*, pp. 238–39.

50. DeMallie, *The Sixth Grandfather: Black Elk's Teachings Given to John G. Neihardt*, p. 236.

51. Walter McClintock, "Saítsiko, the Blackfoot Doctor," p. 83.

52. McClintock, "Saítsiko, the Blackfoot Doctor," p. 85.

53. Wissler, "Ceremonial Bundles of the Blackfoot Indians," p. 77.

54. Wissler, "Ceremonial Bundles of the Blackfoot Indians," pp. 73 and 74; Alfred L. Kroeber, *The Arapaho*, p. 434; Bowers, *Mandan Social and Ceremonial Organization*, p. 175; George B. Grinnell, *The Cheyenne Indians: Their History and Ways of Life*, 1:265–67.

55. Fred W. Voget, *The Shoshoni-Crow Sundance*, p. 105.

56. Robert H. Lowie, "Notes on Shoshonean Ethnography," p. 296.

57. R. F. Fortune, *Omaha Secret Societies*, p. 74.

58. Murie and Parks, *Ceremonies of the Pawnee*, p. 170.

59. Royal Hassrick, *The Sioux: Life and Customs of a Warrior Society*, p. 235.

60. Fletcher, "The Indian and Nature," p. 441.

61. Fortune, *Omaha Secret Societies*, p. 40.

62. A similar attitude can be found among the Woodlands people, as mentioned by A. Irving Hallowell, "Ojibwa Ontology, Behavior, and World View," p. 173:

> I was once told about the puberty fast of a boy who was not satisfied with his initial blessing. He demanded that he dream of all the leaves of all the trees in the world so that absolutely nothing would be hidden from him. This was considered greedy and, while the *pawágan* who appeared in his dream granted his greedy desire, the boy was told that "as soon as the leaves start to fall you'll get sick and when all the leaves drop to the ground that is the end of your life." And this is what happened.

Chapter 10. The Visionary Arts

1. A. Irving Hallowell, "Myth, Culture and Personality," pp. 552–53, has suggested the need to find ways to study the contents of mythic forms that cannot be adequately translated into discursive speech: "Myths and other oral narratives, then, may express meanings that the native [or the ethnographer] cannot easily translate into discursive forms of speech, if he can express them at all." What we need to recognize, therefore, is the existence of meanings that find expression in nondiscursive and nonlinguistic forms. This requires learning how to become more expert in the interpretation of meanings that are expressed in all kinds of symbolic forms.

2. By codetermination I mean to suggest the ways in which symbolic forms work together to determine a particular result. Such a process is by no means mechanical. In its nonverbal structures it represents widely divergent cultural-religious associations. These associations are not forced into any rigid pattern of meanings, but they are interactive and cluster around particular intentional acts. The use of the pipe in ceremonial prayer has divergent but shared meanings, depending on who handles the pipe and how, and on the experience and knowledge of the one who uses it. This understanding in turn is influenced by other situations in which the pipe is used—in the total context of possible use. These uses reflectively create an entire repertoire of actions and associated emotions that, when done with mastery, invoke the presence of the sacred.

3. For the Arikara, see Douglas Parks, *Traditional Narratives of the Arikara*

Indians, 1:94; for the Gros Ventre, see John M. Cooper, *The Gros Ventres of Montana: Religion and Ritual,* p. 23.

4. The Hidatsa Edward Goodbird, *Goodbird the Indian: His Story Told to G. L. Wilson,* p. 23, expressed the idea that the power of the vision was actually in the object itself: "As soon as he was recovered from his fast, he set out to kill an animal like that seen in his vision, and its dried skin, or part of it, he kept as his sacred object, or medicine, for in this sacred object dwelt his god." The significant point to note is that the object is not the "god" but the dwelling place of the power; it resides there but is not exclusively identified with the object. The Absarokee Two Leggings said, "The objects within a medicine bundle are the actual dwelling places of the members of the dreamer's medicine clan"; see Peter Nabokov, *Two Leggings: The Making of a Crow Warrior,* p. 25. The medicine clan is the specific group of powers that aid the visionary. They live there but are not exclusively identified with the bundle—that is, they are present but not confined or held in that place.

5. Clark Wissler, "Ceremonial Bundles of the Blackfoot Indians," p. 104; also John C. Ewers, *The Blackfeet: Raiders of the Northwestern Plains,* p. 163.

6. James O. Dorsey, *A Study of Siouan Cults,* p. 395.

7. Dorsey, *A Study of Siouan Cults,* p. 396.

8. George B. Grinnell, *The Cheyenne Indians: Their History and Ways of Life,* 2:85; Clark Wissler, "Some Protective Designs of the Dakota," p. 50.

9. Peter Nabokov, *Two Leggings: The Making of a Crow Warrior,* p. 110, gives an excellent illustration of the variable symbolic associations of the flute as experienced in the visions of the Absarokee warrior Cold-Wind.

10. William Whitman, *The Oto,* p. 88.

11. James Howard, *The Ponca Tribe,* p. 80.

12. Clark Wissler, "Societies and Ceremonial Associations in the Oglala Division of the Teton-Dakota," p. 92.

13. Clark Wissler, "Ceremonial Bundles of the Blackfoot Indians," p. 84.

14. Frances Densmore, *Teton Sioux Music,* p. 183, n. 1.

15. Robert Smith, *The Art of the Festival,* p. 98, discusses the metonymic structure of imagery in the context of festivals. The image is "captured by the narrative, it stands for it and sums it up." In this case, however, the image refers directly to nonverbal aspects of religious symbolism. While these images can be verbalized, the more important point is that the image invokes the power, its protective presence, its benefit, and its sacred quality simply by being present in a context of belief in the power of imagery.

16. Alfred L. Kroeber, *The Arapaho,* p. 420.

17. Howard Harrod, *Renewing the World: Plains Indian Religion and Morality,* p. 176, mentions that Absarokee women still use certain colors in beadwork as a result of dreams or of old vision color patterns having been passed on to contemporaries.

18. The analysis of colors mentioned in the ethnography of 450 dreams is as follows, numbers representing frequency: black (169), white (161), red (95), yellow (30), blue (26), green (5), brown (3). These figures are only general approximations because of the translation problem. Color equivalency among various language families is highly variable.

19. J. Gilbert McAllister, "The Four Quartz Rocks Medicine Bundle of the Kiowa-Apache," p. 216.

20. John R. Murie and Douglas R. Parks, *Ceremonies of the Pawnee*, p. 364.

21. An example is given by Wissler, "Ceremonial Bundles of the Blackfoot Indians," p. 80, in the Blackfoot vision of Mink Woman and her association of red with human form: "The red color represents the mink in human form as expressive of the sacred quality that gives life and power to the dreamer."

22. George Horse Capture, *The Seven Visions of Bull Lodge*, pp. 30–31.

23. Other types of more traditional body paint are mentioned in a contemporary setting by Peter J. Powell, *Sweet Medicine*, 2:655:

> Dancers who will wear "Dream" or "Vision" paints . . . their designs will be the ones that came from the *Maiyun* [sacred beings] themselves, who first gave them to certain oldtime fasters. In 1961 four of these dancers wore the Lizard paint. One wore the Deer paint, another the paint of the Swifthawk. . . . [Note 15: Originally a Dream design could be painted only by the man who received it.]

I see this use of traditional paint as a consequence of the vision fast's being undertaken rarely or not at all. The old-time paint is retained out of respect for the visions of the past, but if many were fasting and receiving visions, greater variety and innovation would most likely be present.

24. Wissler, "Ceremonial Bundles of the Blackfoot Indians," pp. 72–76 and 82.

25. Alanson Skinner, "Notes on the Eastern Cree and the Northern Saulteaux," p. 77.

26. John Ewers, *The Blackfeet: Raiders of the Northwestern Plains*, p. 166.

27. Robert H. Lowie, "The Assiniboine," p. 49.

28. Grinnell, *The Cheyenne Indians: Their History and Ways of Life*, 1:234.

29. John Ewers, *Murals in the Round: Painted Tipis of the Kiowa and Kiowa-Apache Indians*, p. 33.

30. Ewers, *Murals in the Round: Painted Tipis of the Kiowa and Kiowa-Apache Indians*, p. 27.

31. Alanson Skinner, "Notes on the Eastern Cree and the Northern Saulteaux," p. 70; Densmore, *Teton Sioux Music*, p. 177.

32. Ewers, *Murals in the Round: Painted Tipis of the Kiowa and Kiowa-Apache Indians*, is a particularly fine book that provides many excellent illustrations of the dramatic nature of this type of religious or sacred art.

33. McAllister, "The Four Quartz Rocks Medicine Bundle of the Kiowa-Apache," p. 213. For a single composite article on medicine bundles and their relationship to visions, McAllister's is still one of the best available.

34. Ewers, *The Blackfeet: Raiders of the Northwestern Plains*, p. 163.

35. Examples of this type of bundle are the Buffalo Calf Pipe Bundle of the Sioux, given by *Wope*, which contains the most sacred object of the community (James R. Walker, *Lakota Belief and Ritual*, pp. 148–49), and the Sacred Hat and Sacred Arrow bundles of the Cheyenne, which are believed to have been made hundreds of years ago by Sweet Medicine (see Peter J. Powell, *Sweet Medicine*). A similar type of object is the Omaha Sacred Pole, recently returned to the tribe by the Peabody Museum. All these objects are being cared for by specially designated members of the community.

36. Murie and Parks, *Ceremonies of the Pawnee*, p. 107.

37. Alfred Bowers, *Mandan Social and Ceremonial Organization*, p. 181.

38. James W. Schultz, *Friends of My Life as an Indian*, p. 214. In 1989 I had the opportunity to talk with the niece of the present owner of this bundle, who lives on the Blackfoot reservation near Browning, Montana. She knew the story of the buffalo stone and told me that the bundle was still "alive and well."

39. Murie and Parks, *Ceremonies of the Pawnee*, pp. 190–91.

40. Murie and Parks, *Ceremonies of the Pawnee*, pp. 193–94.

41. William Wildschut, *Crow Indian Medicine Bundles*, p. 90.

42. Wildschut, *Crow Indian Medicine Bundles*, p. 91.

43. Wissler, "Ceremonial Bundles of the Blackfoot Indians," p. 75.

44. Fletcher and La Flesche, *The Omaha Tribe*, p. 565.

45. Densmore, *Teton Sioux Music*, p. 205.

46. Densmore, *Teton Sioux Music*, p. 208.

47. Densmore, *Teton Sioux Music*, p. 210.

48. Walker, *Lakota Belief and Ritual*, pp. 153–55. Other recognized types of Sioux sacred stones were the stones of the sweat lodge, whose power was that of healing and purification. Also, there were various large stones scattered about the plains that would be painted red or green and to which prayers and smoke would be addressed; Densmore, *Teton Sioux Music*, p. 204.

49. Walker, *Lakota Belief and Ritual*, p. 82.

50. Grinnell, *The Cheyenne Indians: Their History and Ways of Life*, 2:136.

51. Ewers, *The Blackfeet: Raiders of the Northwestern Plains*, p. 173.

52. There are many versions of the mythic origins of the various pipes. Cooper, *The Gros Ventres of Montana: Religion and Ritual*, pp. 446–54, gives five different versions for the Gros Ventre. For other Sioux versions, see Walker, *Lakota Belief and Ritual*, pp. 109–12 and 148–50; also Joseph Epps Brown, *The Sacred Pipe: Black Elk's Account of the Seven Rites of the Oglala Sioux*, pp. 3–9.

53. Murie and Parks, *Ceremonies of the Pawnee*, p. 37.

54. Alice Fletcher, *The Hako: A Pawnee Ceremony*, pp. 44–45.

55. Fletcher, *The Hako: A Pawnee Ceremony*, p. 178.

56. Bowers, *Mandan Social and Ceremonial Organization*, p. 182.

57. Alfred Bowers, *Hidatsa Social and Ceremonial Organization*, p. 240.

58. Murie and Parks, *Ceremonies of the Pawnee*, p. 7.

59. Kroeber, *The Arapaho*, p. 436.

60. This observation may reflect the general tendency to regard the warlike actions of the various communities as the outstanding psychological concern and interest for Euro-American historians in an era that had hardly ceased its aggressive and militant oppression of Native American peoples. It is important to recall that this oppression also involved a widespread denial of the value of native religions and a variety of acts passed by the U.S. government curtailing those religious practices. The military aspects of Indian life were given an outstanding place in much of the ethnography.

61. Grinnell, *The Cheyenne Indians: Their History and Ways of Life*, 1:188.

62. Grinnell, *The Cheyenne Indians: Their History and Ways of Life*, 1:202.

63. Dorsey, *A Study of Siouan Cults*, p. 393.

64. Horse Capture, *The Seven Visions of Bull Lodge*, pp. 32–33.

65. An example of a similar emblem is the Great Seal of the United States on the one-dollar bill, which is a circle containing an eagle with

arrows in its right claw and an olive branch in its left. Above its head is a sphere like a sun containing thirteen stars, representing states. It is interesting to note the similarity between this emblem and the symbolism of the thunder war shield. In this case, the war shield has a far longer and more primordial history.

66. Grinnell, *The Cheyenne Indians: Their History and Ways of Life*, 1:196.

67. Ernest Wallace and E. Adamson Hoebel, *The Comanches: Lords of the Southern Plains*, p. 109.

68. Wissler, "Some Protective Designs of the Dakota," p. 30.

69. Grinnell, *The Cheyenne Indians: Their History and Ways of Life*, 1:197.

70. Wissler, "Some Protective Designs of the Dakota," p. 32.

71. For a further discussion of the interwoven complexity of shield symbolism and sacred art, Wissler's "The Whirlwind and the Elk in the Mythology of the Dakotas," and "Some Protective Designs of the Dakota" are highly recommended.

72. H. Alderman, "The Dreamer and the World," p. 342. The author discusses the way in which implements or tools represent instrumentality for the modern dreamer—the means by which the individual interacts with the world. A lack of implements in dreaming may indicate impotence or a sense of existential anxiety with regard to effecting transformation or change favorable for the dreamer in his or her everyday world. Native American visionaries and dreamers demonstrate a remarkable implementality in dreaming; the use of "tools" in the broad sense indicates the sense of effective relatedness to the world so apparent in most visions. The dream object as tool expresses the belief that effective change can be accomplished in the world through the enhanced potency of its symbolic significance. The tool becomes an intermediary between the human situation and the enhancement of the world through the instrumentality of the sacred.

73. Robert G. Ley, "Cerebral Asymmetries, Emotional Experience, and Imagery: Implications for Psychotherapy," p. 51.

74. DeMallie, *The Sixth Grandfather: Black Elk's Teachings Given to John G. Neihardt*, pp. 178–79.

Bibliography

Ahsen, Akhter
  1986 "The New Structuralism: Images in Dramatic Interlock." *Journal of Mental Imagery* 10:1–91.
  1987 "Rewriting the History and Future of the Imagery Movement." *Journal of Mental Imagery* 11:159–281.
  1988 "Prolucid Dreaming: A Content Analysis Approach to Dreams." *Journal of Mental Imagery* 12:1–70.
Albers, Patricia, and Bea Medicine (eds.)
  1981 *The Hidden Half: Studies of Plains Indian Women*. Washington, D.C.: University Press of America.
Albers, Patricia, and Seymour Parker
  1971 "The Plains Vision Experience." *Southwestern Journal of Anthropology* 27:203–33.
Alderman, H.
  1977 "The Dreamer and the World." *Soundings* 60:331–46.
Amiotte, Authur
  1982 "Our Other Selves: The Lakota Dream Experience." *Parabola* 6:26–32.
Applegate, Richard B.
  1978 '*Atishwin: The Dream Helper in Southern California*. New Mexico: Ballena Press.
Bakan, Paul
  1980 "Imagery, Raw and Cooked: A Hemispheric Recipe." *In* Joseph Shorr et al. (eds.), *Imagery: Its Many Dimensions and Applications*. New York: Plenum.
Bakhtin, Mikhail M.
  1978 "The Problem of the Text." *Soviet Studies in Literature* 14:333.
Basso, Ellen B.
  1987 "The Implications of a Progressive Theory of Dreaming." *In* Barbara Tedlock (ed.), *Dreaming Anthropological and Psychological Interpretations*, pp. 86–104. Cambridge: Cambridge University Press.
Bauman, Richard
  1983 *Let Your Words Be Few: Symbolism of the Speaking and Silence Among Seventeenth-Century Quakers*. London: Cambridge University Press.

1984 *Verbal Art as Performance*. Prospect Heights, Il.: Waveland Press.

Benedict, Ruth Fulton

1922 "The Vision in Plains Culture." *American Anthropologist* 24:1–23.

1923 *The Concept of the Guardian Spirit in North America*. American Anthropological Association Memoirs, no. 29. Menasha, Wis.: Banta Publishing Company.

Bloomfield, Leonard

1934 *Plains Cree Texts*. New York: Publications of the American Ethnological Society.

Boas, Franz

1925 "Contributions to the Ethnology of the Kwakiutl." *Columbia University Contributions to Anthropology*, no. 3.

Bohm, David

1980 *Wholeness and the Implicate Order*. London: Routledge and Kegan Paul.

Bourguignon, Erika

1972 "Dreams and Altered States of Consciousness in Anthropological Research." *In* Francis Hsu (ed.), *Psychological Anthropology*. Cambridge, Mass.: Schenkman.

1979 *Psychological Anthropology: An Introduction to Human Nature and Cultural Differences*. New York: Holt, Rinehart and Winston.

Bowers, Alfred W.

1950 *Mandan Social and Ceremonial Organization*. Chicago: University of Chicago Press.

1965 *Hidatsa Social and Ceremonial Organization*. Bureau of American Ethnology, Bulletin no. 194. Washington, D.C.: Smithsonian Institution.

Boyd, Maurice

1982 *Kiowa Voices: Myths, Legends and Folktales*. Two volumes. Fort Worth, Texas: Texas Christian University Press.

Brant, Charles S.

1969 *Jim Whitewolf: The Life of a Kiowa-Apache Indian*. New York: Dover Publications.

Briggs, John P., and David F. Peat

1984 *Looking Glass Universe: The Emerging Science of Wholeness*. New York: Simon and Schuster.

Broughton, Roger T.

1984 "Human Consciousness and Sleep/Waking Rhythms." *In* B. B. Wolman and Montague Ullman (eds.), *Handbook of States of Consciousness*, pp. 461–84.

Brown, Jennifer S., and Robert Brightman

1988 *The Orders of the Dreamed: George Nelson on Cree & Northern Ojibwa Religion & Myth, 1823*. Minnesota Historical Society Press.

Brown, Joseph Epes
1973 *The Sacred Pipe: Black Elk's Account of the Seven Rites of the Oglala Sioux*. Baltimore: Penguin Books.
1989 "Evoking the Sacred through Language, Metalanguage and the Arts." *In* E. D. Blodgett and H. G. Coward (eds.), *Silence: The Words and the Sacred*. Waterloo, Ont.: Wilfrid Laurier University Press.
Bultman, Rudolph
1953 "New Testament and Mythology." *In* Hans Bartsch (ed.), *Kerygma and Myth*. London: S.P.K.E.
Cahen, Roland
1966 "The Psychology of the Dream." *In* G. E. Von Grunebaum and R. Caillois (eds.), *The Dream and Human Societies*, pp. 119–43. Berkeley: University of California Press.
Clements, William M., and Frances M. Malpezzi
1984 *Native American Folklore, 1879–1979: An Annotated Bibliography*. Chicago: Swallow Press.
Cooper, John M.
1957 *The Gros Ventres of Montana: Religion and Ritual*. Washington, D.C.: Catholic University of America Press.
Curtis, Edward S.
1930 *The North American Indian*. Volumes 1–20. Cambridge: The University Press.
D'Andrade, Roy G.
1961 "Anthropological Studies in Dreams." *In* F. L. K. Hsu (ed.), *Psychological Anthropology*. Homewood, Il.: Dorsey Press.
DeMallie, Raymond (ed.)
1984 *The Sixth Grandfather: Black Elk's Teachings Given to John G. Neihardt*. Lincoln: University of Nebraska Press.
DeMallie, Raymond J., and R. H. Lavenda
1977 "Wakan: Plains Siouan Concepts of Power." *In* Raymond D. Fogelson and Richard N. Adams (eds.), *The Anthropology of Power: Ethnographic Studies from Asia, Oceania, and the New World*. New York: Academic Press.
DeMallie, Raymond, and Douglas Parks (eds.)
1987 *Sioux Indian Religion: Tradition and Innovation*. Norman: University of Oklahoma Press.
Dement, William, and Nathan Kleitman
1957 "The Relation of Eye Movements during Sleep to Dream Activity." *Journal of Experimental Psychology* 53:339–46.
Densmore, Frances
1918 *Teton Sioux Music*. Bureau of American Ethnology, Bulletin no. 61. Washington, D.C.: Smithsonian Institution.
1926 *The American Indians and Their Music*. New York: Woman's Press.
1929 *Chippewa Customs*. Bureau of American Ethnology, Bulletin 86. Washington, D.C.: Smithsonian Institution.

1953 "The Belief of the Indian in a Connection Between Song and the Supernatural." Bureau of American Ethnology, Bulletin 151. Washington, D.C.: Smithsonian Institution.

Devereux, George
1951 *Dream and Reality: The Psychotherapy of a Plains Indian*. New York: New York University Press.
1957 "Dream Learning and Individual Ritual Differences in Mohave Shamanism." *American Anthropologist* 59:1036–1045.

Dorsey, James O.
1890 *A Study of Siouan Cults*. Bureau of American Ethnology, Annual Report, no. 11. Washington, D.C.: Smithsonian Institution.

Dubrov, A. P., and V. N. Pushkin
1982 *Parapsychology and Contemporary Science*. New York: Consultants Bureau.

Eastman, Mary
1849 *Dahcotah, or Life and Legends of the Sioux around Fort Snelling*. New York: John Wiley.

Eggan, Dorothy
1949 "The Significance of Dreams for Anthropological Research." *American Anthropologist* 51:171–98.
1966 "Hopi Dreams in Cultural Perspective." *In* G. E. Von Grunebaum and R. Caillois (eds.), *The Dream and Human Societies*, pp. 237–65. Berkeley: University of California Press.

Eliade, Mircea
1970 *Patterns in Comparative Religion*. New York: World Publishing Company.

Ewers, John C.
1958 *The Blackfeet: Raiders of the Northwestern Plains*. Norman: University of Oklahoma Press.
1978 *Murals in the Round: Painted Tipis of the Kiowa and Kiowa-Apache Indians*. Washington, D.C.: Smithsonian Institution Press.

Feinstein, David
1986 "Myth-Making Activity through the Window of the Dream." *Psychotherapy in Private Practice* 4:119–35.

Feinstein, David, and Stanley Krippner
1988 *Personal Mythology: The Psychology of Your Evolving Self*. Los Angeles: Jeremy P. Tarcher.

Fenton, William N.
1968 *Parker on the Iroquois*. Syracuse: Syracuse University Press.

Fire, John, and Richard Erdoes
1972 *Lame Deer: Seeker of Visions*. New York: Simon and Schuster.

Fischer, Roland
1984 "Toward a Neuroscience of Self-Experience and States of Self-Awareness and Interpreting Interpretations." *In* B. B. Wolman and Montague Ullman (eds.), *Handbook of States of Consciousness*, pp. 3–30. New York: Van Nostrand Reinhold.

Fletcher, Alice C.
1884 "The Elk Mystery or Festival: Ogallalla Sioux." *Peabody Museum, Sixteenth and Seventeenth Annual Report* 3:276–88.
1904 *The Hako: A Pawnee Ceremony.* Bureau of American Ethnology, Twenty-second Annual Report. Washington, D.C.: Smithsonian Institution.
1907 "The Indian and Nature." *American Anthropologist* 9:440–43.
Fletcher, Alice C., and Francis La Flesche
1911 *The Omaha Tribe.* Bureau of American Ethnology, Twenty-seventh Annual Report. Washington, D.C.: Smithsonian Institution.
Fogelson, Raymond D., and Richard N. Adams
1977 *The Anthropology of Power: Ethnographic Studies From Asia, Oceania, and the New World.* New York: Academic Press.
Fortune, R. F.
1932 *Omaha Secret Societies.* New York: Columbia University Press.
Foulkes, David
1985 *Dreaming: A Cognitive-Psychological Approach.* New York: Lawrence Erlbaum Associates.
Gilhus, Ingvild S.
1984 "The Phenomenology of Religion and Theories of Interpretation." *Temenos* 20:26–39.
Gill, Sam
1981 *Sacred Words: A Study of Navajo Religion and Prayer.* Contributions to Intercultural and Comparative Studies, 4. New York: Greenwood Press.
Globus, Gordon G.
1987 "Three Holonomic Approaches to the Brain." *In* B. J. Hiley and David F. Peat (eds.), *Quantum Implications,* pp. 372–85. London: Routledge and Kegan Paul.
Goodbird, Edward
1985 *Goodbird the Indian: His Story Told to G. L. Wilson.* St. Paul: Minnesota Historical Society Press. (Original 1914.)
Grinnell, George B.
1914 "The Cheyenne Medicine Lodge." *American Anthropologist* 16:245–56.
1923 *The Cheyenne Indians: Their History and Ways of Life.* 2 Volumes. Lincoln: University of Nebraska Press.
Grof, Stanislav
1985 *Beyond the Brain: Birth, Death, and Transcendence in Psychotherapy.* New York: State University of New York Press.
Hallowell, A. Irving
1934 "Some Empirical Aspects of Northern Salteaux Religion." *American Anthropologist* 36:389–404.
1947 "Myth, Culture and Personality." *American Anthropologist* 49:544–55.
1955 "The Self and Its Behavioral Environment." *In* A. Irving

Hallowell, *Culture and Experience*. Philadelphia: University of Pennsylvania Press.

1966 "The Role of Dreams in Ojibwa Culture." *In* G. E. Von Grunebaum and R. Caillois (eds.), *The Dream and Human Societies*, pp. 267–92. Berkeley: University of California Press.

1975 "Ojibwa Ontology, Behavior, and World View." *In* D. Tedlock and B. Tedlock (eds.), *Teachings from the American Earth: Indian Religion and Philosophy*. New York: Liverwright.

Harrod, Howard L.

1987 *Renewing the World: Plains Indian Religion and Morality*. Tucson: University of Arizona Press.

Haskel, R. E

1986 "Cognitive Psychology and Dream Research: Historical, Conceptual, and Epistemological Considerations." *Journal of Mind and Behavior* 7:131–59.

Hassrick, Royal B., with Dorothy Maxwell and Cile M. Bach

1964 *The Sioux: Life and Customs of a Warrior Society*. Norman: University of Oklahoma Press.

Heesterman, J. C.

1985 *The Inner Conflict of Tradition*. Chicago: University of Chicago Press.

Hewitt, J. N. B.

1895 "The Iroquoian Concept of the Soul." *Journal of American Folklore* 8:107–16.

Hiley, B. J., and David F. Peat (eds.)

1987 *Quantum Implications*. London: Routledge and Kegan Paul.

Hoebel, E. Adamson

1978 *The Cheyennes: Indians of the Great Plains*. New York: Holt, Rinehart and Winston.

Honigmann, John J.

1961 "North America." *In* Francis L. K. Hsu (ed.), *Psychological Anthropology: Approaches to Culture and Personality*. Illinois: Dorsey Press.

Horse Capture, George

1980 *The Seven Visions of Bull Lodge*. Ann Harbor: Bear Claw Press.

Howard, James H.

1965 *The Ponca Tribe*. Bureau of American Ethnology, Bulletin 195. Washington, D.C.: Smithsonian Institution.

Hultkrantz, Ake

1953 *Conceptions of the Soul among North American Indians*. Stockholm: Ethnographic Museum of Sweden, Monograph Series, no. 1.

Hunt, H.

1986 "Some Relations between the Cognitive Psychology of Dreams and Dream Phenomenology." *Journal of Mind and Behavior* 7:213–28.

Irwin, Lee
1990 "Myth, Language and Ontology Among the Huron." *Studies in Religion* 19:413–26.
1992a "Visionary Dialogues: The Huron-Jesuit Relations." *Religion* 22:259–69.
1992b "Cherokee Healing: Myth, Dreams and Medicine." *American Indian Quarterly* 16:237–57.

Jacobi, Jolande
1959 *Complex, Archetype, Symbol in the Psychology of C. G. Jung.* New York: Bollingen Foundation.

James, G. A.
1985 "Phenomenology and the Study of Religion: The Archaeology of an Aproach." *The Journal of Religion* 65:311–35.

Jaspers, Karl, and Rudolph Bultman
1958 *Myth and Christianity.* New York: Noonday Press.

Jones, David E.
1972 *Sanapia: Comanche Medicine Woman.* New York: Holt, Rinehart and Winston.

Jung, Carl G.
1960 "The Transcendent Function." *In The Collected Works of C. G. Jung* 8:67–91.

Kluckhohn, Clyde, and William Morgan
1951 "Some Notes on Navaho Dreams." *In* George B. Wilbur and Warner Muensterberger (eds.), *Psychoanalysis and Culture: Essays in Honor of Geza Roheim,* pp. 120–31. New York: International Universities Press.

Kohl, Johann G.
1985 *Kitchi-Gami: Life among the Lake Superior Ojibway.* St. Paul: Minnesota Historical Society Press. [Original 1860.]

Kracke, Waud
1987 "Myths in Dreams, Thoughts in Images: An Amazonian Contribution to the Psychoanalytic Theory of Primary Process." *In* Barbara Tedlock (ed.), *Dreaming: Anthropological and Psychological Interpretations,* pp. 31–54. Cambridge: Cambridge University Press.

Krippner, Stanley
1986 "Dreams and the Development of a Personal Mythology." *Journal of Mind and Behavior* 7:449–61.

Krippner, Stanley, and L. George
1984 "PSI Phenomena as Related to Altered States of Consciousness." *In* B. B. Wolman and Montague Ullman (eds.), *Handbook of States of Consciousness,* pp. 332–64. New York: Van Nostrand Reinhold.

Kroeber, Alfred L.
1904 *The Arapaho.* New York: Anthropological Papers of the American Museum of Natural History, vol. 18.

1908 "Ethnology of the Gros Ventre." *Anthropological Papers of the American Museum of Natural History,* vol. 1.

Krolick, Stanford

1985 "Through a Glass Darkly: What Is the Phenomenology of Religion?" *International Journal for the Philosophy of Religion* 17:193–99.

Kruger, Dreyer

1982 "The Daseinsanalytic Approach to Dreams." *Journal of Phenomenological Psychology* 13(2):161–68.

La Barre, Weston

1966 "The Dream, Charisma, and the Culture-Hero." *In* G. E. Von Grunebaum and R. Caillois (eds.), *The Dream and Human Societies,* pp. 229–35. Berkeley: University of California Press.

LaBerge, Steven

1985 *Lucid Dreaming.* New York: Ballantine.

La Flesche, Francis

1889 "Death and Funeral Customs among the Omahas." *Journal of American Folklore* 2:3–11.

1891 "The Omaha Buffalo Medicine-Men: An Account of Their Method of Practice." *Journal of American Folklore* 3:215–21.

1932 *A Dictionary of the Osage Language.* Bureau of American Ethnology, Bulletin 109. Washington, D.C.: Smithsonian Institution.

Lewis, Oscar

1941 "Manly-Hearted Women among the North Piegan." *American Anthropologist* 43:173–87.

Ley, Robert G.

1979 "Cerebral Asymmetries, Emotional Experience, and Imagery: Implications for Psychotherapy." *In* A. A. Sheikh and J. T. Shaffer (eds.), *The Potential of Fantasy and Imagination.* New York: Brandon House.

Lincoln, Jackson S.

1935 *The Dream in Primitive Cultures.* Baltimore: Williams and Wilkins.

Linderman, Frank Bird

1930 *Plenty Coups: Chief of the Crows.* Lincoln: University of Nebraska Press.

1932 *Pretty Shield: Medicine Woman of the Crow.* Lincoln: University of Nebraska Press.

Lowie, Robert H.

1909a "The Assiniboine." *Anthropological Papers of the American Museum of Natural History* vol. 4.

1909b "The Northern Shoshone." *Anthropological Papers of the American Museum of Natural History* 2:169–303.

1916 "Dance Associations of the Eastern Dakota." *Anthropological Papers of the American Museum of Natural History* 9:101–42.

1919 "The Tobacco Society of the Crow Indians." *Anthropological Papers of the American Museum of Natural History,* vol. 21, part 2.

1924 "Notes on Shoshonean Ethnography." *Anthropological Papers of the American Museum of Natural History* 20:191–313.
1947 "The Religion of the Crow Indians." *Anthropological Papers of the American Museum of Natural History* 25:309–444.
1966 *The Crow Indians*. New York: Holt, Rinehart and Winston.

Lurie, Nancy O.
1953 "Winnebago Berdache." *American Anthropologist* 55:708–12.

Lynd, James W.
1864 "The Religion of the Dakotas." *Minnesota Historical Society Collections* 2:143–74.

McAllister, J. Gilbert
1965 "The Four Quartz Rocks Medicine Bundle of the Kiowa-Apache." *Ethnology* 4:210–24.
1970 "Dávéko: Kiowa-Apache Medicine Man." *Bulletin of the Texas Memorial Museum*, 17. Austin: University of Texas.

McClintock, Walter
1941 "Saítsiko, the Blackfoot Doctor." *The Masterkey* 15:80–86.

Mails, Thomas E.
1979 *Fools Crow*. New York: Doubleday and Company.

Mandelbaum, David G.
1940 "The Plains Cree." *Anthropological Papers of the American Museum of Natural History*, vol. 37.

Marks, David F.
1985 "Imagery Paradigms and Methodology." *Journal of Mental Imagery* 9:93–106.

Merquior, J. G.
1985 *Foucault*. Berkeley: University of California Press.

Mooney, James, and Frans M. Olbrechts (eds.)
1932 *The Swimmer Manuscript: Cherokee Sacred Formulas and Medicinal Prescriptions*. Bureau of American Ethnology, Bulletin 99.

Morris, Richard
1990 *The Edges of Science: Crossing the Boundary from Physics to Metaphysics*. New York: Prentice Hall.

Murie, John R., and Douglas R. Parks (eds.)
1981 *Ceremonies of the Pawnee*. Parts 1 and 2. Smithsonian Contributions to Anthropology, no. 27. Washington, D.C.: Smithsonian Institution Press.

Nabokov, Peter
1967 *Two Leggings: The Making of a Crow Warrior*. New York: Thomas Y. Crowell.

Niatum, Diane
1975 *Carriers of the Dream Wheel*. New York: Harper and Row.

Noll, Richard
1985 "Mental Imagery Cultivation as a Cultural Phenomenon: The Role of Visions in Shamanism." *Current Anthropology* 26:443–61.

Nye, Wilbur Sturtevant
1962 *Bad Medicine and Good: Tales of the Kiowas*. Norman: University of Oklahoma Press.
Opler, Marvin K.
1959 "Dream Analysis in Ute Indian Therapy." *In* Marvin K. Opler (ed.), *Culture and Mental Health*, pp. 97–117. New York: Macmillan.
Opler, Morris E.
1969 *Apache Odyssey: A Journey between Two Worlds*. New York: Holt, Rinehart and Winston.
Opler, Morris E., and William E. Bittle
1961 "The Death Practices and Eschatology of the Kiowa-Apache." *Southwestern Journal of Anthropology* 17:383–94.
Ornstein, Robert
1986 *The Psychology of Consciousness*. New York: Viking Penguin.
Otto, Rudolph
1969 *The Idea of the Holy*. London: Oxford University Press.
Paper, Jordan
1988 *Offering Smoke: The Sacred Pipe and Native American Religion*. Moscow: University of Idaho Press.
Park, Willard Z.
1934 "Paviotso Shamanism." *American Anthropology* 36:98–113.
1975 *Shamanism in Western North America: A Study of Cultural Relations*. New York: Cooper Square Publishers. (Original 1938.)
Parker, John (ed.)
1976 *The Journals of Jonathan Carver and Related Documents, 1766–1770*. Minnesota Historical Society Press.
Parks, Douglas R.
1991 *Traditional Narratives of the Arikara Indians*. Four volumes. Lincoln: University of Nebraska Press.
Parsons, Elsie C.
1929 *Kiowa Tales*. New York: The American Folklore Society.
Pond, Gideon H.
1864 "Dakota Superstitions." *Minnesota Historical Society Collections* 2:32–62.
Powell, Peter J.
1969 *Sweet Medicine*. Two volumes. Norman: University of Oklahoma Press.
Powers, Marla N.
1986 *Oglala Women: Myth, Ritual, and Reality*. Chicago: University of Chicago Press.
Powers, William K.
1977 *Oglala Religion*. Lincoln: University of Nebraska Press.
1982 *Yuwipi: Vision and Experience in Oglala Religion*. Lincoln: University of Nebraska Press.
1986 *Sacred Language: The Nature of Supernatural Discourse in Lakota*. Norman: University of Oklahoma Press.

Price-Williams, Douglass
    1987 "The Waking Dream in Ethnographic Perspective." *In* Barbara Tedlock (ed.), *Dreaming: Anthropological and Psychological Interpretations*, pp. 246–62. Cambridge: Cambridge University Press.
Radin, Paul
    1916 "The Winnebago Tribe." *Bureau of American Ethnology, Annual Report no. 37*. Washington, D.C.: Smithsonian Institution.
Rechtschaffen, Allan
    1978 "The Single-Mindedness and Isolation of Dreams." *Sleep* 1:97–109.
Riggs, Stephen R.
    1893 *Dakota Grammar, Texts, and Ethnography*. Washington: Department of the Interior, U.S. Geographical and Geological Survey of the Rocky Mountain Region.
Rockwell, David
    1991 *Giving Voice to Bear: North American Indian Myths, Rituals, and Images of the Bear*. Niwot, Colo.: Roberts Rinehart.
Rodnick, David
    1939 "An Assiniboine Horse-Raiding Expedition." *American Anthropologist* 41:611–16.
Rogers, T. B
    1982 "Emotion, Imagery, and Verbal Codes: A Closer Look at an Increasingly Complex Interaction." *In* John C. Yuille (ed.), *Imagery, Memory and Cognition*. New Jersey: Lawrence Erlbaum Associates.
Samuels, Andrew
    1985 *Jung and the Post-Jungians*. Boston: Routledge and Kegan Paul.
Schoolcraft, Henry R.
    1857 "Indian Theory of the Mind during Sleep." *In* Henry R. Schoolcraft, *History of the Indian Tribes of the United States: Their Present Condition and Prospects, and a Sketch of Their Ancient Status*, part 6:664–65. Philadelphia: L. J. B. Lippincott.
Schultz, James Willard
    1923 *Friends of My Life as an Indian*. New York: Houghton Mifflin.
Schultz, James W., and J. L. Donaldson
    1930 *The Sun God's Children*. New York: Houghton Mifflin.
Schlesier, Karl H.
    1987 *The Wolves of Heaven: Cheyenne Shamanism, Ceremonies, and Prehistoric Origins*. Norman: University of Oklahoma Press.
Siskin, Edgar E.
    1983 *Washo Shamans and Peyotists*. Salt Lake City: University of Utah Press. [Original 1941.]
Skinner, Alanson
    1911 "Notes on the Eastern Cree and the Northern Saulteaux." *Anthropological Papers of the American Museum of Natural History* 9:1–177.

1913 "Menomini Social Life and Ceremonial Bundles." *Anthropological Papers of the American Museum of Natural History* 13:1–165.
1914 "Ceremonies of the Plains Cree." *Anthropological Papers of the American Museum of Natural History* 11:513–42.
1915 "Societies of the Iowa, Kansa, and Ponca Indians." *Anthropological Papers of the American Museum of Natural History* 11:681–801.

Slobodin, Richard
1970 "Kutchin Concepts of Reincarnation." *Western Canadian Journal of Anthropology* 2:67–79.

Smith, Robert J.
1975 *The Art of the Festival*. University of Kansas Publications in Anthropology, no. 6. Lawrence: University of Kansas Libraries.

Spier, Leslie
1930 "Klamath Ethnography." *University of California Publications in American Archaeology and Ethnology* 30:1–338.

Stands in Timber, John, and Margot Liberty
1967 *Cheyenne Memories*. New Haven: Yale University Press.

Stevens, Anthony
1982 *Archetypes: A Natural History of the Self*. New York: William Morrow.

Stewart, Kenneth M.
1946 "Spirit Possession in Native America." *Southwestern Journal of Anthropology* 2:323–39.

Stone, Michael H.
1977 "Dreams, Free Association, and the Non-dominant Hemisphere: An Integration of Psychoanalytical, Neurophysiological, and Historical Data." *Journal of the American Academy of Psychoanalysis* 5:255–84.

Swanton, John R.
1905 "Social Condition, Beliefs and Linguistic Relationship of the Tlingit Indians." *Annual Report of the Bureau of American Ethnography* 26:391–485. Washington, D.C.: Smithsonian Institution.

Tart, Charles T.
1972 "States of Consciousness and State-Specific Sciences." *Science* 176:1203–10.
1987 "The World Simulation Process in Waking and Dreaming: A Systems Analysis of Structure." *Journal of Mental Imagery* 11:145–58.

Tedlock, Barbara
1987 *Dreaming: Anthropological and Psychological Interpretations*. Cambridge: Cambridge University Press.

Thwaites, Reuben G.
1901 *The Jesuit Relations and Allied Documents: Travels and Explorations of the Jesuit Missionaries in New France*. 73 vols. Cleveland: Burrows Brothers.

Tolaas, Jon
1984 "Transformatory Framework: Pictorial to Verbal." *In* B.B. Wolman and Montague Ullman (eds.), *Handbook of States of Consciousness*, pp. 31–67. New York: Van Nostrand Reinhold.

Tooker, Elizabeth
1964 *An Ethnography of the Huron Indians, 1615–1649*. Bureau of American Ethnology, Bulletin 190. Washington, D.C.: Smithsonian Institution.

Turner, Victor
1969 *The Ritual Process: Structure and Anti-Structure*. New York: Cornell University Press.
1981 "Social Dramas and Stories about Them." *In* W. J. T. Mitchell (ed.) *On Narrative*, pp. 137–64. Chicago: University of Chicago Press.

Ullman, Montague D.
1984 "Access to Dreams." *In* B. B. Wolman and Montague Ullman (eds.), *Handbook of States of Consciousness*, pp. 524–52. New York: Van Nostrand Reinhold.

Ullman, Montague D., and Stanley Krippner
1973 *Dream Telepathy: Experiments in Nocturnal ESP*. Baltimore: Penguin.

Vestal, Stanley
1934 *Warpath: The True Story of the Fighting Sioux Told in a Biography of Chief White Bull*. New York: Houghton Mifflin.

Voget, Fred W.
1984 *The Shoshoni-Crow Sun Dance*. Norman: University of Oklahoma Press.

Walker, Deward E.
1967 "Nez Perce Sorcery." *Ethnology* 6:66–96.

Walker, James R.
1917 "The Sundance and Other Ceremonies of the Oglala Division of the Teton Dakota." *Anthropological Papers of the American Museum of Natural History* 16:51–223.
1980 *Lakota Belief and Ritual*. Edited by R. DeMallie and E. Jahner. Lincoln: University of Nebraska Press.
1983 *Lakota Myth*. Lincoln: University of Nebraska Press.

Wallace, Anthony
1947 "The Dream in Mohave Life." *Journal of American Folklore* 60:252–58.
1956 "New Religions among the Delaware Indians, 1600–1900." *Southwestern Journal of Anthropology* 12:1–21.
1958 "Dreams and the Wishes of the Soul: A Type of Psychoanalytic Theory among the Seventeenth-Century Iroquois." *American Anthropologist* 60:234–48.

Wallace, Ernest, and E. Adamson Hoebel
1952 *The Comanches: Lords of the Southern Plains*. Norman: University of Oklahoma Press.

Wallis, Wilson D.
1947 "The Canadian Dakota." *Anthropological Papers of the American Museum of Natural History* 41:1–225.

Weitzner, Bella
1979 "Notes on the Hidatsa Indians Based on Data Recorded by the Late Gilbert L. Wilson." *Anthropological Papers of the American Museum of Natural History*, vol. 56, part 2.

Weltfish, Gene
1938 "The Vision Story of Fox Boy." *International Journal of American Linguistics* 9:73.
1965 *The Lost Universe: The Way of Life of the Pawnee.* New York: Ballantine.

Whitman, William
1937 *The Oto.* New York: Columbia University Press.

Wilber, Ken (ed.)
1982 *The Holographic Paradigm and Other Paradoxes: Exploring the Leading Edge of Science.* Boulder: Shambala Press.

Wildschut, William
1960 *Crow Indian Medicine Bundles.* New York: Museum of the American Indian, Heye Foundation.

Wissler, Clark
1905 "The Whirlwind and the Elk in the Mythology of the Dakotas." *Journal of American Folklore* 18:257–68.
1907a "Some Dakota Myths." *Journal of American Folklore* 20:121–31; 195–206.
1907b "Some Protective Designs of the Dakota." *Anthropological Papers of the American Museum of Natural History* 1:21–53.
1912 "Ceremonial Bundles of the Blackfoot Indians." *Anthropological Papers of the American Museum of Natural History* 7:65–298.
1916 "Societies and Ceremonial Associations in the Oglala Division of the Teton-Dakota." *Anthropological Papers of the American Museum of Natural History* 9:1–100.

Index